Plagues and Peoples

Also by William H. McNeill

Europe's Steppe Frontier 1500–1800:
  A Study of the Eastward Movement in Europe
The Rise of the West:
  A History of the Human Community
A World History
The Shape of European History
Venice: The Hinge of Europe 1081–1797

Plagues and Peoples

William H. McNeill

1976
ANCHOR PRESS/DOUBLEDAY
GARDEN CITY, NEW YORK

The map, "The Spread of the Black Death in Europe,"
is reprinted by permission
of the *Annales: Economies, Sociétés, Civilisations*
and appeared in the *Annales*, 17,
in the article "Autour de la Peste Noire:
Famines et Épidémies dans L'Histoire du XIVᵉ Siècle"
by Elizabeth Carpentier (1962, pp. 1062–92).

LIBRARY OF CONGRESS CATALOGING IN PUBLICATION DATA

MCNEILL, WILLIAM HARDY, 1917–
  PLAGUES AND PEOPLES.

  INCLUDES BIBLIOGRAPHICAL REFERENCES AND INDEX.
  1. EPIDEMICS—HISTORY. 2. CIVILIZATION—HISTORY.
I. TITLE.
RA649.M3   614.4'9
ISBN: 0-385-11256-4
LIBRARY OF CONGRESS CATALOG CARD NUMBER 76-2798

Contents

57513

Acknowledgments

This book was composed in the spring and summer of 1974 and corrected in the spring of 1975. In between, a rough draft was circulated to the following readers for their expert criticism: Alexandre Bennigsen, James Bowman, Francis Black, John Z. Bowers, Jerome Bylebyl, L. Warwick Coppleson, Alfred W. Crosby, Jr., Philip Curtin, Allen Debus, Robert Fogel, Ping-ti Ho, Laverne Kuhnke, Charles Leslie, George LeRoy, Stuart Ragland, Donald Rowley, Olaf K. Skinsnes, H. Burr Steinbach, John Woods. The manuscript also benefited from a panel discussion at a meeting of the American Association for the History of Medicine, May 1975, at which Saul Jarcho, Barbara G. Rosenkrantz, John Duffy, and Guenter B. Risse commented on what they had read. Subsequently, in the autumn of 1975, Barbara Dodwell read Chapter IV and Hugh Scogin worked over Chinese data for me; between them they led me to adjust the way I understand the propagation of the Black Death. Fortunately it proved possible to insinuate appropriate adjustments into the text at the last minute.

This episode illustrates how tentative many of the assertions and suggestions of this book are and must remain until epidemiologically informed researches have been undertaken in Chinese and other ancient records. Suggestions and corrections from the entire array of readers permitted improvement of the original version in numerous details and steered me away from some silly errors; but needless to say, I remain responsible for what appears below, including any and all residual errors.

A generous grant from the Josiah Macy, Jr., Foundation permitted time away from normal academic duties for the completion of this essay. I was assisted by Edward Tenner, Ph.D., who looked things up for me in European languages, and by Joseph

Cha, Ph.D., who consulted Chinese and Japanese texts on my behalf and compiled the roster of Chinese epidemics that appears in the Appendix. Without their help the task would have taken longer and, in particular, my remarks about the Far East would have been far sketchier. Marnie Veghte twice typed the text with cheerful accuracy and admirable speed. Charles Priester of Anchor Press/Doubleday asked suitably pointed questions to provoke me to improve the original manuscript in important ways.

To all who thus assisted in bringing this book to birth, I am sincerely grateful.

William H. McNeill
15 December 1975

Plagues and Peoples

Introduction

Nearly twenty years ago, as part of my self-education for writing *The Rise of the West: A History of the Human Community*, I was reading about the Spanish conquest of Mexico. As everyone knows, Hernando Cortez, starting off with fewer than six hundred men, conquered the Aztec empire, whose subjects numbered millions. How could such a tiny handful prevail? How indeed? All the familiar explanations seemed inadequate. If Montezuma and his friends first thought the Spaniards were gods, experience soon showed otherwise. If horses and gunpowder were amazing and terrible on first encounter, armed clashes soon revealed the limitations of horseflesh and of the very primitive guns the Spaniards had at their disposal. Cortez's skill in finding allies among the Indian peoples of Mexico and rallying them against the Aztecs was certainly important, but his Indian allies committed themselves to the Spanish side only when they had reason to think Cortez would win.

The extraordinary story of the conquest of Mexico (soon to be followed by Pizarro's no less amazing conquest of the Inca empire in South America) was really only part of a larger puzzle. Relatively few Spaniards ever were able to cross the ocean to the New World, yet they succeeded in impressing their culture on an enormously larger number of Amerindians. The inherent attraction of European civilization and some undeniable technical superiorities the Spaniards had at their command do not seem enough to explain wholesale apostasy from older Indian patterns of life and belief. Why, for instance, did the old religions of Mexico and Peru disappear so utterly? Why did villagers not remain loyal to deities and rituals that had brought fertility to their fields from time immemorial? The exhortation

of Christian missionaries and the intrinsic appeal of Christian
faith and worship seem insufficient to explain what happened,
even though, in the eyes of the missionaries themselves, the
truth of Christianity was so evident that their success in con-
verting millions of Indians to the faith seemed to need no explanation.

A casual remark in one of the accounts of Cortez's conquest
—I no longer can tell where I saw it—suggested an answer to
such questions, and my new hypothesis gathered plausibility
and significance as I mulled it over and reflected on its implications afterward. For on the night when the Aztecs drove Cortez
and his men out of Mexico City, killing many of them, an
epidemic of smallpox was raging in the city. The man who had
organized the assault on the Spaniards was among those who
died on that *noche trista,* as the Spaniards later called it. The
paralyzing effect of a lethal epidemic goes far to explain why
the Aztecs did not pursue the defeated and demoralized Spaniards, giving them time and opportunity to rest and regroup,
gather Indian allies and set siege to the city, and so achieve
their eventual victory.

Moreover, it is worth considering the psychological implications of a disease that killed only Indians and left Spaniards un-
harmed. Such partiality could only be explained supernaturally,
and there could be no doubt about which side of the struggle
enjoyed divine favor. The religions, priesthoods, and way of life
built around the old Indian gods could not survive such a demonstration of the superior power of the God the Spaniards wor-
shiped. Little wonder, then, that the Indians accepted Christianity and submitted to Spanish control so meekly. God had
shown Himself on their side, and each new outbreak of infectious disease imported from Europe (and soon from Africa as
well) renewed the lesson.

The lopsided impact of infectious disease upon Amerindian
populations therefore offered a key to understanding the ease of
the Spanish conquest of America—not only militarily, but culturally as well. But the hypothesis swiftly raised other questions.

Introduction

How and when did the Spaniards acquire the disease experience that served them so well in the New World? Why did the Amerindians not have diseases of their own with which to mow down the invading Spaniards? Tentative answers to such questions soon began to uncover a dimension of human history that historians have not hitherto recognized: the history of humanity's encounters with infectious diseases, and the far-reaching consequences that ensued whenever contacts across disease boundaries allowed a new infection to invade a population that lacked any acquired immunity to its ravages.

Looked at in this way, world history offered a number of parallels to what happened in the Americas in the sixteenth and seventeenth centuries. This book describes the main lines of these fateful encounters. My conclusions will startle many readers, since events but little noticed in traditional histories assume central importance for my account. This is because the long line of learned scholars whose work it was to sift surviving records from the past has not been sensitive to the possibility of important changes in disease patterns.

To be sure, a couple of spectacular examples of what can happen when an unfamiliar infection attacks a population for the first time have never been expunged from European memory. The Black Death of the fourteenth century was the chief example of this phenomenon, and the cholera epidemics of the nineteenth century constitute a second, far less destructive, but more recent and better-documented instance. Historians, however, never saw these as belonging to a more general class of critically important epidemiological breakthroughs because earlier examples of disastrous encounters with new diseases lay buried deeper in the past, where records were so imperfect that both the scale and the significance of what happened were easy to overlook.

In appraising ancient texts, historians were naturally governed by their own experience of epidemic infection. Living amid disease-experienced populations, where relatively high levels of immunity to familiar infections damped any ordinary epidemic outbreak very quickly, critically trained historians were impelled to discount as exaggeration any remark about massive die-off from infectious disease. Failure to understand the profound difference between the outbreak of a familiar disease amid an experienced population and the ravages of the same infection when loosed upon a community lacking acquired immunities is, indeed, at the bottom of the failure of previous historians to give adequate attention to the whole subject. Assuming that infections had always been present in much the same fashion as they were in Europe before the advent of modern medicine, there seemed nothing much to say about epidemics, and historians tended, therefore, to pass such matters by with only the sort of casual mention I found in the account of Cortez's victory.

History of epidemics became the province of antiquarians, who took pleasure in recording essentially meaningless data simply because it was there. Yet there remained the Black Death, together with a number of instances when a sudden outbreak of disease in an army abruptly altered military circumstances, and sometimes determined the outcome of a campaign. Such episodes could not be left out, but their unpredictability made most historians uncomfortable. We all want human experience to make sense, and historians cater to this universal demand by emphasizing elements in the past that are calculable, definable, and, often, controllable as well. Epidemic disease, when it did become decisive in peace or in war, ran counter to the effort to make the past intelligible. Historians consequently played such episodes down.

To be sure, there were a number of outsiders, like the bacteriologist Hans Zinsser, who played devil's advocate, picking out instances when disease did make a difference. Thus Zinsser's eminently readable book, *Rats, Lice and History*, showed how outbreaks of typhus often upset the best-laid plans of kings and captains. But such books did not try to fit disease experience into any larger picture of human history. For them as for others, occasional disastrous outbreaks of infectious disease remained sudden and unpredictable interruptions of the norm, essentially beyond historical explanation and therefore of little interest to serious professional historians whose job it was to explain the past.

This book aims to bring the history of infectious disease into the realm of historical explanation by showing how varying patterns of disease circulation have affected human affairs in ancient as well as in modern times. Many of my suggestions and inferences remain tentative. Careful examination of ancient texts by experts in many different and difficult languages will be needed to confirm and correct what I have to say. Such scholarly work requires a thesis to test, a target to shoot down. The speculation and guesswork I have indulged in ought to serve this purpose, and in the meantime, it can draw ordinary readers' attention to important gaps in older ideas about the human past.

Quite apart from details of what I have to say, everyone can surely agree that a fuller comprehension of humanity's ever-changing place in the balance of nature ought to be part of our understanding of history, and no one can doubt that the role of infectious diseases in that natural balance has been and remains of key importance.

A Few Key Concepts

Before proceeding with the story, a few remarks about parasitism, disease, pestilential infection, and related concepts may help to avoid confusion.

Disease and parasitism play a pervasive role in all life. A successful search for food on the part of one organism becomes for its host a nasty infection or disease. All animals depend on other living things for food, and human beings are no exception. Problems of finding food and the changing ways human communities have done so are familiar enough in economic histories. The problems of avoiding becoming food for some other organism are less familiar, largely because from very early times human beings ceased to have much to fear from large-bodied animal predators like lions or wolves. Nevertheless, one can properly think of most human lives as caught in a precarious equilibrium between the microparasitism of disease organisms and the macroparasitism of large-bodied predators, chief among which have been other human beings.

Microparasites are tiny organisms—viruses, bacteria, or multi-celled creatures as the case may be—that find a source of food in human tissues suitable for sustaining their own vital processes. Some microparasites provoke acute disease and either kill their host after only a brief period of time, or provoke immunity reactions inside his body that kill them off instead. Sometimes, too, one of these disease-causing organisms is somehow contained within a particular host's body so that he becomes a carrier, capable of infecting someone else without being noticeably sick himself. There are, however, other microparasites that regularly achieve more stable relations with their human hosts. Such infections no doubt take something away from their host's bodily energies, but their presence does not prevent normal functioning.

Macroparasites exhibit similar diversity. Some kill at once, as lions and wolves must do when feeding on human or any other kind of flesh; others allow the host to survive indefinitely.

In very early times, the skill and formidability of human hunters outclassed rival predators. Humanity thus emerged at the very top of the food chain, with little risk of being eaten by predatory animals any more. Yet for a long time thereafter cannibalism almost certainly remained a significant aspect of the interaction of adjacent human communities. This put the successful human hunters exactly on a level with a pride of lions or a pack of wolves.

Later, when food production became a way of life for some human communities, a modulated macroparasitism became possible. A conqueror could seize food from those who produced it, and by consuming it himself become a parasite of a new sort on those who did the work. In specially fertile landscapes it even proved possible to establish a comparatively stable pattern of this sort of macroparasitism among human beings. Early civilizations, in fact, were built upon the possibility of taking only a part of the harvest from subjected communities, leaving enough behind to allow the plundered community to survive indefinitely, year after year. In the early stages the macroparasitic basis of civilization remained harsh and clear; only later and by slow degrees did reciprocal services between town and countryside develop importance enough to diminish the one-sidedness of tax and rent collection. To begin with, though, the hard-pressed peasantries that supported priests and kings and their urban hangers-on received little or nothing in return for the food they gave up, except for a somewhat uncertain protection from other, more ruthless and shortsighted plunderers.

The reciprocity between food and parasite that has under-girded civilized history is matched by parallel reciprocities within each human body. The white corpuscles, which constitute a principal element in defenses against infection, actually digest intruders. Organisms they are unable to digest become parasites, digesting in their turn whatever they find nourishing within the human body.[1]

This is, however, only one facet of the exceedingly complex processes that affect the success or failure of any particular organism in invading and proliferating within a particular human being. In fact, despite all the advances of medical research in the past hundred years or so, no one fully understands their interaction. At every level of organization—molecular,[2] cellular, organismic, and social—one confronts equilibrium patterns. Within such equilibria, any alteration from "outside" tends to provoke compensatory changes throughout the system so as to minimize over-all upheaval, though there are always critical limits which, if transgressed, result in the breakdown of the previously existing system. Such a catastrophic event may involve dissolution into simpler, smaller parts, each with equilibrium patterns of its own; or, on the contrary, may involve incorporation of smaller parts into some larger or more complex whole.

The two processes may in fact combine, as in the familiar case of animal digestion, whereby the feeder breaks down the cells and proteins of its food into simpler parts only to combine them into new proteins and the cells of its own body.

Simple cause-and-effect analysis is inadequate for such systems. Since many variables are simultaneously at work, interacting constantly and altering their magnitudes at irregular rates, it is usually misleading to concentrate attention on a single "cause" and try to attribute a particular "effect" to it. Study of simultaneity among multiple processes is presumably a better way to approach an understanding. But the conceptual and practical difficulties here are enormous. Recognition of patterns, and observation of their endurance or dissolution is, at most levels of organization, about as much as people are capable of; and at some levels, including the social, there is profound uncertainty and dispute about which patterns are worth attending to, or can, in fact, be reliably detected. Divergent terminologies direct attention to different patternings; and finding a logically convincing test, acceptable all around, that can determine whether one such system of terms is superior to its rivals, is often impossible.

Yet the slow processes of evolution presumably apply to human societies and their symbolic systems as much as to human bodies, so that when logic cannot decide, survival eventually will. Terms that direct attention to the critically useful facets of a situation clearly do have enormous survival value for human beings. It is this aspect of our capacity to communicate with one another that has allowed *Homo sapiens* to become such a dominant species. Yet no system of terms is ever likely to exhaust or completely comprehend all aspects of the reality around us. We have to do the best we can with the language and concepts we inherit, and not worry about obtaining a truth that will satisfy everyone, everywhere, and for all time to come.

Just as language is a social and historical product, so, too, within wide limits is the very concept of disease. Holy men whom Americans today would consign to hospitals for the men-

tally ill abound in the historic record. Conversely, nearsighted-
ness and a dull sense of smell, which we regard as compatible
with good health, would probably have been classed as crippling diseases by our hunting ancestors. But despite such variability, there remains a firm and universal nucleus to the concept of disease. A person who can no longer perform expected
tasks because of bodily disorder will always seem diseased to his
fellows; and many such bodily disorders arise from encounters
with parasitic organisms.

To be sure, different human beings and entire communities
exhibit widely varying levels of susceptibility and/or immunity
to infections. Such differences are sometimes hereditary, but
more often they are the result of past exposures to invading organisms.[3] Adjustment of our defenses against disease occurs
constantly, not only within individual human bodies but also
among entire populations. Levels of resistance and immunity
rise and fall accordingly.[4]

Just as human individuals and populations undergo continual
alteration in response to infectious disease, so also the various
infectious organisms that provoke disease undergo a process of
adaptation and adjustment to their environment. Characteristically, conditions within the bodies of their hosts constitute a
very important part of that environment, though not the whole
of it. After all, a recurrent problem for all parasites, including
disease organisms, is how to get from one host to another in a
world in which such hosts are almost never contiguous entities.

Prolonged interaction between human host and infectious organism, carried on across many generations and among suitably
numerous populations on each side, creates a pattern of mutual
adaptation which allows both to survive. A disease organism
that kills its host quickly creates a crisis for itself, since a new
host must somehow be found often enough, and soon enough,
to keep its own chain of generations going. Conversely, a human body that resists infection so completely that the would-be
parasite cannot find any lodgment, obviously creates another
kind of crisis of survival for the infectious organism. In fact,

many disease partnerships have probably failed to last into our time because of one or the other of these extremes; and if some self-confident public health officers are to be believed, a number of famous and formerly important disease organisms are today in danger of extinction, thanks to widespread application of vaccination and other public health measures all round the globe.[5]

Optimal conditions for host and parasite occur, often though not necessarily always, when each can continue to live in the other's presence for an indefinite period of time with no very significant diminution of normal activity on either side. Numerous examples of this sort of biological balance exist. Human beings carry a massive population of bacteria in their lower intestines, for instance, with no noticeable ill effects. Our mouths and skins abound with organisms that normally make no substantial difference to us. Some of these creatures may assist digestion; others are believed to have a role in preventing harmful organisms from multiplying freely within our bodies. But firm data on what might be called the ecology of human infection and infestation are generally lacking.[6]

Nevertheless, from an ecological point of view we may say that many of the most lethal disease-causing organisms are poorly adjusted to their role as parasites. In some cases, they are still in early stages of biological adaptation to their human hosts; though one must not assume that prolonged co-existence necessarily tends toward mutual harmlessness.[7]

The malarial plasmodium, for instance, is probably among the oldest of human (and pre-human) parasites[8]; yet it continues to inflict severe and debilitating fevers upon its human hosts. At least four different forms of the plasmodium infect human beings, and one of these, *Plasmodium falciparum*, is far more virulent than the others. Conceivably, *Plasmodium falciparum* entered human bloodstreams more recently, and has not had time to adjust as well to human hosts as the other forms of malarial infection. In this case, however, evolutionary adjustment between host and parasite is complicated by the diversity of hosts to which the infectious organism must accommodate itself to complete its life cycle. Accommodation that would allow the malarial plasmodium to live indefinitely within the red blood corpuscles of a human being would make no provision for successful transmission from host to host.

The pattern that in fact prevails involves the periodic breakup and destruction of millions of red corpuscles, provoking fever in the human host and allowing the plasmodia to move through the bloodstream as free-moving organisms for a day or two until they re-establish themselves as parasites within new red corpuscles. This provokes fever and debilitating weakness in the human host; but it also permits the plasmodium to perpetuate itself by "hitching a ride" aboard mosquitoes that happen to suck in the free-living form of the plasmodium with a meal of human blood. Once arrived in a mosquito's stomach, the plasmodia exhibit different behaviors, culminating in sexual replication. The result, after a few days, is a new generation of plasmodia which travel to the mosquito's salivary glands, ready to penetrate a new human host in the course of the mosquito's next meal.

So far as can be detected, the malarial plasmodia do not trouble the mosquitoes that carry them from human host to human host in this remarkable way. The mosquitoes' lives seem not to be shortened nor their activity diminished by the parasite that feeds on their tissues while completing its life cycle. There is an obvious reason for this. If the plasmodium is to reach a new human host, the mosquito carrying it must be vigorous enough to fly normally. A seriously sick mosquito simply could not play its part in perpetuating the malarial cycle by carrying the parasite to a new human host successfully. But a weak and feverish human being does not interfere with the cycle in the slightest. Hence it is not surprising that this very ancient form of infection should be harmless to mosquitoes and still preserve its malignancy among humans.

Some other important human infections are like malaria inasmuch as the infectious organism must accommodate itself to more than one host. If the alternate host is somehow more important to the parasite, adaptation toward a stable biological balance will concentrate on adjustment to its non-human host. Such infections, when transferred to men, may therefore remain violently destructive to human life indefinitely. This is the case with bubonic plague, for example, since *Pasteurella pestis*, as the parasite in question is called, normally infects rodents and their fleas and only occasionally invades human bodies. In communities of ground-burrowing rodents, the infection can endure indefinitely. Patterns of infection and recovery, often involving more than one species of rodent host sharing the same burrows, are very complex and not fully known. Among some of the burrowing rodents that live in large underground "cities," however, an encounter with *Pasteurella pestis* is a childhood disease much as smallpox or measles used to be among human city dwellers above ground. Accommodation, in other words, between rodent host and this parasitic bacillus has achieved reasonably stable patterns. It is only when the disease invades previously unexposed rodent and human populations that extraordinary consequences ensue, such as those which made visitations of bubonic plague especially awful for our ancestors.

Schistosomiasis (transmitted via snails), sleeping sickness (transmitted via tsetse flies), typhus (transmitted via fleas and lice), and a number of other diseases remain formidable to humans because of the complexities of parasitic adjustment to two or more different hosts. Typhus is a particularly instructive case. The same or closely similar strains of the rickettsial organisms responsible for typhus inhabit certain species of ticks in a stable fashion, i.e., pass from generation to generation with no apparent ill effect upon either the tick or the parasite. Rats and their fleas, however, react to typhus infection by recovering, i.e., they reject the invading organism from their systems after a period of illness. When, however, typhus parasites transfer their activity to human lice and to human bodies, the result is always lethal to the louse and often lethal to the person. Such a pattern suggests successive transfers, from a stable co-existence with ticks to a less stable adjustment to rats and rat fleas, and to a highly unstable and presumably, therefore, recent transfer to humans and to human lice.[9]

There are, however, other human diseases that pass directly from host to host with no intermediary carrier and with minimal delay. Tuberculosis, measles, smallpox, chicken pox, whooping cough, mumps, influenza fall into this class. They constitute, indeed, a roster of infectious diseases with which civilized peoples remain thoroughly familiar. For all except tuberculosis and influenza, a single infection induces prolonged, often lifelong, immunity. As a result, these diseases have commonly afflicted children, and still do where vaccinations and other artificial methods have not altered the natural patterns of disease propagation.

Such childhood diseases need not be very serious, in the sense that nursing care can usually assure recovery. Yet these same infections, when invading a human population without any previous exposure to them, are likely to kill a high proportion of those who fall sick. Young adults in the prime of life characteristically die more frequently than other age groups. In other words, when invading virgin populations, these are the infections capable of destroying or crippling entire human communities, in the way that smallpox and a succession of other diseases did to Aztec and Inca civilizations.

Other diseases—whether chronic slow infections, mental disorders, or the debilities that come with aging—undoubtedly account for a greater sum of human suffering. They constitute a sort of "background noise" against which human life has always been lived. In recent times, such afflictions have increased in importance because we live longer than our ancestors did. But the pattern of disease with which we are familiar differs radically from the disease experience of our ancestors. Among them the sporadic outbreak of pestilence, in any of its dread forms, was a terrifying and ever-present possibility. Although statistical and clinical data allowing precise definition of which infections killed how many people, when and in what places are unattainable before the nineteenth century—and remain spotty even then—we may still observe major changes in patterns of pestilential infection. This, in fact, is the subject of this book.

I

Man the Hunter

Before fully human populations evolved, we must suppose that like other animals our ancestors fitted into an elaborate, self-regulating ecological balance. The most conspicuous aspect of this balance was the food chain, whereby our forebears preyed upon some forms of life and were, in their turn, preyed upon by others. In addition to these inescapable relations among large-bodied organisms, we must also suppose that minute, often imperceptible parasites sought their food within our ancestors' bodies, and became a significant element in balancing the entire life system of which humanity was a part. Details cannot be reconstructed; indeed the whole question of the descent of man remains obscure, since the various pre-human and proto-human skeletal remains that have been discovered (mainly in Africa) do not tell a complete story. Africa may not have constituted humanity's only cradleland. Forms of life ancestral to man may have also existed in the tropical and sub-tropical parts of Asia, evolving along roughly parallel lines with the humanoid populations whose bones and tools have been discovered so abundantly at Olduvai Gorge and in other parts of sub-Saharan Africa.

Human hairlessness, however, points unequivocally to a warm climate where temperatures seldom or never went below freezing. Accurate depth perception based on overlapping fields of vision, in conjunction with the grasping hand, and our obvious kinship with apes and monkeys who still spend much of their time in trees, point toward an arboreal habitat for human ancestors. Dentition suggests an omnivorous diet, in which nuts and fruits, grubs, and perhaps some kinds of vegetable shoots were more important than animal flesh. But what about disease and parasites?

The sort of infections that prevail among monkeys and arboreal apes today may resemble the parasitic populations with which these remote ancestors of humankind co-existed. Though important details remain unclear, the array of parasites that infest wild primate populations is known to be formidable. In addition to various mites, fleas, ticks, flies, and worms, wild apes and monkeys apparently play host to an impressive roster of protozoa, fungi, and bacteria, not to mention more than 150 so-called arbo-viruses (i.e., arthropod-borne viruses, conveyed from one warm-blooded host to another by insects or other arthropods).[1]

Among the organisms that infect monkeys and apes in the wild are fifteen to twenty[2] species of malaria. Humankind normally supports only four kinds of malaria, but apes can be infected with human strains of malaria plasmodia, and people can likewise suffer from some of the kinds of malaria found among monkeys and apes. Such speciation, in addition to the specialization of habitat for different kinds of anopheles mosquitoes between the treetops, middle altitude and ground level of tropical rain forests,[3] certainly suggests a very long evolutionary adjustment among the three parties concerned: primate, mosquito, and plasmodium. Moreover, given the present-day distribution of malarial organisms, and what is known about the geography of malaria in older times, sub-Saharan Africa appears to have been a principal and perhaps the exclusive center for the development of this form of parasitism.[4]

Among all the diverse natural environments of the earth, tropical rain forests are the most variegated in the sense that more diverse forms of life share this kind of habitat than occupy drier, cooler regions. A corollary to this fact is that no single species of plant or animal dominates the forest—not even humankind, at least until very recently. Many tiny organisms that cannot endure freezing temperatures or low humidity thrive in tropical rain forests. In the warmth and moisture of those environments, single-celled parasites can often survive for long periods of time outside the body of any host. Some potential parasites can exist as free-living organisms indefinitely. This means that scant populations of potential hosts can still experience widespread infection and infestation. Even if contacts between the parasite and a possible host are rare occurrences because there are few hosts to be found in the forest, the parasite can wait. Applied to human populations, this means that even when our ancestors were few and scarce in the balance of nature, it was possible for an individual to pick up a full complement of parasites in the course of a normal lifetime. This remains true today; so much so that the principal obstacle to human dominion over the rain forests is still the rich variety of parasites lying in wait for intruders.[5]

Does this mean that our pre- and proto-human ancestors were perpetually sick? Not really, for the myriad tropical forms of parasitism are characteristically slow to advance toward critical intensity, just as they are slow to recede. Another way of saying the same thing is that tropical rain forests support a highly evolved elaborate natural balance at every level: between parasites and hosts, among rival parasites, and between host and the things he eats. We may safely assume that millions of years ago, before humans began to alter the ecological context of the world's tropical rain forests, the balance between eater and eaten was stable, or nearly so, for long periods of time.

Hence the wide variety of foods our remote ancestors consumed was undoubtedly matched by the wide variety of para-

17

sites that shared this food with them, in one way or another, without necessarily producing symptoms we would recognize as illness. Mild parasitic invasions may have, at times, diminished our ancestors' strength and endurance. Low-grade infections and infestations probably flared up into fatal complications whenever serious injury or some other severe stress (famine, for instance) upset the host's internal physiological balances. In the absence of some such serious disturbance, however, a tolerable state of health can be supposed, such as exists among wild primates of the forest today.

As long as the biological evolution of humankind's ancestors kept pace with the evolution of their parasites, predators, and prey, no very important alteration in this sort of tightly woven web of life could occur. Evolutionary development, proceeding through genetic variation and selection, was so slow that any change in one partner was compensated for by changes in the other partner's respective genetic and/or behavioral patternings. When humankind began to respond to another sort of evolution, however, elaborating learned behavior into cultural traditions and systems of symbolic meaning, these age-old biological balances began to confront new sorts of disturbances. Cultural evolution began to put unprecedented strains upon older patterns of biological evolution. Newly acquired skills made humanity increasingly capable of transforming the balance of nature in unforeseen and far-reaching ways. Accordingly, the disease liability of emerging humankind also began to change dramatically.

The first discernible upheaval of this kind resulted from the development of skills and weapons suitable for killing the sorts of large-bodied herbivores that abounded on the grasslands of the African savanna (and perhaps in similar landscapes in Asia). No definite date can be offered for this transition: it may have begun as much as four million years ago.

The first pre-human primates who came down from the trees

and started to prey upon the antelope and related species probably could catch only the weak or very young. They may have had to compete with hyenas and vultures for carrion left by more efficient predators like lions. Among such pre-human primate populations hovering around the fringes of a concentrated food resource like that offered today by the vast herds of herbivores on the African savanna,[6] any genetic change that improved hunting efficiency was sure to pay off handsomely. Enormous reward awaited any group possessing muscular and mental skills that permitted more effective co-operation in the hunt. Emergent humanity reaped these rewards by developing patterns of communication that allowed increasingly effective mutual support in moments of crisis, and by elaborating tools and weapons to augment an unimpressive musculature and puny teeth and claws. In such circumstances, new traits that paid off cumulated rapidly—rapidly, that is, by the spacious standards of biological evolution. Any fresh variation, permitting more of what had begun to work well already, enlarged the food supply and increased chances for survival.

This sort of evolutionary spurt is known among biologists as "orthogenic," and is often associated with a transition to a new ecological niche.[7] No one can expect to disentangle all the genetic changes that this process provoked among pre-human populations. When variations could be so extravagantly successful, however, displacement of one humanoid population by another even more effective group of hunters must have occurred frequently. Survival was more likely for the more formidable in battle as well as for the more efficient in the hunt.

A major landmark in the resulting evolutionary development was the elaboration of language. Genetic changes governing the formation of brain, tongue, and throat were necessary to open the way for articulated language; language in turn allowed vastly improved social co-ordination. Talking things over and thereby enacting and re-enacting roles allowed human beings to practice and perfect skills ahead of time, so as to achieve otherwise unattainable precision in hunting and in other co-operative activities. With language, systematic teaching of the arts of life to others became possible, while those arts themselves became susceptible to extraordinary elaboration, since words could be used to classify things, order them, and define appropriate reactions to all sorts of circumstances. Language, in short, made hunters fully human for the first time, inaugurating a new dimension of social-cultural evolution which soon put vast and hitherto unmatched strains upon the ecological balance within which humanity arose.

What of disease amid this relatively rapid evolution? Clearly any change of habitat, such as that involved in coming down from the trees to walk and run in open grasslands, implies a substantial alteration in the sort of infections one is likely to encounter. To be sure, some infections presumably remained almost unaffected. This would be the case for those transmitted by close bodily contact, as is true, for instance, of most of the intestinal bacteria. Other parasites, such as those requiring moist conditions for successful transfer from one host to another, must have become less abundant, finding conditions on the savanna far less propitious. As the rain forest types of infestation and infection thinned out, however, new parasites, and fresh diseases, especially those contracted from association with the herds of the savanna, must have begun to affect the bodies of burgeoning humankind.

We cannot say just what these infestations and infections may have been. Various kinds of worms, for instance, that infest herbivores today may transfer their parasitism to humans when, in eating meat, we inadvertently consume the eggs or some encysted form of the parasite. This must have happened anciently, too.

A more important exposure was to the trypanosome that today causes sleeping sickness in many parts of Africa. This organism dwells as a "normal" parasite in many species of antelope and is transferred from one host to another by the tsetse fly. It produces no noticeable signs of sickness in the fly or in the host animal, and is, therefore, an example of a stable, well-adjusted, and presumably very ancient parasitism. Injected into a human body, this same organism provokes drastic debility. Indeed, one species of this trypanosome is usually lethal to its human host within a few weeks.

It is, in fact, mainly because sleeping sickness was and remains so devastating to human populations that the ungulate herds of the African savanna have survived to the present. Without modern prophylaxis, humans simply cannot live in regions where the tsetse fly abounds. Hence, until very recently, the vast herds of these regions remained the prey of lions and of other well-adapted predators, but were spared more than casual contact with that far more destructive newcomer among the beasts of prey: humankind. If, as seems almost certain, the trypanosome of sleeping sickness existed among the ungulate herds before our ancestors left their trees, the presence of this parasite must have set sharp limits upon the zones within which earliest humankind was able to take advantage of the abundance of game available on African grasslands. Conversely, within the tsetse's range, something resembling a pre-human ecological balance survives to the present.[8]

Incidentally, it is not absurd to class the ecological role of humankind in its relationship to other life forms as a disease. Ever since language allowed human cultural evolution to impinge upon age-old processes of biological evolution, humankind has been in a position to upset older balances of nature in quite the same fashion that disease upsets the natural balance within a host's body. Time and again, a temporary approach to stabilization of new relationships occurred as natural limits to the ravages of humankind upon other life forms manifested themselves. Yet sooner or later, and always within a span of time that remained minuscule in comparison with the standards of biological evolution, humanity discovered new techniques allowing fresh exploitation of hitherto inaccessible resources, thereby renewing or intensifying damage to other forms of life. Looked at from the point of view of other organisms, humankind therefore resembles an acute epidemic disease, whose occasional lapses into less virulent forms of behavior have never yet sufficed to permit any really stable, chronic relationship to establish itself.

That the first fully human hunters became the dominant predators in the savanna lands of Africa (and perhaps in similar regions of Asia) was only a modest presage of what was to come. No doubt, at the time, it was drastic enough, catapulting what had been one of the less conspicuous forms of primate life all the way to the apex of the food chain. As skillful and formidable hunters, humankind soon had little to fear from any animal rival. Our earliest fully human ancestors thus escaped one of the elemental checks upon population growth. Slaughter of man by man probably took over an equivalent demographic role, at least from the time when all suitable territory within the favorable savanna lands had been pre-empted by human hunting bands and they began to rival one another. Other social controls on population growth may also have come into operation, e.g., abandonment of unwanted infants. At any rate, present-day hunters and gatherers have customary ways of keeping their numbers within the limits of available food supplies; and such customs are likely to be very old.[9]

Within the African cradleland itself, human hunters established a relatively stable relation to the environment. Big-game hunting by humans started in Africa something like half a million years ago, although the full force of human bands, armed with weapons of stone and wood, may not have been felt much before 100,000 B.C. Despite occasional crises such as must have accompanied the extinction of a number of valuable species of game during ensuing millennia,[10] human hunting bands continued to share the landscape with rich and varied populations of other forms of life. Indeed, even when agriculture later led to an enormous increase in the number of people and precipitated a drastic environmental change, many parts of Africa remained wild and uncultivated. Hunting bands, relegated in recent millennia to marginal regions unsuited for agriculture, continue to pursue traditional styles of life in parts of that continent even to this day.

In other words, compensatory adjustments by other forms of life hemmed in human communities in such a tough and complex way that even after fully human skills had been achieved, the new efficiency attainable through cultural evolution was not sufficient to overpower and revolutionize the ecological system within which humanity had evolved. Probably the most significant factor in blunting the initial impact of humanity upon other forms of life was the peculiar richness and elaboration of African infestations and infections—an elaboration of parasitism that evolved along with humanity itself and tended to intensify as human numbers increased.[11]

Many of the parasitic worms and protozoa that abound in Africa do not provoke immune reactions, i.e., the formation of antibodies in the bloodstream. This allows a sensitive and quite automatic ecological balance to assert itself, whereby if human numbers increase, the rate of infection also increases. Opportunities for transfer from one host to another multiply with increased human density, so that, if and when a critical threshold is surpassed, infection can suddenly develop into runaway hyperinfection. Such epidemic situations seriously interfere with normal activity. Chronic symptoms of lassitude, internal pains, or the like, may, if they become nearly universal in a human community, seriously hamper food-getting, or childbearing and rearing. This in turn can soon reduce a population until the local density sinks safely below the threshold necessary for hyperinfection. Then, as more individuals escape the debilitating effects of parasitic infection, human vigor can begin to pick up. Food-getting and other activities return to normal until some other form of infection asserts its power, or the population density again transgresses the point at which hyperinfection can recur.

All such ecological disturbances of course have affected human prey as well as human parasites. Hunters who became too numerous would also find it harder and harder to discover suitable game. Undernourishment might therefore conspire with parasitic hyperinfestation to reduce human energies and child-rearing capacities until a more nearly stable balance again established itself.

Moreover, all the interdependent forms of life simultaneously have responded to fluctuations in climate and other changes in the physical environment. Drought, grass fires, torrential rains, and other emergency conditions set limits for all forms of life; and these limits stood generally far below population possibilities at other, more favorable times. The ecological system, in other words, maintained a loose, fluctuating balance which, despite local and temporary departures from the norm, effectively resisted radical alteration. The establishment of human hunters at the top of the food chain, preying upon others, but too formidable to be preyed upon by large-bodied rivals, did not, in and of itself, do much to alter these age-old ecological relations. In triumphantly claiming a new niche, humanity did not, therefore, transform the system as a whole.

The interactions that produced and sustained such fluctuating balances were (and remain) extremely complex. Despite several generations of scientific observation, the interrelationships of disease, food supply, human densities, habit patterns, not to mention insect vectors of disease and the number and distribution of alternate hosts for disease-causing organisms, are not fully understood in Africa, or anywhere else for that matter. Moreover, conditions in contemporary Africa do not exactly match the patterns of infection and infestation that must have existed when all men were hunters and before human agriculture intruded upon older natural balances.

Yet the multiplicity of life forms in tropical Africa is an undeniable fact; and the toughness with which the biological balances of that continent have resisted efforts to import methods of agricultural production that worked in temperate zones is also a matter of record. In fact, until relatively recent times (say five thousand years ago), human communities in Africa played a comparatively modest role amid the abundance of other life forms. Humans were the chief predators, to be sure, but remained relatively rare in the balance of nature, like lions and other large-bodied beasts of prey with which human hunters had to compete for their food.

Anything else would, in fact, be surprising. If, as seems probable, humankind originated in Africa, there was time while humanoids slowly evolved into fully human populations, for surrounding life forms to adjust themselves to the risks and possibilities that human activities presented. Conversely, the extraordinary variety of human parasites that exist in Africa suggests that Africa was the principal cradle for humankind, for nowhere else did the adjustment between human and non-human forms of life achieve anything like the same biological elaboration.

What about the rest of the world, beyond the African rain forest and grasslands? Formidable humanoid hunters certainly existed in far scattered regions of the Old World, beginning perhaps as much as one and a half million years ago. Finds in China, Java, Germany attest substantial skeletal differentiation; but discoveries are too few to allow any definite connections to be made with the more abundant human and pre-human remains that have been found in Africa. Parallel evolution from some sort of ancestral primate stock in different regions of southern and southeastern Asia is possible, since the rewards for an enlarged brain, erect posture and tool-using hands were substantial even in environments less well endowed with big-game animals than the African savanna lands.

Arguing from insufficient evidence can be misleading. Archaeological study of the vast areas concerned is still sketchy, and discovery of even a single new site, like Olduvai Gorge in Africa, might alter the over-all picture profoundly. Nevertheless, what little is known seems to indicate that pre-human and proto-human populations in Eurasia lagged behind the African efflorescence of humanoid populations. This remained the situation until the rather abrupt appearance of fully modern types of human beings sharply altered pre-existing ecological balances over the entire earth beginning sometime between 100,000 and 50,000 years ago.

Evidence remains too scanty to pinpoint exactly where *Homo sapiens* first evolved. Bone fragments, whose classification as exemplifying *Homo sapiens* is debatable, date back in East Africa about 100,000 years. Elsewhere traces of fully modern types of humankind remain subsequent to 50,000 B.C. Moreover, as modern forms of *Homo sapiens* appeared, pre-existing populations, like the well-known Neanderthal of western Europe, disappeared, leaving little or no trace.[12]

Within Africa, the appearance of this eminently successful type of human population did not cause alterations as drastic as were to occur elsewhere. All the same, the extinction of a number of large game animals and of rival humanoid forms, if correctly attributable to *Homo sapiens*, demonstrates what human hunters were capable of. Far more spectacular results occurred when humanity learned how to keep warm in cold climates by domesticating fire and putting other creatures' skins and furs on their own backs.

The grand invention of clothes allowed bands of hunters to attack animal populations of northern grasslands and forests.

The consequences were analogous to what happened when our primal ancestors first came down from the trees. That is, a new, or rather a series of new, ecological niches opened before the newcomers; and as they learned to exploit the new food possibilities that their skill opened up to them, a very rapid, global transformation of ecological relationships ensued. Between about 40,000 B.C. and 10,000 B.C., human hunting groups occupied all the main land masses of the earth, except for Antarctica. Hunting bands entered Australia between 40,000 and 30,000 years ago; some 5,000 to 15,000 years later other bands managed to cross the Bering Strait from Asia and entered the Americas. Within a few thousand years, human populations expanded across the entire climatic spectrum of North and South America, reaching Tierra del Fuego about 8000 B.C.

Never before had a dominant, large-bodied species been able to spread all around the globe. Humans could accomplish this feat because they learned how to create micro-environments suitable to the survival of a tropical creature under widely varying conditions. Invention of different sorts of clothing and housing did the trick, insulating the human body from extremes of climate and assuring survival despite freezing temperatures. In other words, cultural adaptation and invention diminished the need for biological adjustment to diverse environments, thereby introducing a fundamentally disruptive, persistently changeable factor into ecological balances throughout the land masses of the entire earth.

Decisive as cultural adaptation to differing natural environments was for humankind's extraordinary expansion between 40,000 and 10,000 B.C., there was another factor of considerable importance. In leaving tropical environments behind, our ancestors also escaped many of the parasites and disease organisms to which their predecessors and tropical contemporaries were acustomed. Health and vigor improved accordingly, and multiplication of human numbers assumed a hitherto unparalleled scale.[13]

Humanity's place within the balance of nature in tropical regions differed fundamentally from what developed in temperate and Arctic climatic zones. As we have just seen, in sub-Saharan Africa humankind continued to confront biological checks that remained powerfully effective even after human hunting skills had upset the older balances of nature among large-bodied creatures. But when human communities learned to survive and flourish in temperate climes, they faced a simpler biological situation. In general, lower temperatures meant less propitious conditions for life. As a result, the forms of plants and animals adapted to temperate and northern climates were fewer in number than those that pullulated in tropical climes. Consequently a less richly articulated web of life greeted human hunters when first they burst upon the scene. Moreover, temperate ecological balances soon proved to be much more easily disrupted by human agency. The initial absence or near-absence of organisms capable of living parasitically on or inside human bodies was a passing phenomenon. In time, biologically and demographically significant diseases developed among human communities of temperate climes too, as we shall soon see. But the vulnerability of ecological balances to human manipulation remained a permanent feature of the extra-tropical scene.

Thus humankind's biological dominion in temperate climes assumed a different order of magnitude from the start. As a stranger and newcomer to temperate ecological systems, humanity was in a situation like that rabbits met when introduced into Australia. Lacking both natural predators and natural parasites in the new environment, and finding, at least to begin with, abundant food, the rabbit population of Australia grew enormously and soon began to interfere with human efforts to raise sheep. Similar swarmings of imported forms of life—pigs, cattle, horses, rats, together with a broad spectrum of plants—occurred in the Americas when Europeans first arrived as well. But these initial runaway population explosions soon created their own correctives.[14]

In a long enough time perspective, perhaps the same will be true of humankind's expansion into the diverse and novel ecological environments of the temperate world. But on the sort of time scale we are accustomed to, in which centuries and millennia rather than eons matter, ordinary biological adjustments among diverse species have not been enough to check the multiplication of humankind. The reason is that cultural rather than biological adaptations generated and sustained the entire adventure, so that, as one particular pattern of human exploitation of the environment began to encounter difficulties, thanks to exhaustion of one or another key resource, human ingenuity found new ways to live, tapping new resources, and thereby expanded our dominion over animate and inanimate nature, time and again.

Riches in the form of woolly mammoths, giant sloths, and other large and inexperienced animals that awaited human slaughter did not endure for long. Indeed, one calculation suggests that skilled and wasteful human hunters took a mere thousand years to exterminate most large-bodied game in North and South America. According to this vision of the American past, hunters gathered in large, organized groups along a moving frontier where large-bodied game could be found. Within a few years they so depleted the herds that they had to move on, ever southward, until most American species of big game had been completely destroyed.[15] Such a catastrophic pattern could of course only arise when skilled hunters collided with totally inexperienced game animals. In the Old World no such dramatic confrontation ever occurred. There, hunting skills were applied more gradually to the large-bodied herds of the North, if only because with each advance northward, the hunters had to adjust to a harsher climate and more arduous winters. In the Americas, on the contrary, the movement was from north to south, from severity to mildness. The result was a far more sudden and widespread extermination of large-bodied game than occurred in the Old World.

Subsequent discoveries of new techniques allowed people to re-enact this frontier phenomenon of easy exploitation and rapid depletion of resources over and over again. Current oil shortages outside the Middle East are only the most recent example of humanity's spendthrift ways. Yet as a result of the Stone Age occupancy of the temperate and sub-Arctic parts of the globe, humankind also entered into a far more enduring new pattern of co-existence with other forms of life—a pattern that was to play an important role in later history. Human distribution across diverse climatic zones created what may be called a parasitic gradient among the different communities that resulted. The general thinning out of the variety of life forms that took place as climates became colder and/or drier implies, after all, a diminution in the number and variety of parasitic organisms capable of afflicting human beings. Conditions for successful transfer from host to host became more difficult as temperatures (and humidity) dropped and as the seasons of warmth and sunlight shortened. The effect was to create a gradient of infection and infestation such that populations from warmer, wetter climes could travel to cooler and/or drier regions with little likelihood of encountering unfamiliar parasites, whereas infections and infestations lurking in southern and warmer or wetter lands constituted a standing threat to intruders from the cooler North or drier desert.

The gradient may be described conversely as follows: the further human populations penetrated into cold and/or dry climates, the more directly their survival depended on their ecological relations with large-bodied plants and animals. Balances with minute parasitic organisms, so important in the tropics, became comparatively insignificant.

This difference has an important corollary. Nearly all microparasites are too small to be seen with the unaided human eye, and this meant that until the invention of the microscope and other elaborate aids to human powers of observation, no one was able to understand or do much to control encounters with such organisms. Despite the intelligence which served humankind so well in dealing with things it could see and experiment with, relations with microparasites remained until the nineteenth century largely biological, that is, beyond or beneath human capacity for conscious control.

In places where microparasites were less pervasive and significant, however, intelligence could play freely upon the parameters of human life that mattered most. As long as men and women could see food and foe, they could invent new ways to cope with both; and by so doing eventually became no longer the rare predator that a hunting mode of life alone allowed. Instead human numbers proliferated into millions in landscapes where only a few thousand hunters had been able to exist. Escape from the tropical cradleland, therefore, had far-reaching implications for humanity's subsequent role within the balance of nature, giving a much wider scope to cultural invention than had been attainable within the tighter web of life from which naked humanity had originally emerged.

Obviously, local conditions were capable of distorting this general pattern. Densities of human populations, the character and quality of available water supply, food, and shelter, together with the frequency and range of contacts among individuals all could affect disease patterns significantly. Great cities were, until recently, always unhealthy, even when situated in cool or dry climates. Generally speaking, though, all such local disturbances of ecological relations have worked within a biological gradient characterized by an increase in the variety and frequency of infections as temperatures and moisture increased.[16]

While it lasted, the expansion of Paleolithic hunting bands throughout the temperate and sub-Arctic zones of the earth constituted a period of unprecedented biological success for humankind. But by the time all available hunting grounds had been occupied, the most suitable game animals in older regions had been depleted and in some cases entirely destroyed by overkill.

Depletion of big-game food resources obviously created a crisis of survival for hunters at different times in different parts of the world. Such crisis coincided with radical changes of climate associated with the retreat (since about 20,000 B.C.) of the most recent ice cap. These two factors presented human hunting communities with a series of severe environmental challenges. Wherever older ways ceased to work, the response was intensification of the search for food and experimentation with new sorts of things to eat. Exploitation of the sea marges, for example, led to the development of boats and fishing; gathering of edible seeds led other groups to develop agriculture.

Paleolithic hunters and gatherers in a rough way presumably recapitulated the experience of the earliest humanoids in their tropical cradleland. That is, once the obvious possibilities of new ecological niches had been exploited, a kind of rough equilibrium set in, whereby checks of various kinds supervened to halt the growth of human populations. What these were varied from place to place, community to community, and time to time. Nonetheless, it seems probable that outside the tropical zones where humanity had itself evolved, disease organisms were not very important. Parasites that could spread from host to host by direct bodily contact, like lice, or the spirochete of yaws, could survive in temperate climates within small and migratory hunting communities. As long as the infection acted slowly and did not incapacitate the human host too severely or too suddenly, such parasitisms could and probably did travel with hunting communities from humanity's tropical cradle-lands throughout the earth. But the array of such infections and infestations was vastly diminished from what had thriven in the tropical luxuriance of humanity's oldest habitat.

As a result, ancient hunters of the temperate zone were most probably healthy folk, despite what appear to be comparatively short life spans.[17] That they were healthy is also supported by what is known about the life of contemporary hunting peoples in Australia and the Americas. Except for formidable illnesses traceable to recent contacts with the outside world, these peoples, too, seem to have been quite free from infectious disease and from infestation by multicelled parasites.[18] Anything else would be very surprising, for there was not enough time for the slow work of biological evolution to devise organisms and patterns of transfer from host to host suitable for cool and dry conditions such as would be needed to maintain a tropical level of infection and infestation among the small and relatively isolated communities of hunters who penetrated the world's temperate and sub-Arctic climates.

Before such adjustments could affect human life, new and fateful inventions again revolutionized humanity's relationships with the environment. Food production permitted a vast and rapid increase in the number of people, and soon sustained the rise of cities and civilizations. Human populations, once concentrated into such large communities, offered potential disease organisms a rich and accessible food supply that was quite as unusual, in its way, as the big game of the African savanna had been for our remoter ancestors. Micro-organisms in their turn could expect good hunting under the new conditions created by the development of human villages, cities and civilizations. How they took advantage of the new possibilities offered by human aggregation into large communities will be the theme of the next chapter.

II

Breakthrough to History

The numerous extinctions of large-bodied game animals that began in Africa about 50,000 years ago, spread to Asia and Europe about 20,000 years ago and became especially pronounced in the Americas some 11,000 years ago must have been a severe blow to human hunters whose skills had concentrated on killing big animals.[1] Indeed, the disappearance of one species of large-bodied prey after another probably led to sharp local reductions in human numbers. It was one thing for a band to feed on a single mammoth for a week or more, and quite a different task to kill sufficient small game, day after day, to keep the same number of human beings alive. Simultaneously, climatic changes altered the balance of nature, both in northern regions along the fringes of the retreating glaciers, and in the subtropics where a northward shift of the trade winds spread desiccation across what had earlier been good hunting territory in the African Sahara and adjacent parts of western Asia.

Everywhere, therefore, ancient hunters had to readjust their habits to make fuller use of whatever they could find in changing landscapes. When large-bodied animals disappeared, other foods had to be searched out. Under these pressures, our ancestors became omnivorous again like their distant primate forebears, feeding on an expanded number of plant and animal species. In particular, the food resources of shore and sea were for the first time systematically exploited, as numerous middens of discarded mollusk shells and far less conspicuous fishbones

35

attest. Not only that; new ways of preparing food were developed. Certain groups learned, for instance, that by prolonged soaking, they could remove poisonous chemicals from olives and cassava, thus making them edible. Other vegetable matter could also be rendered more palatable or digestible by grinding, cooking, fermenting.[2]

All these palliatives were, however, soon eclipsed by the development of food production, through domestication of animals and plants. Many communities in different parts of the earth moved in this direction, with results that varied in accordance with what was available in a wild state to start from. Generally speaking, although the New World was remarkably impoverished in domesticable animals, it did have a number of useful plants, whereas the Old World offered to human ingenuity both a wide range of domesticable animals and an impressive array of potential food plants.

Details of early domestications remain unclear. One must assume a process of mutual accommodation between humanity and the various domesticable species. This involved rapid and sometimes far-reaching changes in the biological character of domesticated plants and animals as a result of both accidental and deliberate selection for particular traits. Conversely, one can assume that a radical, if rarely deliberate, selection among human beings occurred as well. Individuals who refused to submit to the laborious routines of farming, for instance, must often have failed to survive, and those who could not or would not save seed for next year's planting, and instead ate all they had, were quickly eliminated from communities that became dependent on annual crops.

Herdsmen and farmers, together with their varying array of domesticated animals and plants, fitted into the wild background of plant and animal life in different ways, depending on climate, soils and human skills (or lack thereof). Results varied markedly from village to village, field to field, and even, for that matter, within a single field.

Nevertheless, there are some general phenomena worth noting. First of all, as men made over natural landscapes by causing some animals and plants to multiply, others were displaced. The general effect was to reduce biological variety and to make local plant and animal populations more uniform. Simultaneously, food chains shortened as human action reduced the roles of rival predators and reserved an increased amount of food for the consumption of a single species: *Homo sapiens*.

Shortening natural food chains involved humankind in never-ending effort. Protecting herds and crops from animal predators was not a serious problem for skilled hunters, though it required perpetual vigilance. Protection from other men, however, was a different matter, and efforts to achieve safety from human marauders provided the chief stimulus to political organization—a process by no means completed yet.

More significant for human life, because it involved more continual effort by a larger proportion of the entire population, was the work of reducing weeds, i.e., trying to eliminate rival species competing with domesticated varieties of plants and animals for living space. Weeding by hand may indeed have been the first form of "agriculture," but human powers achieved a new range when people learned how to remodel natural environments more radically, widening the ecological niche available to their preferred crops by eliminating natural climax vegetation. Two methods proved effective: artificial flooding of land naturally dry, and mechanical alteration of soil surfaces by digging and plowing.

Flooding allowed humans to drown out the competing species. When the agricultural year could be arranged so that part of the time fields lay under water while at other times the water was allowed to run off so that the land dried out, weeds were not much of a problem. Few plant species could thrive under alternating extreme conditions of wet and dry; fewer still could survive when farmers deliberately adjusted periods of flood and drought to suit the needs of the desired crop by simply opening and closing cunningly arranged sluices. Of course, only crops that flourish under shallow water benefited by such a regime: rice above all. But other less valuable root crops can be raised in this fashion also.

The mechanical disturbance of soil by digging-stick, hoe, spade, or plow is far more familiar to Westerners, since this was the type of agriculture that established itself in the ancient Near East and spread thence to Europe. It also prevailed at the other centers of early agricultural development in the Americas and Africa. An initial phase—slash-and-burn cultivation—depended on destroying deciduous forest by girdling the trees. This allowed sunlight to flood the forest floor and sustain the growth of grains in an environment from which competing grasses were absent. This style of cultivation, however, even when supplemented by burning the dead trees and scattering ashes on the soil to renew fertility, was not stable. Air-borne seeds soon established a lush growth of thistles and similar weeds in forest clearings. Given a year or two in which to establish themselves, these intruders were fully capable of crowding out the crop. Only by moving on to start anew with a first year's weed-free crop on virgin land could the most ancient Near Eastern, Amerindian, and African farmers keep going.

These initial limitations were transcended in the ancient Near East by the invention of plowing, not long before 3000 B.C. Plowing allowed effective weed control, year in and year out, so that fields could be cultivated indefinitely. The secret was simple. By substituting animal for human muscles, the plow allowed ancient Near Eastern farmers to cultivate twice the area they needed for cropland, so that when the extra land was fallowed (i.e., plowed during the growing season so as to destroy weeds before seeds had formed), it created a suitably empty ecological niche into which next year's crop might safely move without being too severely infested by locally formidable weed species.

It is a testimony to humanity's animistic propensities that most textbooks still explain how fallowing allows the earth to restore fertility by having a rest. A moment's thought will convince anyone that whatever processes a geological weathering and consequent chemical change occur in a single season would make no noticeable difference for the following year's plant growth. To be sure, in the case of "dry farming," soil kept in a bare fallow can store moisture that would otherwise be dispersed into the air by passage of water from the soil through the roots and leafy parts of plants. In regions where deficient moisture limits crop yields, a year's fallowing can, therefore, increase fertility by letting subsoil moisture accumulate. Elsewhere, however, where moisture is not the critical limit to plant growth, the great advantage of fallowing is that it allows farmers to keep weeds at bay by interrupting their natural life cycle with the plow.

Digging (or flooding) would of course achieve similar results; but in most environments human muscles did not alone suffice to break up enough land in a year to allow a family to subsist on the crop that could be harvested from only half of the cultivated area, while the rest was fallowed. Special soils and ecological conditions did allow some exceptions. The two most significant were (1) North China, where friable and fertile loess soil permitted human populations to subsist on crops of millet without the assistance of animal strength hitched to the plow; and (2) the Americas, where the high calorie yield per acre of maize and potatoes as compared with the Old World crops like wheat, barley, and millet, led to similar results even on soils less easily tilled than the loess of China.[8]

One must admire the skill with which humankind discovered and exploited the possibilities inherent in remodeling natural landscapes in these radical ways, increasing human food supply many times over, even though it meant permanent enslavement to an unending rhythm of work. To be sure, the plow used animal strength to pull the share through the soil, and the plowman's life was generally less toilsome than the lot that fell to the rice farmer of East Asia, who used his own muscles for most of the tasks of water and soil engineering required to create and maintain paddy fields. But toil—persistent, unending, and fundamentally at odds with humankind's propensities as shaped by the hunting experience—was nevertheless the lot of all farming populations. Only so could man the farmer successfully distort natural ecological balances, shorten the food chain, magnify human consumption and multiply human numbers until what had been a relatively rare creature in the balance of nature became the dominant large-bodied species throughout the broad regions of the earth susceptible to agriculture.

The struggle with weeds (including what we may call weed animals, like weevils, rats, and mice) was conducted with the help of tools, intelligence, and experiment; and though unending, it led to a series of victories for humanity. There was, however, another side to the agriculture distortion of natural ecological balances. Shortening the food chain and multiplying a restricted number of domesticated species of plants and animals also created dense concentrations of potential food for parasites. Since most successful parasites were too small to be seen, for many centuries human intelligence could not cope very effectively with their ravages.

Prior to the dawn of modern science and the invention of the microscope, therefore, our ancestors' victories over weeds and rival large-bodied predators, remarkable as they were, met a counterforce in the extended opportunities small-bodied parasitic predators found in the altered landscapes successful farmers created. Hyperinfestation by a single or a very few species is,

indeed, a normal response to any abrupt and far-reaching alteration of natural balances in the web of life. Weed species live by
exploiting the gaps disasters create in normal ecological systems. Weeds remain rare and inconspicuous amid undisturbed
natural vegetation, but are able rapidly to occupy any niche
created by destruction of local climax cover. Since few species
are equipped to exploit such opportunities efficiently, the result
is hyperinfestation of the denuded landscape by a limited number of different kinds of weeds. Yet weeds do not prevail for
long in nature. Complex compensatory adjustments soon
manifest themselves, and in the absence of fresh "external" disturbances of a far-reaching sort, a more or less stable and variegated flora will re-establish itself, usually looking much like
what had been destroyed at the start.

But as long as human beings continued to expend effort to
alter natural landscapes and fit them for agriculture, they
prevented re-establishment of natural climax ecosystems, and
thereby kept open the door for hyperinfestation.[4] As we have
seen, when dealing with relatively large-bodied organisms that
humans could see and manipulate, observation and experiment
soon allowed early farmers to keep weeds (as well as animal
pests like mice) under control. But human intelligence
remained for thousands of years only fumblingly effective in
dealing with disease-causing micro-organisms. As a result, the
ravages of disease among crops, herds, and peoples played a
significant part in human affairs throughout historic time. In
fact, the effort to understand what happened in a way that humans could not do before modern medical discoveries made
clear some of the important patterns of disease propagation is
the *raison d'être* of this book.

So far so good. But when one seeks to descend from this
level of generalization and ask what sorts of disease arose or extended their sway in what parts of the world and at what times
and with what consequences for human life and culture, uncer-

tainty blocks any adequate answer. Even if one excludes diseases affecting crops and domestic animals, exact information is
lacking wherewith to create a history of human infections.

It is easy to see that settling down to prolonged or permanent occupancy of a single village site involved new risks of
parasitic invasion. Increased contact with human feces as they
accumulated in proximity to living quarters, for instance, could
allow a wide variety of intestinal parasites to move safely from
host to host. By contrast, a hunting band, perpetually on the
move with only a brief sojourn in any one location, would risk
little from this kind of infectious cycle. We should expect that
human populations living in sendentary communities were
therefore far more thickly infested with worms and similar parasites than their hunting predecessors or contemporaries in the
same climatic zones. Other parasitic organisms must have
found it easy to move from host to host via contaminated
water supplies. This, too, was far more likely to happen when
human communities remained in one location permanently
and had to rely on the same water sources for all household
needs year in and year out.

All the same, the small village communities characteristic of
earliest agriculture may not always have fallen prey to particularly heavy parasitic invasion. Near Eastern slash-and-burn cultivators moved from place to place several times in a lifetime;
Chinese millet farmers and Amerindian cultivators of maize,
beans, and potatoes were scattered rather thinly and lived in
small hamlets during pre-civilized times. Infections and infestations of various sorts presumably established themselves in
these communities, and, although the parasite population must
have differed from place to place, within each village or hamlet
nearly everyone probably acquired about the same assortment
of parasites in youth. Such, at any rate, is the case today among
primitive cultivators.[5] Yet such infections cannot have been a
very heavy biological burden, since they failed to inhibit

human population growth of unexampled magnitude. Within only a few hundred years, in all the historically significant regions where valuable food crops were successfully domesticated,[6] human population density became ten to twenty times greater than hunting densities had ever been in the same areas.

Insofar as early agriculture depended on irrigation, as was the case in Mesopotamia and Egypt as well as in the Indus River valley and in the Peruvian coastal region, more elaborate social controls than those ordinarily needed in a simple, more or less isolated village, were required. Planning of canals and dikes, co-operation in their maintenance, and above all, allocation of irrigation water among competing users, all invited or required some sort of authoritative leadership. Cities and civilization resulted, characterized by far wider co-ordination of effort and specialization of skills than anything village life permitted.

But irrigation farming, especially in relatively warm climates, came near to recreating the favorable conditions for the transmission of disease parasites that prevailed in tropical rain forests whence humanity's remote ancestors had presumably emerged. Abundant moisture—even more abundant than that commonly available in rain forest environments—facilitated transfer of parasites from host to host. Where suitably warm and shallow water, in which potential human hosts constantly waded about, provided a satisfactory transfer medium, parasites did not need resistant cysts, or other life forms that could withstand dry conditions for lengthy periods of time.

Ancient forms of parasitism may have differed slightly from those of today, but organic evolution moves very slowly when measured by human and historical standards. A mere five thousand years ago, therefore, parasitic forms of life exploiting the special conditions created by irrigation agriculture were probably almost identical with those that still make life difficult for modern irrigation and rice paddy farmers.

A good deal is known about these parasites. The most important of them is the blood fluke that causes schistosomiasis, a nasty, debilitating disease, affecting perhaps as many as 100 million people today. The fluke's life cycle involves mollusks and men as alternate hosts; and the organism moves from one to the other through water, in tiny free-swimming forms.[7] The infection is sometimes fatal to snails (the commonest mollusk host), but among chronically exposed human populations it peaks in childhood and persists in less acute form thereafter. As in the case of malaria, the parasitic life cycle is remarkably elaborate. The fluke has two distinct free-swimming forms that seek their respective hosts, mollusk or man as the case may be, only to undertake extraordinary migrations within the host's body after initial penetration. This complexity, as well as the chronic character of the disease it produces in its human hosts, suggests that a lengthy evolution lies behind the modern blood fluke's behavior. The parasitic pattern, like malaria, may have originated in African or Asian rain forests; but the modern distribution of the disease, being very broad,[8] does not offer any firm basis for deciding when and where it may have spread to the regions of the world where it now flourishes. Ancient Egyptian irrigators suffered from the infection as early as 1200 B.C., and probably long before then.[9] Whether ancient Sumer and Babylonia were similarly infected cannot be said for sure, though contacts between the two river valleys would make such a condition probable.[10] In distant China, too, a recently discovered and usually well-preserved corpse buried in the second century B.C. carried a complement of blood flukes and worms, even though the actual cause of death was a heart attack.[11] In view of modern experience of how swiftly the infection builds up in irrigated landscapes where human cultivators spend long hours wading in the shallows,[12] it seems probable that ancient irrigation and schistosomiasis were closely linked throughout the Old World from very early times.

Whatever the ancient distribution of schistosomiasis and

similar infections may have been, one can be sure that wherever they became widespread they tended to create a listless and debilitated peasantry, handicapped both for sustained work in the fields and digging irrigation channels, and for the no less muscularly demanding task of resisting military attack or throwing off alien political domination and economic exploitation. Lassitude and chronic malaise, in other words, of the kind induced by blood fluke and similar parasitic infections,[13] conduces to successful invasion by the only kind of large-bodied predators human beings have to fear: their own kind, armed and organized for war and conquest. Although historians are unaccustomed to thinking of state building, tax collection, and booty raids in such a context, this sort of mutual support between micro- and macroparasitism is, assuredly, a normal ecological phenomenon.

How important parasitic infection of agricultural field workers may have been in facilitating the erection of the social hierarchies of early river valley civilizations cannot be estimated very plausibly. But it seems reasonable to suspect that the despotic governments characteristic of societies dependent on irrigation agriculture may have owed something to the debilitating diseases that afflicted field workers who kept their feet wet much of the time, as well as to the technical requirements of water management and control which have hitherto been used to explain the phenomenon.[14] The plagues of Egypt, in short, may have been connected with the power of Pharaoh in ways the ancient Hebrews never thought of and modern historians have never considered.

As long as their invisibility prevented parasites from being recognized, human intelligence was quite literally blindfolded in trying to cope with the manifestations of infectious disease. Yet men did sometimes work out dietary and sanitary codes that may have reduced the risk of infection. The most familiar case is the Jewish and Moslem prohibition of pork. This appears inexplicable until one realizes that hogs were scavengers in Near Eastern villages, quite capable of eating human feces and other "unclean" material. If eaten without the most thorough cooking, their flesh was easily capable of transferring a number of parasites to human beings, as modern encounters with trichinosis attest. Nonetheless, the ancient prohibition of pork presumably rested rather on an intuitive horror of the hogs' behavior than on any sort of trial and error; and any benefit to human health that may have resulted from observing the taboo cannot be detected from available records.

Similar sentiments lay behind the expulsion of lepers[15] from ordinary society. This was another ancient Jewish rule that must have reduced exposure to disease transmitted by skin-to-skin contact. Washing, whether in water or with sand, plays a prominent part in Moslem as well as Hindu ritual; and that, too, may sometimes have had the effect of checking the spread of infections.

On the other hand, ceremonial bathing shared by thousands of pilgrims gathered to celebrate some holy festival offers human parasites a specially favorable chance to find new hosts. In Yemen, for example, ablution pools attached to a mosque were found to harbor snails infected with schistosomiasis[16]; and in India the propagation of cholera was (and is) largely a function of religious pilgrimage.[17] Traditional rules even when sanctified by religion and immemorial practice were not, therefore, always effective in checking the propagation of diseases; and practices that actually conduced to their spread could and did become just as holy as other rules that had positive health value.

It was, of course, not merely worms and other multicelled parasites that found conditions created by agriculture propitious for their spread among humankind. Protozoan, bacterial, and viral infections also had an expanded field for their propagation as flocks, crops, and human populations all multiplied.

Effects were characteristically indirect, unforeseen and unforeseeable; and save in rare instances it is impossible to reconstruct all the circumstances that may have allowed a new disease pattern to assert itself.

There are, however, some exceptions. In western Africa, for instance, when agriculture began to spread into rain forest environments, slash-and-burn methods of cultivation clearly put new strains on older ecological balances. An unexpected result was to give malaria a new, epidemic intensity. What seems to have happened is this: clearings multiplied breeding places for a kind of mosquito, *Anopheles gambiae*, that feeds by preference on human blood. Indeed, *Anopheles gambiae* can properly be described as a weed species that proliferates enormously in the gashes human agriculture creates in the African rain forest. With the advance of agriculture, it supplants other mosquito species accustomed to feeding on creatures other than man. As a result, the man-mosquito malarial cycle attains an unexampled intensity, affecting practically every human being who ventures into these forest clearings.[18]

African cultivators were nevertheless able to persist in their effort to tame the rain forest for agriculture; not, however, without genetic adaptation whereby the frequency of a gene that produces sickle-shaped red corpuscles in heterozygous individuals increased markedly. Such cells are less hospitable to the malarial plasmodium than normal red blood cells. Consequently, the debilitating effects of malarial infection are reduced in individuals who have this kind of red corpuscle.

But the cost of such protection was very high. Individuals who inherit the sickling gene from both parents die young. Resulting heavy child mortality is further increased by the fact that those born entirely without the sickling gene are liable to lethal malarial infection. Indeed, in the most intensively malarial regions of West Africa, half the infants born among populations bearing the sickle-cell trait are biologically vulnerable.

Since the agricultural penetration of the rain forest is still in process, the contemporary distribution of malaria, *Anopheles gambiae* and the sickling trait permit a plausible reconstruction of the unusually drastic consequences the alteration of older ecological patterns entailed, and continues to entail, in that environment.[19]

In central and eastern Africa, events in the nineteenth and twentieth centuries connected with ill-conceived efforts by European colonial administrators to alter traditional patterns of herding and cultivation also illustrate the unexpected side effects that sometimes arise from agricultural expansions into new regions. These efforts, in fact, precipitated veritable epidemics of sleeping sickness in parts of Uganda, the Belgian Congo, Tanganyika, Rhodesia, and Nigeria; and the end result, as colonial regimes came to an end, was a land more thickly infested with death-dealing tsetse flies than before government policy set out to utilize what looked like good agricultural land more effectively.[20]

Obviously human attempts to shorten the food chain within the toughest and most variegated of all natural ecosystems of the earth, the tropical rain forests and adjacent savanna regions of Africa, are still imperfectly successful, and continue to involve exceptionally high costs in the form of exposure to disease. That, more than anything else, is why Africa remained backward in the development of civilization when compared to temperate lands (or tropical zones like those of the Americas), where prevailing ecosystems were less elaborated and correspondingly less inimical to simplification by human action.

Ecosystems in the regions of the earth where early and historically important agricultural societies first developed were all intrinsically less resistant to human alteration than in tropical Africa. In temperate zones, fewer and less formidable parasites lay in wait to take advantage of any notable increase in human numbers. But because the major breakthrough and principal alterations of natural balances took place five to ten thousand years ago, it is no longer possible to infer or observe, as one still can do in Africa, the disease costs which particular agricultural inventions and territorial expansion may have involved.

We can, nevertheless, infer one important general alteration in disease exposure that came, sooner or later, to all civilized communities. Eventually agricultural populations became dense enough to sustain bacterial and viral infections indefinitely, even without benefit of an intermediate non-human host. This cannot ordinarily happen in small communities, since unlike multicelled parasites, bacterial and viral invasions provoke immunity reactions within the human body. Immunity reactions impose drastic alternatives upon the host-parasite relationship. Whenever they dominate the interaction of host and parasite, either speedy death of the infected person or full recovery and banishment of the invading organism from the host's body tissues ensues—at least for a period of time of months or years until the immunizing antibodies fade from the bloodstream so as to permit reinfection.

As usual in biology, things are not quite so simple as such a statement implies. Individual resistance to infection is not simply and solely a matter of the formation of antibodies. In some cases, moreover, even infections that do provoke antibodies may linger on for years or even throughout a lifetime. Individual "carriers," like the famous "Typhoid Mary," may harbor a disease organism indefinitely and experience no very noticeable ill effects themselves while communicating the infection to others with drastic, even fatal, results. In still other cases, an infection may become "latent," that is, withdraw to some region of the host's body and hide there for lengthy periods of time.

One of the most remarkable patterns of latency allows the chicken pox virus to disappear for as much as fifty years, by retreating into the tissues of the efferent nerves, only to reappear as an affliction of the elderly known as shingles. In this way, the virus neatly solves the problem of maintaining an unbroken chain of infection within a small human community. Even if every available human host gets the chicken pox and develops immunity so that the disease disappears, still, decades later, when a new generation of susceptible human beings has had time to come into existence, the infection can recur, creeping down the efferent nerve paths to the skin of an elderly member of the community, and there manifesting itself as shingles. Transferred to a new host, however, the virus provokes the familiar childhood symptoms of chicken pox. Both the mildness of the disease for most people and the remarkable latency pattern it exhibits suggest that this is an old viral infection among humankind. In this respect chicken pox is unlike the other common childhood diseases of modern times.[21]

Diseases that lack such a technique of survival and yet confront the drastic alternatives created by antibody reactions within the host's body have to rely on numbers for their survival. Numbers, that is, of potential hosts, among whom, if the total size of the community is sufficient, there will always be someone who has not yet had the disease and therefore remains susceptible to infection. Such parasites, are, in all probability, rank newcomers in the time scale of biological evolution, even if ancient and immemorial on the time scale of human history. Only in communities of several thousand persons, where encounters with others attain sufficient frequency to allow infection to spread unceasingly from one individual to another, can such diseases persist. These communities are what we call civilized: large, complexly organized, densely populated, and without exception directed and dominated by cities. Infectious bacterial and viral diseases that pass directly from human to human with no intermediate host are therefore the diseases of civilization par excellence: the peculiar hallmark and epidemiological burden of cities and of countryside in contact with cities. They are familiar to almost all contemporary humankind as the ordinary diseases of childhood: measles, mumps, whooping cough, smallpox, and the rest.[22]

Contemporary global diffusion of childhood diseases required several thousand years to establish itself, and a good part of the subject matter of this book will be a consideration of critical thresholds in that diffusion process. Moreover, one must suppose that the initial establishment of these diseases (or of infections ancestral to those we know today) was itself a gradual process, involving numerous false starts and lethal encounters in which either the human hosts or the invading parasite died out locally, and thus broke off the chain of infection before it could become a normal, endemic, more or less stable element in the biological balances of civilized human life.

Most and probably all of the distinctive infectious diseases of civilization transferred to human populations from animal herds. Contacts were closest with the domesticated species, so it is not surprising to find that many of our common infectious diseases have recognizable affinities with one or another disease afflicting domesticated animals. Measles, for example, is probably related to rinderpest and/or canine distemper; smallpox is certainly connected closely with cowpox and with a cluster of other animal infections; influenza is shared by humans and hogs.[23] Indeed, according to a standard handbook,[24] diseases human populations share today with domestic animals number as follows:

Poultry	26
Rats and mice	32
Horse	35
Pig	42
Sheep and goats	46
Cattle	50
Dog	65

There are many overlaps in this tabulation, since a single infection often afflicts several animal species as well as humans. Moreover, because some infections are rare while others occur commonly, a mere listing of the variety is not very significant. Nevertheless, the number of overlaps does suggest how ramified our disease relations with domesticated animals have become. It also appears obvious that the sharing of infection increases with the degree of intimacy that prevails between man and beast.

In addition to diseases derived from or shared with domesticated animals, human populations may become diseased by intruding upon one or another disease cycle established among wild animals. Bubonic plague, at home among burrowing rodents, yellow fever at home among monkeys, and rabies at home among bats are examples of the more lethal of such infections.[25]

Novel transfers of parasites from one host to another have not ceased to occur, and even in recent times such events have sometimes had abrupt and drastic consequences. Rinderpest invaded Africa in 1891, for instance, where it killed off very large numbers of domesticated cattle as well as antelope and other wild species; but its ravages were so severe and sudden —up to 90 per cent die-off occurred—that the disease did not establish itself as an endemic.[26] Instead, it disappeared after a few years, presumably from lack of susceptible surviving populations of ungulates to infect. In 1959 a new human disease, called O'nyong nyong fever, appeared in Uganda, probably as a result of the transfer of a virus from monkeys. The disease spread rapidly and widely, but in this case its effects upon human beings were mild, and recovery (with the development of suitable immunity) came quickly. As a result, O'nyong nyong fever, like rinderpest among African antelopes, failed to establish itself as an endemic human infection. Instead, it disappeared as mysteriously as it had come, presumably by retreating back into the treetops, where it was properly at home.[27] A decade later, in 1969, another fever, far more lethal than the Ugandan outbreak, manifested itself in Nigeria. Termed Lassa fever from the hospital station where it was first noticed by western-trained doctors, the new disease was eventually (by 1973) traced back to rodents, the normal hosts for the parasite in question. Appropriate preventive measures were thereupon taken to check further spread of the disease.[28]

As human numbers increased in particular regions of the earth with the domestication of both plants and new species of animals, we must therefore imagine a long series of episodes like these. Infections must have been transferred repeatedly to humankind from animal reservoirs, and particularly from the domesticated species with which human populations began to have extended and intimate contacts. Such infections can, of course, run multilaterally. Human beings, for example, can sometimes infect their domesticated animals. Likewise, infections can be exchanged between domesticated herds and wild populations, both within and across species lines, as chance contacts and the susceptibility of potential hosts dictate.

In other words, disease-producing parasites were quite as successful as people in taking advantage of new opportunities for occupying novel ecological niches that opened up as a result of human actions that distorted natural patterns of plant and animal distribution. Human success meant larger numbers of fewer kinds of plants and animals: an improved feeding ground, therefore, for parasites able to flourish by invading a single species, even if, as was true for almost all viral and most bacterial infections, the invading organisms could only flourish for a few days or weeks before antibodies blocked their continuance within any one individual host's body.

Before proceeding further with disease history, it is worth pointing out the parallels between the microparasitism of infectious disease and the macroparasitism of military operations.

Only when civilized communities had built up a certain level of wealth and skill did war and raiding become an economically viable enterprise. But seizing the harvest by force, if it led to speedy death of the agricultural work force from starvation, was an unstable form of macroparasitism. Nevertheless such events happened often enough, and deserve to be compared with parasitic invasions like the African rinderpest of 1891 that also destroyed the hosts in such numbers as to inhibit the establishment of any stable, ongoing infectious pattern.

Very early in civilized history, successful raiders became conquerors, i.e., learned how to rob agriculturalists in such a way as to take from them some but not all of the harvest. By trial and error a balance could and did arise, whereby cultivators could survive such predation by producing more grain and other crops than were needed for their own maintenance. Such surpluses may be viewed as the antibodies appropriate to human macroparasitism. A successful government immunizes those who pay rent and taxes against catastrophic raids and foreign invasion in the same way that a low-grade infection can immunize its host against lethally disastrous disease invasion. Disease immunity arises by stimulating the formation of antibodies and raising other physiological defenses to a heightened level of activity; governments improve immunity to foreign macroparasitism by stimulating surplus production of food and raw materials sufficient to support specialists in violence in suitably large numbers and with appropriate weaponry. Both defense reactions constitute burdens on the host populations, but a burden less onerous than periodic exposure to sudden lethal disaster.

The result of establishing successful governments is to create a vastly more formidable society vis-à-vis other human communities. Specialists in violence can scarcely fail to prevail against men who have to spend most of their time producing or finding food. And as we shall soon see, a suitably diseased so-

54

ciety, in which endemic forms of viral and bacterial infection continually provoke antibody formation by invading susceptible individuals unceasingly, is also vastly more formidable from an epidemiological point of view vis-à-vis simpler and healthier human societies. Macroparasitism leading to the development of powerful military and political organization therefore has its counterpart in the biological defenses human populations create when exposed to the microparasitism of bacteria and viruses. In other words, warfare and disease are connected by more than rhetoric and the pestilences that have so often marched with and in the wake of armies.[29]

Initially, most transfers of bacterial and viral parasitism were probably unstable, in the same way that the recent careers of rinderpest and O'nyong nyong fever in Africa were unstable. Many times, we may imagine, human populations were sharply cut back by some new, localized epidemic. Over and over again the exhaustion of available and susceptible human hosts must have driven invading disease organisms from new grazing grounds in the tissues of early farming folk. Even so, a ready basis for reinfection remained because in all probability domesticated animals were already chronic bearers of viral and bacterial infections capable of invading and reinvading people.

The reason for supposing that such animals as cattle, horses, and sheep may have been chronic bearers of infection can be traced to the condition of their natural existence in the wild. They were gregarious, and pastured on the grasslands of Eurasia in vast herds long before human hunters became numerous enough to make much difference in their lives. Constituting large populations of a single species, they provided exactly the condition required to allow bacterial and viral infection to become endemic, since in a sufficiently large population there is always another susceptible and available host to perpetuate the chain of infection. Indeed, the evolution of herds and parasites was presumably lengthy enough for reasonably stable biological balances to arise. Hence, a number of viral and bacterial infections probably became rife among wild herds of cattle, sheep and horses without provoking more than mild symptoms. Such infections were presumably "childhood diseases" of the herds, affecting susceptible young beasts endlessly but almost harmlessly. Transferred to human populations, however, such infectious organisms must have usually become virulent, since initially human bodies lacked any acquired immunities to the new invaders, whereas any substantial population of their accustomed hosts would enjoy at least partial protection from the start.[30]

Eventually, however, and at different times in different places, we must assume that various viral and bacterial parasites successfully transferred to human populations, and established an ongoing relationship with their new hosts. Rapid and semi-catastrophic initial adjustments were undoubtedly required in many, perhaps in all, cases. Heavy die-off of hosts and of disease organisms may have occurred repeatedly until the development of acquired immunities in the new host population and adaptations on the part of the parasite permitted the infection to become endemic. There seem to be no good examples of such a process taking place among human populations in modern times, but the fate of rabbits in Australia when exposed to an exceedingly virulent new infection may be used to illustrate the manner in which a virus infection acts when it penetrates a new population and then survives to become endemic.

The story is indeed dramatic. English settlers introduced rabbits to Australia in 1859. In the absence of natural predators, the new species spread rapidly throughout the continent becoming very numerous and, from the human point of view, a pest that ate grass that sheep might have otherwise consumed. The Australian wool pack was thereby reduced; so were the profits of innumerable ranchers. Human efforts to reduce the number of rabbits in Australia took a new turn in 1950 when the virus of myxomatosis (a distant relative of human small-pox) was successfully transferred to the rabbit population of that continent. The initial impact was explosive: in a single season an area as great as all of western Europe was infected. The death rate among rabbits that got the disease in the first year was 99.8 per cent. In the next year, however, the death rate went down to a mere 90 per cent; seven years later mortality among infected rabbits was only 25 per cent. Obviously, very rigorous and rapid selection had occurred among rabbits and among viral strains as well. Samples of the virus derived from wild rabbits became measurably milder in virulence with each successive year. Despite this fact, rabbit population has not recovered its former level in Australia and may not do so for a long time—perhaps never. In 1965 only about one fifth as many rabbits lived in Australia as had been there before myxomatosis struck.[31]

Before 1950 myxomatosis was a well-established disease among rabbits in Brazil. The virus provoked only mild symptoms among the wild-rabbit population of that country and exhibited a comparatively stable pattern of endemic incidence. It might be supposed, therefore, that the adaptation involved in transfer from Brazilian to Australian rabbits was less than the adaptation required for a parasite from some different host species to *Homo sapiens*. But this is not really the case, since despite their common name the rabbits of the Americas are of a different genus from those of Europe and Australia. Hence the shift to a new host that took place in 1950 under the eyes of experts resembled the presumed pattern whereby important human diseases once broke away from an animal host species and began to infect humankind.

Whether or not a new disease begins as lethally as myxomatosis did, the process of mutual accommodation between host and parasite is fundamentally the same. A stable new disease pattern can arise only when both parties manage to survive

57

their initial encounter and, by suitable biological and cultural[32] adjustments, arrive at a mutually tolerable arrangement. In all such processes of adjustment, bacteria and viruses have the advantage of a much shorter time between generations. Genetic mutations that facilitate the propagation of a disease organism safely from host to host are consequently able to establish themselves much more rapidly than any comparable alterations of human genetic endowment or bodily traits can occur. Indeed, as we shall see in a later chapter, historical experience of later ages suggests that something like 120 to 150 years are needed for human populations to stabilize their response to drastic new infections.[33]

By way of comparison, the nadir of the rabbit population in Australia occurred in 1953, three years after the initial outbreak of myxomatosis. Given the brevity of rabbit generations—observed as six to ten months from birth to parenthood in Australia[34]—this three-year span was equivalent to 90 to 150 years on a human scale, if we calculate a human generation to be 25 years. In other words, comparable generational time may be needed for humans and for rabbits to adjust to an initially lethal new disease.

The entire process of adjustment between host and parasite may be conceived as a series of wavelike disturbances to pre-existing biological equilibria. The initial disturbance is likely to be drastic, as happened among Australian rabbits in 1950. In many cases, transfer of parasitism to a new host species is too drastic to persist very long. Assuming, however, that the new infection is able to survive indefinitely, a fluctuating balance then asserts itself, with periods of unusual frequency of infection alternating with periods when the disease wanes and may almost disappear. These fluctuations tend to stabilize themselves into more or less regular cycles—that is, as long as some new major intrusion from "outside" does not alter the emerging equilibrium pattern between host and parasite. A multitude of factors enters into any such cyclic equilibrium. Seasonal changes in temperatures and moisture, for instance, tend to concentrate childhood diseases in modern cities of the temperate zone in spring months.

The number of susceptible persons in a population is also fundamental, as are the ways in which they congregate or remain apart. School and military service, for example, have been the two most significant ways susceptible youth congregate in modern times. Any parent can attest the role of primary schools in propagating childhood diseases in contemporary western societies: in the nineteenth century, before inoculations became standard, draftees into the French army from the countryside suffered—sometimes seriously—from infectious disease to which their city-bred contemporaries were almost immune, having already been exposed. As a result, robust peasant sons had a far higher death rate in the army than did undernourished weaklings drafted from urban slums.[35]

The size of dose required to infect a new host, the length of time during which the infection may be transferred from one person to another, modes of such transfer, and customs affecting opportunities for exchanging infections, all play roles in determining how many get sick and when. Not infrequently a disease requires a massive, megalopolitan concentration of human hosts to survive indefinitely. In such a population the chance of encountering enough susceptible new hosts so as to keep a chain of infection going is obviously greater than when potential hosts are scattered thinly across a rural landscape. Yet when enough susceptible persons exist in rural communities, such a disease can sally forth from its urban focus and run like a terrifying brushfire from village to village, household to household. Such outbreaks, however, fade away as rapidly as they arise. As the local supply of susceptible hosts runs out, the infection dies and disappears, except in the urban center whence it had initially emerged. There, enough susceptibles will remain for the infectious organism to keep itself alive until disease-inexperienced individuals again accumulate in the rural landscape and another epidemic flare-up becomes a possibility.

All these complex factors sometimes shake down to relatively simple over-all patterns of incidence. Careful statistical study of the way measles propagates itself in modern urban communities shows a wave pattern cresting in periods of time just under two years. Moreover, it has recently been demonstrated that to keep this pattern going, measles requires a population with at least 7,000 susceptible individuals perpetually in its ranks. Given modern birth rates, urban patterns of life and the custom of sending children to school, where measles can spread very rapidly through a class of youngsters meeting the virus for the first time, it turns out that the minimal population needed to keep measles going in a modern city is about half a million. By scattering out across a rural landscape, a smaller population suffices to sustain the chain of measles infection. The critical threshold below which the virus cannot survive falls between 300,000 and 400,000 persons. This can be demonstrated by the way the measles infection behaves among island populations ranking above and below this critical mass.[36]

No other disease current in our own time exhibits so precise a pattern, and none, probably, requires such large human communities for its survival. Comparably exact studies for other common childhood diseases have not been made, largely because artificial immunization procedures have altered patterns of infection in far-reaching ways in all modern countries. Yet notable changes in virulence as well as in the frequency of the most common childhood diseases have occurred as recently as the nineteenth century, when European governments first started to collect statistics on the incidence of separate infectious diseases. In other words, the adjustment between the disease-causing organisms and their human hosts was (and is) still evolving very rapidly, in response to the altering circumstances and conditions of human life.

Searching historic records for evidence of when and where the ancestors of our modern childhood diseases first invaded human populations can be quite frustrating. First of all, ancient medical terminology cannot easily be fitted to modern classifications of disease. Symptoms alter, and undoubtedly have altered, so much as to be unrecognizable. At first onset, a new disease often exhibits symptoms that later disappear when the host population in question has had time to develop resistance.

The fulminating symptoms that syphilis initially exhibited in Europe is a familiar example of this phenomenon from the past. Similar episodes can be observed today whenever a new disease invades a previously isolated community for the first time. Symptoms can, indeed, be such that they completely disguise the nature of the disease from all but expert bacteriological analysis. Thus, for example, when tuberculosis first arrived among a tribe of Canadian Indians, the infection attacked organs of their bodies which remained unaffected among whites. Symptoms—meningitis and the like—were far more dramatic, and the progress of the disease was far more rapid, than anything associated with tuberculosis infections among previously exposed populations. In its initial manifestations, only microscopic analysis allowed doctors to recognize the disease as tuberculous. By the third generation, however, the tuberculosis infection tended to concentrate in the lungs, as mutual accommodation between hosts and parasites began to approximate the familiar urban pattern.[37]

The process of adaptation between host and parasite is so rapid and changeable that we must assume that patterns of infection prevailing now are only the current manifestations of diseases that have in fact altered their behavior in far-reaching ways during historic times. Yet in view of the figure of half a million needed to keep measles in circulation in modern urban communities, it is noteworthy that a recent estimate of the total population of the seat of the world's oldest civilization in ancient Sumeria comes out to exactly the same figure.[38] It seems safe to assume that the Sumerian cities were in close enough contact with one another to constitute a single disease pool; and if so, massed numbers, approaching half a million, surely constituted a population capable of sustaining infectious chains like those of modern childhood diseases. In subsequent centuries, as other parts of the world also became the seats of urban civilizations, ongoing infectious chains became possible elsewhere. First here, then there, one or another disease organism presumably invaded available human hosts and made good its lodgment in the niche increasing human density had opened for it.

Person to person, "civilized" types of infectious disease could not have established themselves much before 3000 B.C. When they did get going, however, different infections established themselves among different civilized communities in Eurasia. Proof of this fact is that when communications between previously isolated civilized communities became regular and organized, just before and after the Christian era, devastating infections soon spread from one civilization to another, with consequences for human life analogous to, though less drastic than, what happened to rabbits in Australia after 1950.

Closer consideration of these events will be reserved for the next chapter. Here it seems only needful to reflect briefly about the general historical consequences of the establishment of these distinctively civilized sorts of diseases in a few centers of unusually dense human population between 3000 and 500 B.C.

First and most obvious: patterns of human reproduction had to adjust to the systematic loss of population that resulted from exposure to diseases that flourished under civilized conditions. Until very recently cities were unable to maintain their numbers without a substantial inflow of migrants from surrounding countrysides. Urban health hazards were simply too great, for, in addition to infectious person-to-person diseases transmitted as childhood diseases usually are—by breathing in droplets of infectious matter sneezed or coughed into the atmosphere—ancient cities suffered from an intensified circulation of diseases transmitted through contaminated water supplies, plus a full array of insect-borne infections. Any breakdown of transportation bringing food from afar threatened famine, and local crop failures were often difficult to compensate for. In view of all this it is not surprising that cities could not maintain themselves demographically, but had to depend on migrants from the countryside to replenish the losses arising from famine, epidemic, and endemic diseases.

A civilized pattern of life therefore required rural cultivators not only to produce more food than they themselves consumed in order to feed urban dwellers, but also to produce a surplus of children whose migration into town was needed to sustain urban numbers. Rural reproductive surpluses had also to be capable of bearing losses resulting from macroparasitism, i.e., from war and raiding, and from the famine such activities nearly always provoked. Only occasionally and for limited periods of time was anything like a stable balance attained between rural birth rates and occupational niches available in urban contexts for the surplus from the countryside. Open and accessible frontiers—so important for European history in the past four centuries—were also unusual, though when land was available, surplus rural population could and did migrate to the frontier and thereby enlarge the agricultural base of the society instead of trying the risky (though to a few, spectacularly rewarding) path of migration into town.

Until after 1650, when population statistics begin to assume a degree of reliability, it seems impossible even to guess at the magnitudes involved in this pattern of population flow. Nevertheless, such patterns clearly asserted themselves from the time cities first formed. The striking way, for example, in which Sumerian-speakers gave way to Semitic-speakers in ancient Mesopotamia during the third millennium B.C.[39] is probably a direct consequence of this kind of population movement. Speakers of Semitic tongues presumably migrated into Sumerian cities in such numbers that they swamped speakers of the older language. Sumerian lingered on as a language of learning and priestcraft, but for everyday purposes, the Semitic Akkadian took over. This linguistic shift might have resulted from a spurt of urban growth, or more likely from an unusually heavy die-off of established urban populations because of disease, war or famine, although which of these factors or combination of factors may have been at work in ancient Sumer is not known.

A nineteenth-century parallel may be useful. From the 1830s and especially after 1850, rapid urban growth together with the ravages of a new disease, cholera, disrupted cultural patterns of long standing in the Hapsburg monarchy.[40] Peasant migrants into the towns of Bohemia and Hungary had long been accustomed to learn German, and in a few generations their descendants became German in sentiment as well as in language. This process began to falter in the nineteenth century. When the number of Slav- and Magyar-speaking migrants living in the cities of the monarchy passed a certain point, newcomers no longer had to learn German for everyday life. Presently nationalist ideals took root and made a German identity seem unpatriotic. The result was that Prague became a Czech- and Budapest a Magyar-speaking city within half a century.

Early civilizations that were linguistically more uniform obviously did not register the process of migration into town by linguistic change as ancient Mesopotamia and the nineteenth-century Hapsburg monarchy did. Nonetheless, the reality of urban population wastage in very ancient as well as in more recent times cannot be doubted. The mere existence of cities and the intensified patterns of disease circulation they created must have led to this result, with only as much delay as was needed for disease organisms to discover and work themselves into the enriched environment urbanized humanity presented for their nutriment.

How the flow of surplus population from the countryside was provoked and sustained is not at all clear. To be sure, the country was often healthier, since various forms of infection rife in cities were less likely to reach rural dwellers. On the other hand, when an epidemic did penetrate the countryside it could have more drastic consequences than were likely among an already diseased and therefore partially immune urban population. Moreover, many peasantries were chronically undernourished and therefore especially vulnerable to any infection that happened along. Clearly, peasantries subjected to civilized control did not automatically find it easy to raise more children than were needed to keep the family operation going, any more than they found it easy to produce more food than they themselves required for survival.

Yet universally they accomplished both of these tasks. Civilizations could not have persisted without a flow of migrants as well as a flow of food from countryside to city. It is, therefore, altogether probable that moral codes encouraging a high rural birth rate were a necessary underpinning for civilized patterns of society. At any rate, the various means by which hunting and gathering communities regulated their numbers have not prevailed among civilized peasantries. Instead, in most if not all peasant societies, early marriage and a long string of children has been regarded as a sign of moral excellence and divine favor, as well as the best of all possible assurances against a helpless old age, since if one child should die another can still take on the responsibility for looking after the old folks when they are no longer able to support themselves. These attitudes were also connected with recognition of individual and familial property rights to land. Such rights were often, in turn, defined or reinforced by governmental policy with respect to rent and taxes.

Exactly how cultural, social, and biological factors acted and reacted upon each other, however, is impossible to tell. All we can be sure of is that successful civilizations all managed to assure a flow of persons as well as of goods from the countryside into the cities, and they did so through combining the sanctions of religion, law and custom.

As will be readily appreciated in our age of explosive population growth, the civilized reproductive norm ran the risk of provoking acute rural overpopulation. Any prolonged slackening of career opportunities for the peasant surplus—in cities, armies, or by emigration to some frontier region—soon had the effect of ponding excess population back in villages. To forestall rural overpopulation, alternative careers had to involve high death rates, yet without deterring large numbers of men and women from accepting the risks involved, whether they did so voluntarily or involuntarily, knowingly or in ignorance, of the probable upshot of leaving home.

To keep a stable demographic balance under such circumstances was and is exceedingly difficult. Urban and military die-off must match rural growth rates, and the whole community must simultaneously succeed in defending itself against "outside" invasion so massive as to upset its internal demographic pattern.

A genuinely stable macroparasitic pattern conforming to these specifications has rarely existed for long in any part of the world. Instead, civilized history has characteristically exhibited sharp fluctuations up and down, as periods of peace and prosperity induced population growth in excess of macroparasitic powers of absorption (i.e., destruction); whereupon an increase in death rates asserted itself through the breakdown of public order. Peasant revolt, civil war, foreign raid and rapine, together with accompanying intensification of famine and disease, could always be counted on to reduce populations catastrophically whenever less drastic regulators of peasant numbers failed to maintain a satisfactory balance.

Characteristically, heightened death rates would cut back peasant numbers far below previous levels before successful political consolidation would again allow rural population growth to assert itself. Obviously, "outside" invasions—whether by disease organisms or by armed men—were capable of interrupting such cycles; so could unusual climatic conditions that resulted in heavy crop losses. Indeed, in most of the civilized world such "outside" factors were so powerful and so frequent as to mask any close correlation between the oscillation of peasant numbers and the level of public peace. Only in China, where external political-military forces were weaker because geographic barriers insulated the civilized human mass from important foreign pressures most of the time, did this cycle manifest itself unmistakably; though even there, extraneous factors were never entirely absent and sometimes held back population recovery for centuries at a time.

Civilized societies had another way of consuming surplus population from the countryside. By mounting attacks on neighboring regions, kings and armies were sometimes able to expand the territories under their control and open frontier lands for their subjects to settle and exploit. Such enterprises, indeed, offered an all but infallible solution to any danger of overpopulation at home, since a notable increase in the number of deaths could always be expected from wars of conquest, whether they were successful or not.

Trade, too, sometimes allowed the support of otherwise surplus population. Until recent centuries, however, the cost of transportation overland was so high that significant numbers of people could prosper through trade only by locating themselves near the sea or along navigable rivers. Nevertheless, from the earliest days of civilization ships could and did bring food and other useful commodities from afar to a number of ports. By exchanging manufactures and other goods for food and raw materials, civilized merchants and seamen could engage in mutually advantageous trade with foreigners. But it was as difficult to maintain trade balances in a steady state as it was to maintain a stable demographic balance within a single political community. Hence, sharply alternating expansion and contraction was the rule in trade as well as in politics and war.

With such multiple instabilities built in, it seems clear that civilized society has not yet attained anything like a well-adjusted ecological balance on the macroparasitic level. Like a disease invading an inexperienced host population, the incidence of civilized forms of macroparasitism have fluctuated sharply through recorded history—sometimes killing off excessive numbers of the peasants and other workers who sustained the system by their labor, and at other times failing to hold the number of mouths at a figure to match available food.

Despite innumerable local setbacks, however, the areas subject to civilized patterns of organization did tend to increase across the centuries. Yet the number of discrete civilizations always remained modest, though whether one counts a total of half a dozen or two dozen depends on the criteria used to distinguish one style of civilized life from another. Such small numbers reflect the fact that civilizations do not characteristically expand by stimulating the elaboration of pre-existing local institutions, ideas, and skills to new heights of sophistication. Instead, civilizations regularly export key cultural elements from an already elaborated center onto new ground. Often, perhaps always, it was easier to borrow and imitate than to create anew. There was, however, another factor in the situation that goes far to explain the comparative ease with which civilized societies expanded into new territories, one that was a result not of conscious policies or of macroparasitic patterns, but of the dynamics of microparasitism. A moment's reflection will show what these were.

When civilized societies learned to live with the "childhood diseases" that can only persist among large human populations, they acquired a very potent biological weapon. It came into play whenever new contacts with previously isolated, smaller human groups occurred. Civilized diseases when let loose among a population that lacked any prior exposure to the germ in question quickly assumed drastic proportions, killing off old and young alike instead of remaining a perhaps serious, but still tolerable, disease affecting small children.[41]

The disruptive effect of such an epidemic is likely to be greater than the mere loss of life, severe as that may be. Often survivors are demoralized, and lose all faith in inherited custom and belief which had not prepared them for such a disaster. Sometimes new infections actually manifest their greatest virulence among young adults, owing, some doctors believe, to excessive vigor of this age-group's antibody reactions to the invading disease organism.[42] Population losses within the twenty-to-forty age bracket are obviously far more damaging to society at large than comparably numerous destruction of either the very young or the very old. Indeed, any community that loses a substantial percentage of its young adults in a single epidemic finds it hard to maintain itself materially and spiritually. When an initial exposure to one civilized infection is swiftly followed by similarly destructive exposure to others, the structural cohesion of the community is almost certain to collapse. In the early millennia of civilized history, the result was sporadically to create a fringe of half-empty land on the margins of civilized societies. Simple folk brought into contact with urban populations always risked demoralizing and destructive disease encounters. Survivors were often in no position to offer serious resistance to thoroughgoing incorporation into the civilized body politic.

To be sure, warfare characteristically mingled with and masked this epidemiological process. Trade, which was imperfectly distinct from warlike raiding, was another normal way for civilized folk to probe new lands. And since war and trade relations have often entered civilized records, whereas epidemics among illiterate and helpless border folk have not, historians have hitherto failed to take anything like adequate notice of the biological weapon urban conditions of life implanted in the bloodstreams of civilized peoples. Absence of documentation should not, however, deter us from recognizing the force of the epidemiological superiority civilized conditions of life created among those who had survived the local mix of childhood diseases.

Nonetheless, even when local populations had been decimated and demoralized by exposure to one or more diseases of civilization, effective obstacles to civilized encroachment on neighboring territory sometimes remained. If the land was too dry, too cold, too wet or too hilly for the agricultural methods familiar to the civilized community, then settlement was inhibited, and local peoples might have a chance to recover biologically, or be reinforced by some other population filtering in from more distant regions. If contacts became chronic between a civilized center and such a border zone, repeated exposure would deprive civilized diseases of most of their terrors. Occasional disasters might still occur in these borderlands if a new form of infection appeared, if human density increased to a point at which new patterns of disease propagation could sustain themselves, or if too long a period of time elapsed between exposures to forms of infection whose permanent hearth remained in the cities of civilization.

But when no geographic or climatic barrier prevented the established methods of civilized cultivation from spreading into borderlands, peoples shattered by exposure to novel diseases were unlikely to be able to resist further encroachment. The process, in fact, resembles ordinary animal digestion rather closely. First, the structural organization of neighboring communities was broken down by a combination of war (cf. mastication) and disease (cf. the chemical and physical action of stomach and intestines). Sometimes, no doubt, a local population suffered total extinction, but this was not typical. More often, the shattering initial encounters with civilization left substantial numbers of culturally disoriented individuals on the land. Such human material could then be incorporated into the tissues of the enlarged civilization itself, either as individuals or as small family and village groupings. After mingling for a while with emigrants and refugees from the civilized interior, such populations became indistinguishable from other rural and remote elements of the civilized body politic. The way in which human digestion regularly breaks down the larger chemical structures of our food in order to permit molecules and atoms to enter into our own bodily structures seems closely parallel to this historical process.

Observed from the civilized side of the frontier, an initial die-off and disruption of local social defenses opened the way for an overabundant civilized peasantry to move onto new ground and there find a fresh chance to thrive. For the most part this phenomenon remained sporadic and local. Suitable lands and surplus manpower were by no means always available. But it happened often enough across the centuries to allow recurrent bursts of expansion on the part of pre-existing civilized societies. In fact, it is fundamentally because of this phenomenon that civilized societies throughout history have so persistently tended to expand their geographical size.

Of course, collisions between expanding civilizations occurred too, beginning in relatively early times, when Mesopotamian and Egyptian imperial governments started to clash in

Syria and Palestine after about 1300 B.C. Moreover, the epidemiological and cultural "digestion" of one society by another has sometimes dissolved civilized communities as well. This was the fate of Amerindian civilizations after 1500. It happened also to ancient Egypt and Mesopotamia in the course of their gradual incorporation into imperial structures stretching beyond their original borders—a process completed only after the Moslem conquests of the seventh century A.D.

Some readers will boggle at this series of assertions and *a priori* deductions, especially when applied to civilized societies *en bloc* and without taking account of local differences and alterations across time. Undoubtedly there were such differences. But surviving records are incapable of discerning them, since the few who could write were completely unaware of the biological process I have tried, even if clumsily, to anatomize. We must reconcile ourselves to the fact that until modern times, when the phenomenon assumed unparalleled proportions as a result of European oceanic explorations that broke through innumerable epidemiological barriers, surviving records simply do not take notice of what happened to the weak and unfortunate neighbors of civilized peoples.

Writers, naturally enough, tended to assume that the expansion of civilization (*their* own, of course) was only to be expected, since its charms and value were self-evident. Modern historians often unthinkingly assume the same thing. But given the normal attachment human beings feel for the ways of life to which they have been brought up, it is doubtful whether intact foreign communities ever opted for incorporation into an alien body social, even when the encroaching community possessed obvious and undeniable superiorities of skill, wealth and knowledge.

To be sure, barbarians often enough triumphed as conquerors only to be conquered in their turn by the seductions of civilized ways. Such invaders probably seldom foresaw what would happen to their inherited life style, and they often struggled against civilized corruption when they finally began to recognize what was happening. Moreover, as conquerors and rulers, they always had far more attractive prospects than any available to poor and humble folk on the borderlands, whose appointed role was to be assimilated into the most oppressed class of civilized society. Such peoples may therefore be presumed to have always resisted incorporation into civilized society insofar as it lay within their power.

If one tries to correct, therefore, for the built-in biases of available sources, the success civilizations so regularly demonstrated in incorporating border peoples into the fabric of metropolitan society needs explanation. Only if one gives appropriate weight to the epidemiological patterns described above does the expansion of civilized cultural frontiers become intelligible. Nothing else seems in the least adequate, or to accord with ordinary human behavior.

For my argument India offers a sort of test case. In that subcontinent, a civilized level of society arose initially in the semiarid Northwest, where the Indus River runs through increasingly desert lands from the high Himalayas to the sea. Such a landscape was similar to that of ancient Mesopotamia and Egypt, and the irrigation agriculture that supported Indus civilization was probably very like that of the two ancient Middle Eastern civilizations. The basic pattern of Indian history was defined by massive barbarian (Aryan) invasions after 1500 B.C., followed by a slow reassertion of civilized patterns of life. This, too, closely conforms to the rhythms of ancient history as experienced in the other river valley civilizations.[43]

Divergence becomes unmistakable after about 800 B.C., however, when civilized social structures re-established themselves in northwestern India. These urban communities bordered to the south and east upon a landscape occupied by various "forest peoples" who lived, at least usually, in small, self-contained communities of a sort that in temperate zones were extremely vulnerable to epidemiological undoing by civilized diseases. There is no reason to think that civilized diseases were not just as disruptive in India as they were in more northerly parts of Eurasia. But the forest peoples in India did not crumple up and disintegrate as might have been expected. Instead, they had their own epidemiological riposte to the biological armament of civilization. Various tropical diseases and parasitic infestations that flourished in moist and warm climates protected them against the temperate zone pattern of civilized encroachment. As was true later in Africa, death and debility lurked in too many forms to allow massive or rapid invasion of moist, warm regions by civilized personnel from India's drier North and West. A sort of epidemiological standoff ensued. Forest folk might be decimated by infections arising from contacts with civilized peoples, but civilized intruders were equally vulnerable to contacts with the tropical diseases and infestations familiar among the forest folk.

The upshot is well known. Instead of digesting the various primitive communities that had occupied southern and eastern India in the manner that was normal north of the Himalayas, Indian civilization expanded by incorporating ex-forest folk as castes, fitting them into the Hindu confederation of cultures as semi-autonomous, functioning entities. Local cultural and social traditions were therefore not destroyed before being fitted into Indian civilized social structures. Instead, a vast variety of primitive rites and practices survived for centuries. Every so often such elements surfaced within the Indian literate record, when orally transmitted ideas and rituals attracted the attention of literate individuals and were duly written down, elaborated or distorted so as to fit into the pullulating complexity of historic Hinduism.

Other elements and attitudes of course entered into the definition and maintenance of the caste principle in Indian society. Yet the taboos on personal contact across caste lines, and the elaborate rules for bodily purification in case of inadvertent infringement of such taboos, suggest the importance fear of disease probably had in defining a safe distance between the various social groups that became the castes of historic Indian society. Only after a prolonged process of epidemiological encounter, during which antibody immunities and tolerances of parasitic infestation were gradually equalized (or initial differences sharply reduced) did it become safe for Aryan-speaking intruders to live side by side with speakers of Tamil and other ancient tongues. Genetic blending (despite caste rules against intermarriage) no doubt accompanied this epidemiological exchange, and a fairly rigorous selective survival must have altered gene assortments among the forest peoples as well as among intrusive representatives of civilized styles of life.

Yet all such homogenizing processes fell short of the drastic "digestive" pattern characteristic of the other Old World civilizations. Consequently, the cultural uniformity and sociological cohesion of the Indian peoples has remained relatively weak in comparison to the more unitary structures characteristic of the northerly civilizations of Eurasia. One may, of course, attribute this peculiarity of the Indian style of civilization to chance or to conscious choices. Chance and choice may indeed have played a role in defining the caste principle; but the unique epidemiological situation confronting Indian civilization in its early phases of expansion must also have a great deal to do with making castes what they became, thereby defining the structure of Indian civilized society in a different way than prevailed elsewhere.

The situation in the Americas was different in another way. Civilized diseases of the kind that arose in the major Eurasian centers of urban life failed to establish themselves before 1500 in Mexico and Peru. Otherwise Montezuma would surely have had a more efficacious epidemiological revenge on the invading Spaniards than in fact manifested itself. It seems best, however, to reserve a more careful consideration of American disease patterns until a later chapter, when the epidemiological consequences of European arrival in America will become the subject of our consideration.

Here it remains to summarize the results of all these inferences and arguments based on modern notions of infectious disease. Despite the lack of conclusive literary or archaeological evidence, it seems sure that the major civilized regions of the Old World each developed its own peculiar mix of infectious, person-to-person diseases between the time when cities first arose and about 500 B.C. Water-borne, insect-borne, and skin-to-skin infections also had a much expanded scope within the crowded cities and adjacent regions of dense agricultural settlement. Such diseased and disease-resistant civilized populations were biologically dangerous to neighbors unaccustomed to so formidable an array of infections. This fact made territorial expansion for civilized populations much easier than would otherwise have been the case.

Exact boundaries between the different disease pools cannot be ascertained. No doubt the geographic range of any particular infection varied from year to year, depending on movement of people, fluctuations of virulence, and patterns of incidence within the civilized centers themselves. The result was acutely unstable. The novel biological balances—both micro- and macroparasitic—which civilized social structures had created were liable to further disturbance with every significant alteration of transport and communication, since none of the important new infections had reached geographical or other natural limits. Exploration of how these balances altered in the period from 500 B.C. to A.D. 1200 will be the theme of the next chapter.

III

Confluence of the Civilized Disease Pools of Eurasia: 500 B.C. to A.D. 1200

By 500 B.C. different micro- and macroparasitic balances had established themselves in each civilized region of Eurasia, and unstable accommodations between human hosts and the new civilized diseases had begun to manifest themselves in some and probably in all of the major civilized centers.

Exact definition of disease balances is altogether impossible, even for the oldest and best-known of these centers, in the Middle East. Here the original irrigation core had been supplemented after about 2000 B.C. by the establishment of cities and organized states on rain-watered land. Civilized patterns of social organization thereafter became endemic wherever good agricultural soil was to be found. A broad belt of civilized lands therefore arose on both the eastern and western flanks of Mesopotamia; a more slender fringe also expanded Egyptian influence into both eastern and northern Africa.

The ebb and flow of empires these circumstances permitted is well known. Akkadian, Babylonian, Kassite, Mittanian, Hittite, Egyptian, Assyrian, Chaldean, and Persian conquerors succeeded one another amid tumultuous war and recurrent influxes of barbarians from the borderlands. Successive imperial structures tended to grow ever larger and better organized, expanding toward natural limits set by those conditions of soil and climate that restricted peasant agriculture. With the establishment of the Persian empire in the sixth century B.C., these limits were approximately reached. By 500 B.C., the borders of that empire—on the north, south, and east—abutted on steppe and desert lands where prevailing methods of cultivation would not have brought in lush enough crops to bear the cost of an expanded imperial administration.

To be sure, on the west a narrow Aegean gateway offered a prospect of expansion onto fresh and sufficiently fertile ground for supporting the imperial style of macroparasitism. But when Xerxes' armies tried to make this possibility real, 480–479 B.C., they met defeat, as much from difficulties of supply as from the valor of the leagued Greek cities that resisted the Persian invasion. A similar gateway existed far to the southeast in the Indian Doab, a fertile region between the upwaters of the Indus and Ganges. The Persians made no recorded attempt to force this gate, however, and when Alexander of Macedon did try in 326 B.C., his troops mutinied and refused to follow. As a matter of fact, a disease gradient that assured severe losses to any army invading from beyond the Himalayas was probably more effective in guarding this gateway than any merely human obstacle.

Can we also say that microparasitism achieved a kind of natural limit within the expanded circuit of Middle Eastern civilized society by about 500 B.C.? Perhaps the forms of parasitism appropriate to irrigation farming and dependent on the specialized exposures to infection and infestation resulting from frequent wading in irrigation water had attained a fairly stable balance by 500 B.C. Irrigation farming was at least 3,000 years old by then, and communication between its major centers in Egypt, Mesopotamia and the Indus Valley was sufficient to have permitted a thorough homogenization of parasitic organisms across the 2,000–3,000 years during which these valleys had maintained contact with each other. Absence of evidence in written sources of any notable change in worm and related forms of infestation can scarcely be taken as confirmatory, since those who wrote paid practically no attention to the life conditions of the peasantry, and medical texts are completely opaque when it comes to translating ancient terms into modern disease classifications.

Written evidence does, however, clearly attest the appearance of epidemic diseases in the ancient Middle East. Among the disasters mentioned in the Babylonian *Epic of Gilgamesh* as preferable to the Flood was visitation from the god of pestilence, and an Egyptian text of about the same age (ca. 2000 B.C.) compares fear of Pharaoh with fear of the god of disease in a year of pestilence.[1] In China, too, the most ancient decipherable writings, dating back to the thirteenth century B.C., show familiarity with infectious epidemic disease. "Will this year have pestilence and will it be deaths?" asked an ancient ruler of Anyang.[2] His expert diviners thereupon recorded the question in a form that modern scholars can read on the sheep's shoulderblade used in ritually seeking an answer from the spirits.

Biblical texts are of substantially later date but may preserve oral traditions going back to about the same time. There may therefore well have been an historical basis for the plagues of Egypt described in the Book of Exodus. It is there stated that among the plagues Moses brought down upon Egypt were "sores that break into pustules on man and beast."[3] Furthermore, a lethal visitation upon Egypt's first-born in a single night left "not a house where there was not someone dead."[4] One may also cite an epidemic visited on the Philistines as punishment for their seizure of the Ark[5]; the pestilence that punished David's sin of numbering the people, and killed, if the text of the Bible is to be believed, 70,000 out of 1,300,000 able-bodied men in Israel and Judah[6]; and the fatal visitation

79

that "slew in the camp of the Assyrians one hundred and eighty-five thousand"[7] overnight, and caused the Assyrian king, Sennacherib, to withdraw from Judah without capturing Jerusalem.

Such passages make it certain that the writers of the Old Testament, when they put the text into its present form between 1000 and 500 B.C., were quite familiar with the possibility of a sudden outbreak of death-dealing disease, and interpreted such epidemics as acts of God. Modern translators regularly used the term plague for such events, since the principal disease that continued to manifest itself in this catastrophic fashion in Europe until the eighteenth century was bubonic plague.[8] There is, however, no good reason for supposing these ancient epidemics were outbreaks of bubonic plague. Any of the familiar civilized infections—whether propagated via the respiratory tract, like measles, smallpox,[9] and influenza, or via the alimentary canal, like typhoid and dysentery—could have produced the sort of sudden outbreak of mortality recorded in the Bible.

All one can properly conclude therefore is that diseases of this type were familiar to ancient Middle Eastern populations well before 500 B.C. and must have played roles of some importance in reducing population density from time to time and in affecting the course of military events. But the ravages of such diseases clearly were not enough to disrupt armies regularly nor to keep population below levels necessary for empire-building. Otherwise the Assyrian and Persian empires could not have flourished as they did between the ninth and fifth centuries B.C. It follows that epidemic diseases of the sort that attracted the attention of biblical writers were neither severe nor frequent enough to threaten the fabric of civilized society with disruption. In other words, from the point of view of the disease organisms, they were on the way to arriving at a mutually tolerable accommodation to their human hosts. Animal reservoirs (as with bubonic plague) may of course have played a role in allowing some infections to survive between epidemic outbreaks, but human populations of the ancient Middle East were certainly large enough to sustain the ancestors of modern childhood diseases on a fluctuating endemic basis.

In a few major centers of population and communication, where human chains of infection had an optimal chance of becoming permanently established, some of these diseases were probably becoming common childhood afflictions according to the pattern familiar today. Epidemic outbreaks would then occur mainly in outlying regions, where population density was insufficient to sustain the infection on a long-lasting basis, but where unusual conditions (often connected with military operations) might trigger a sudden outbreak of infection, intense enough and sufficiently disastrous to human life to attract the attention of the learned priests and scribes who shaped the biblical texts in which such events are referred to.

If these deductions are correct, civilized infectious diseases were only a little behind the diseases incident to irrigation agriculture in achieving a balance with their host populations in the ancient Middle East. As the locus of the oldest civilizations of the earth and one of the largest concentrations of human population in the world as of 500 B.C., the Middle East offered adequate time and opportunity for microparasitic as well as macroparasitic balances to approach stability within conditions defined by village and city life. More particularly: since the earliest surviving literary references to epidemic disease date back to about 2000 B.C., there had been sufficient time by 500 B.C. for some reasonably stable patterns of infectious diseases to establish themselves in the anciently civilized, much fought over, and densely populated regions of the Middle East.[10]

By contrast, greater instability prevailed in fringe areas where three different natural environments—the Yellow River flood plain, the monsoon lands of the Ganges Valley, and the Mediterranean coastlands—had all become capable of supporting civilized social structures much more recently than was the case in the Middle East. Accordingly, in 500 B.C. ecological balances were still precarious in these regions, and there is reason to suppose that disease patterns were far less firmly fixed than in the Middle East.

Ecological instability can be attested in the first place by the comparatively massive population growth that was under way in each of these environments both before and after 500 B.C. Evidence is circumstantial but no less certain on that account. Without large-scale increase in human numbers the territorial expansion that each of these civilizations underwent would have been impossible. In each case, moreover, population growth was associated with far-reaching technical adjustments in patterns of agriculture and with appropriate elaboration of the respective macroparasitic political and cultural structures that gave each civilization an enduring and characteristic form throughout subsequent history.[11]

In the Far East, Chinese peasants began to make real progress in farming the flood plain of the Yellow River from about 600 B.C. This involved extending agricultural operations beyond the semi-arid environment of the loess soils where earlier Chinese agriculture had been at home, and shifting from millet to rice as the staple crop. A vast labor of diking, draining, canalization, and reclamation of swamp and marsh had to be carried through before the vast flood plain could be transformed into an almost unbroken carpet of rice paddies, each with a regulated access to water. In addition, the cultivated area as a whole had to be defended against dangers of flood and drought by an extensive and elaborate system of engineering works designed to control the tumultuous waters of the Yellow River.

This stream is one of the most geologically active large rivers in the world. Recently (geologically speaking) it annexed important tributaries from other drainage systems, and in making its way through the loess country in its middle course, the river erodes vast quantities of soil, cutting its channel deeper every year. When silt-laden waters then debouch upon the almost flat flood plain, the current slows so that massive deposition succeeds the no less massive erosion upstream. As a result, in the flood plain the river builds up its bed rather rapidly. This made for trouble when men started to restrain the stream with artificial dikes. To be sure, the dikes could be built a little higher each year to match the deposition in the river's bottom. But the result was that soon the great river began to flow seaward across the fertile flood plain above the level of the surrounding land. Enormous human effort was required to keep it there, since any runlet finding a pathway through a dike could quickly grow into a rushing torrent if not checked in time. Even a few hours might suffice to tear a gaping hole in the dike; and whenever massive gaps did occur, the entire river spilled out from its artificial bed, seeking a new, lower channel for itself. Several times the great river has thus shifted course by hundreds of miles, debouching either north (as at present) or south of the Shantung highlands.[12]

The geological instability of the Yellow River was exacerbated but not created by human activity; and it will take geologic time spans for the river to achieve a more stable adjustment of its flow. Other dimensions of the ecological instabilities affecting early China were nearer the human scale. At the political level, for instance, the enlarged food resources produced by rice paddy cultivation sustained centuries of warfare among rival princes, until in 221 B.C. a single conqueror mastered the whole Yellow River flood plain as well as a broad band of adjacent territory both north and south of the river. After one brief bout of further civil war, a new dynasty, the

Han, emerged to supremacy in 202 B.C., and remained in at least nominal control of all China until A.D. 221.

Internal peace secured by an imperial bureaucratic administration probably diminished the costs to the peasantry inherent in earlier chronic warfare. Yet the Han peace also meant consolidation of a double layer of human macroparasites upon peasant rice (and millet) fields. Private landowners, who extracted rents, and official representatives of the Emperor, who extracted taxes, from the same peasant population obviously were in competition, yet they also supported each other most effectively. Their interests were basically the same, for in fact, the members of the imperial bureaucracy were recruited in large part from the landowning rentier class.

There was, however, another powerful factor in the macroparasitic balance that began to define itself in ancient China. As Chinese landowners consolidated claims on the peasantry, a distinctive set of ideas and ideals of conduct also took root among the landlord and official classes. These are commonly called Confucian because the sage Confucius (traditional dates 551–479 B.C.) did a great deal to articulate and define the new ideals. The propagation of Confucian culture among imperial officials and private landowners internalized an ethic that strenuously restrained arbitrary or innovative use of power. One critically important consequence was to keep exactions imposed upon the peasantry within traditional and, under most circumstances, tolerable limits.

As a result, by the time of the Emperor Wu-ti (140–87 B.C.), a remarkably stable and long-lasting balance was achieved within Chinese society between peasant farmers and the two social classes most directly parasitic upon them. This balance survived, with some important elaboration but no real structural breaks, until the twentieth century. Overall, we can be sure that the demands of landlord and official tax collector, heavy though they were, did not take more from the Chinese farmers than they were capable of producing over and above the minimum required for their own survival. Otherwise the slow, majestic march of the Chinese population throughout the Yellow River flood plain and adjacent regions, and then southward into and beyond the Yangtze Valley, could not have occurred; nor could the Chinese peasantry have offered a persistently expanding base (despite innumerable local and some general and long-lasting setbacks) for the imposing cultural and imperial structures of traditional China.

Existing literature does not permit anyone to follow the pace of this Chinese advance with any exactitude. Yet massive development of the South did not occur until after the end of the Han Dynasty. In other words, almost a thousand years elapsed from the time when the taming of the Yellow River flood plain got seriously under way before comparable development took place in the valley of the Yangtze River.[13]

At first glance this relatively slow pace of Chinese settlement in more southerly parts of what is today China may seem surprising. Political-military obstacles were relatively unimportant. Agricultural conditions favored settlement, since milder climates meant longer growing seasons, and more abundant rainfall removed the risk of drought that often endangered crops on unirrigated land in the North. Moreover, the fact that the Yangtze passes through lakes after it emerges from the mountains of the West means that no troublesome quantities of sediment clog its lower reaches. The awkward buildup of the river bed, characteristic of the Yellow River, was thus absent. Correspondingly, dikes and artificial networks for water distribution escape the extraordinary pressures they encounter in the North. The awesome, recurrent, and inescapable technical disasters that distinguished the history of the Yellow River valley simply do not occur.

Despite these obvious and real advantages, an invisible and unrecorded but, one must still believe, very potent obstacle stood in the way of the swift and successful development of rice paddies and urban life in lands to the south of the historic cradle of Chinese civilization: for in moving southward and into better farming regions, Chinese pioneers were also climbing a rather steep disease gradient!

The climatic shift involved is comparable to the difference between New England and Florida, but the lie of the land and prevailing wind patterns make the transition sharper than any climatic gradient occurring along the East Coast of North America. A mountain barrier shelters the Yangtze Valley from the cold and dry northwest winds that pour across the Yellow River valley from the Mongolian plateau in winter, constituting the winter monsoon. Correspondingly, in summer, when the monsoon winds blow the opposite way, warm, moist air sucked in from the South China Sea assures abundant precipitation in the Yangtze region. But these summer winds shed most of their moisture while crossing the mountain barrier before reaching the Yellow River valley, so that rainfall there is frequently insufficient to ward off damaging drought on unirrigated fields.

The result is a sharp climatic difference between northern and central China. Among other things, the warmer, moister condition of the South allowed a greater variety of parasites to flourish than could survive in the North. Throughout the Yellow River flood plain, the severe winters killed off parasites that lacked dormant forms capable of resisting prolonged freezing. Important insect carriers of disease were similarly inhibited from establishing themselves because they could not survive the cold and dry conditions of the North. Nothing of the kind occurs in the Yangtze Valley south of the sheltering mountains. Populations accustomed to disease conditions of the North therefore faced formidable problems in adjusting to the markedly different patterns of parasitism that prevailed farther south.

The earlier shift from dry farming on loess soils to irrigation farming in the Yellow River flood plain must also have exposed Chinese peasants to new and perhaps initially formidable disease risks. But whatever microparasitic adjustments occurred in connection with this change went hand in hand with far more conspicuous and time-consuming adjustments of a technical and macroparasitic kind. Centuries of effort were required to learn the arts of water management on a scale suitable for taming the Yellow River, and problems of political consolidation and modulation of human macroparasitism upon the peasantry were no less critical and time-consuming. Any adjustments to intensified disease risks could and did therefore occur simultaneously with these other more conspicuous transformations of Chinese society and techniques.

Which process was the critical one? It is of course impossible to say for sure, but the macroparasitic side seems to have been the slower to come into balance. The reason for making such a judgment is that political-military stability did not come to China until the very end of the third century B.C. Before that time, organized violence mounted in intensity throughout the Warring States epoch of Chinese history (403–221 B.C.), climaxing with the conquest of the entire Chinese area by a still semi-barbarous state of Ch'in in 221 B.C. By the time the macroparasitic balances of ancient China attained a new imperial definition under the Han Dynasty (202 B.C.–A.D. 221) Chinese peasants already had four centuries of experience with the conditions of rice paddy farming behind them. Such a length of time gave ample opportunity for the epidemiological consequences of irrigation agriculture to stabilize themselves in the Yellow River valley, generations or even centuries before the macroparasitic side came into balance.

Clearly, whatever intensification of infection and infestation occurred when Chinese farmers began to spend a significant part of their working time in shallow standing water—and there must have been striking consequences of such a change from the semi-arid conditions of loess farming—the new patterns of disease did not forestall a steady increase in human numbers. Otherwise manpower for building and maintaining an ever-expanding network of dikes and water channels, not to mention the manpower for increasingly massive armies, would simply not have been available. When, however, engineering techniques along with the administrative and moral bases for stable imperial government had been achieved by the end of the third century B.C., nothing remained to inhibit the rapid development of central and southern China except the disease barrier. The power of that barrier is attested by the five to six additional centuries that elapsed before massive occupation of the Yangtze Valley by Chinese settlers became an accomplished fact. Put very simply, too many immigrants from the cooler, drier North died to permit a more rapid buildup.

All these assertions remain uncomfortably abstract and *a priori*. As in the case of the Middle East, there is little hope of discovering from ancient texts exactly what the humanly dangerous parasites may have been. Still, ancient writers often betray keen awareness of the disease risks of the South. Thus, Ssu-ma Ch'ien, the founder of Chinese historiography, who lived from about 145 to 87 B.C., tells us: "In the area south of the Yangtse the land is low and the climate humid; adult males die young."[14] He also comments on the abundance of land suitable for cultivation and the sparcity of population in the region. This is authoritative testimony, for Ssu-ma Ch'ien made a personal tour of the country to prepare himself for writing his history. In later literature, the unhealthiness of the South was taken for granted. Special handbooks for southern travelers prescribed suitably exotic regimens and medicines for the malignant diseases encountered there.[15] These did not help very much, as the remarkable short tenure of office and high mortality recorded for officials sent to the South attests.

Modern disease distributions, so far as they can be plotted on the map of China, also confirm the expectation that a richer variety of infection and infestation flourishes in the warmer and wetter South. A number of modern disease boundaries fall between the Yellow River and the Yangtze, and climatic patterns certainly suggest that such a disease gradient is age-old.[16] The form in which ancient Chinese medical texts have come down to us, however, tends to hide regional differentiations, for the long list of distinct diseases Chinese medical writers recognized were organized around the seasons at which they were most prevalent. Some, such as malaria, can be confidently recognized today; for many others such identification with modern classifications of infection is as difficult as it is to translate Galen's language into twentieth-century medical terminology.[17]

Malaria, although occurring occasionally in the North, is a modern health problem only in the South.[18] In fact it may have constituted the principal obstacle to early Chinese expansion southward. Another mosquito-borne disease, dengue fever, which is closely related to yellow fever though not as lethal in modern times, also affects southern parts of China. Like malaria, dengue fever may have been present from time immemorial, lying in wait for immigrants from more northerly climes among whom prior exposure had not built up any sort of natural resistance. Fevers, including regularly recurring fevers that must have been malarial, figure very prominently in ancient Chinese medical writings, a fact that supports the notion that such afflictions mattered a good deal in the early centuries of Chinese expansion.[19] Chinese *materia medica* of the nineteenth century also embraced several effective febrifuges—so much so that imported quinine scarcely seemed superior, even in the eyes of European doctors.[20]

Schistosomiasis is another major health problem of southern and central China in modern times. It, too, has probably always conformed to climatically defined boundaries. The recent discovery of a corpse from the second century B.C. so well preserved that evidence of chronic schistosomiasis could be positively discerned[21] proves that this affliction had established itself in China before Chinese pioneers were able to develop the Yangtze Valley to anything like the levels familiar in the North.

All in all, one may say that the Chinese met with striking success—technical and political as well as epidemiological—in penetrating the difficult environment of the Yellow River flood plain in the centuries after about 600 B.C. They achieved a no less striking success after about 200 B.C. in arriving at a tolerable and unusually stable macroparasitic balance between food producers and those who lived off peasant harvests. At the microparasitic level, however, far-reaching adjustments within the vast regions to the South were still under way during the pre- and post-Christian centuries. The Yangtze Valley and other territories under Chinese political domination from 211 B.C. (or earlier) could not be fully incorporated into the Chinese body social because of disease barriers until after the fall of the Han Dynasty (A.D. 221), when, as we shall presently see, other drastic and far-reaching disease adjustments also occurred.

In India, information about the early agricultural development of the middle Ganges Valley and of adjacent regions closer to the Bay of Bengal is practically nil. Rice cultivation became important at an early time—but just when seems impossible to tell. Nor is it even clear how important irrigation was. In the Ganges Valley monsoon rains were fully adequate for most agricultural purposes without bothering to tap the Ganges' waters. Irrigation was, however, essential for multiple cropping in a single year, since in summer and fall monsoon rains cease, and artificial means for bringing water to the fields became necessary if the land were not to lie idle until the rains returned. Multiple cropping has been widespread in recent centuries; how ancient it may be has never been satisfactorily established.

What is known is that powerful and extensive kingdoms developed in the Ganges Valley beginning about 600 B.C. Soon after Alexander's invasion (327–325 B.C.), one such state, ruled by Chandragupta Maurya (ca. 321–297 B.C.), united the entire region into a single imperial structure, and his successors extended their authority throughout most of the Indian subcontinent. Early in this political development, Prince Gautama, the Buddha (traditional dates: 563–483 B.C.), played a role strikingly parallel to that of his Chinese contemporary, Confucius. For like Confucius in China, Buddha in India articulated a world view and exemplified a style of life that became widely influential.

As compared to China, however, both the political and the intellectual structures that arose in the Ganges region before and after 500 B.C. remained unstable, and never were consolidated into an enduring whole. One of the reasons—and perhaps a very pervasive factor in all Indian history—was the heavy microparasitism characteristic of a climate as warm and wet as that of the Ganges Valley and of the rest of India's best agricultural lands.

The cities and states around which subsequent Indian civilization crystallized were located in an environment very different from the semi-desert in which the earlier Indus civilization had been based. That civilization, indeed, occupied a region of India where the climate resembled that of Mesopotamia or Egypt. In the Indus Valley rain was scant and agriculture depended on irrigation. In the Ganges Valley, on the other hand, the monsoons brought abundant rain for part of the year, and the shelter of the Himalayas meant that temperatures practically never approached freezing. Such a climate is, in fact, wetter and warmer than the climate of the Yangtze Valley that Chinese farmers had such difficulty in penetrating because of the intensified risks of infection. Classical Indian civilization thus took form under climatic and (presumed) disease conditions that the early Chinese found too much to bear.

Today the Ganges region sustains cholera, malaria, and dengue fever together with a great variety of multicelled parasites, as well as the more universal diseases of cities and civilization that are familiar in cooler climes. What disease organisms may have circulated in ancient times cannot be said for sure, but the climate of the Ganges Valley certainly must have permitted a rich array of parasites to arise as soon as dense human populations came into existence.

Adjustment to survival in such a land had its advantages, of course. For people accustomed to the Ganges environment, other similarly situated river valleys of southeastern Asia—the Brahmaputra, Salween, and Mekong in particular—lay open to pioneer exploration and development. Accordingly, a "Greater India" arose overseas between about 100 B.C. and A.D. 500 through the efforts of Indian merchants and missionaries, who provided models of civilized living to the indigenous rulers and peoples of those parts. Some of the islands of Indonesia also shared in this development. The geographic range and cultural significance of Indian expansion overseas in these centuries is hard for heirs of a civilization that scarcely extended beyond the narrow confines of the Mediterranean to appreciate. We are, after all, accustomed to view Asia through maps of a far different scale from those of ancient Greece, whose "Magna Graecia" in Sicily and southern Italy was of trifling size in comparison to the Greater India of southeastern Asia and Indonesia.

On the other hand, a heavy load of infestation and infection must have reduced individual vigor and capacity for physical labor to a significant degree. Insofar as this was so, peasant families were less able to produce a surplus of food for the support of kings, landlords, armies, and administrators. From a distance India looked wealthy, since its exports were gems and spices, but in spite of that reputation it seems likely that the subcontinent as a whole was always comparatively poor inasmuch as a rather slender margin existed in most times and places between what an average peasant family could produce and what it needed for survival.

The matter can be thought of as a sort of energy balance. Food extracted from peasants for the support of rulers, soldiers, and city folk, as well as food consumed by microparasites within their own bodies, represents a net withdrawal of energy available to the food producers themselves. More going to one kind of parasite leaves less for others, and if it was true that Indian peasants carried more microparasites than was the case north of the Himalayas, then Indian cities and rulers simply had less surplus energy available to them—whether stored in the form of taxable grain or other food, or simply as peasant muscle power that could be conscripted for war or public works.

This was probably an important reason why Indian empires were fragile, evanescent structures. India's political and military weakness made invasion and conquest relatively easy for a long succession of foreigners who came from the Northwest, where the protecting mountain barrier was most easily penetrable. Indian diseases were, in fact, a more reliable protection against such intruders than organized human defenses, since troops from beyond the Himalayas were liable to very heavy die-off when they met the microparasites of the northern Indian plains for the first time. The military and political history of the subcontinent, from the time of Aryan invasions of the fifteenth to twelfth centuries B.C. until the eighteenth century A.D., turned very largely upon the balance between invaders' military prowess and the ravages unfamiliar diseases brought to their ranks.

Two other leading traits of Indian civilization can also be connected with the prevalence of disease. As suggested above

93

in Chapter II, the caste organization of Indian society may have partly been a response to the kind of epidemiological standoff that arose when intrusive Aryans, who had probably learned to live with some acute "civilized" diseases—e.g., perhaps smallpox—encountered various "forest folk" who had acquired tolerances for formidable local infections that flourished in the warmth and moisture of southern and eastern India. And, of course, insofar as the caste principle of personal identity became normative, it tended to weaken the power of the state. Political loyalty scarcely extended across caste lines. Rulers became just another, particularly bothersome, caste from whom prudent men of different caste withdrew as much as possible.

In addition, the transcendentalism that became characteristic of Indian religions accorded well with the circumstances of poverty-stricken, disease-ridden peasants. Unlike Confucianism, which supported and modulated the Chinese imperial structure, the two great Indian religions of Buddhism and Hinduism were fundamentally apolitical. Both, at least in theory, rejected worldly pomp, wealth, and power as mere illusion, along with everything else perceptible to the senses. Confucius had tried to regulate and control the macroparasitism of the upper classes by defining a decorum that would restrain the exercise of power; Indian teachers, on the other hand, turned their backs on politics and society—in a sense despairing of it—and enjoined upon their followers a penurious way of life, minimizing their material demands on the environment in order to invite a liberating mystic vision more effectually. Starving holy men who sought systematically to repress their senses and bodily processes so as better to attain transcendent bliss surely constituted a cultural elite optimally compatible with the slender capacity of a hard-pressed peasantry to support those who did not themselves produce food.

An ideal of escape from the suffering of existence, such as Buddha preached, and the renunciation of worldly goods and attachments that he recommended, obviously also weakened political identities and diminished the significance and scope of politics. But no calculus seems possible of the roles played in weakening Indian states by otherworldly attitudes and values, by the autonomy of castes, or by technical limitations of Indian agriculture. A *fortiori,* the significance of disease in shaping each of these aspects of Indian civilization cannot be measured or exactly defined. The point rather is that everything fitted together in mutually supportive fashion to constitute a very effective and enduring adjustment to the special conditions of civilized life in the Indian subcontinent.

If we compare Indian with Chinese circumstances, then, the material demands of Indian political and cultural elites upon the peasantry seem to have been significantly less than comparable classes in China could safely extract from a less heavily diseased peasant population. Fragile and evanescent state structures and ascetic otherworldly ideals of life may, therefore, have been necessary adaptations to the narrower range of material surplus attainable in a society where microparasitism was more pervasive than in climates where freezing winter weather inhibited various forms of infection and infestation.

Indian civilization, in fact, arose in a climate analogous to that of the African savanna lands, where rains prevail for only part of the year but where warm temperatures are uninterrupted. Such a climate had in all probability been humankind's cradleland, and across the millennia of anthropoid evolution toward humanity, African parasites had also been able to evolve, keeping pace with any and every increase in the prevalence of their protohuman and fully human hosts. A more nearly stable ecological balance therefore prevailed in regions of the world suited to human nakedness than was the case farther north. Risk of the fulminating sort of macroparasitism we call civilization was correspondingly reduced. But since some of Africa's more serious biological obstacles to the multiplication of human numbers—sleeping sickness, for instance—did not extend into India, the possibility of sustaining the macroparasitic social classes needed for civilization did exist there, at least marginally.

Yet despite all the drains upon the energy at their disposal, whether micro- or macroparasitic, a small surplus must have remained at the disposal of both the Indian and Chinese peasantries during the first millennium B.C. This allowed their multiplication, which in turn led to colonization of new regions, and to the elaboration of economic as well as of political and cultural structures near the major centers of population. Without such a growth of peasant numbers the two civilizations could not have developed as they did, and as long as the peasant base continued to expand without meeting insurmountable and lasting checks, the ecological disbalance favoring the rise of civilization continued to exist both in India and China.

A similar disbalance existed during the first millennium B.C. in the Aegean basin, and more generally throughout the Mediterranean coastlands. As in China and India, farmers in the most active Aegean centers of cultural development were also exploring the potentialities of a new sort of cultivation. The Aegean system was, however, more complicated in the sense that it required exchange of products between economically differentiated regions; and this, in turn, rested upon the availability of cheap transport, i.e., large-scale movement of goods by ship. This exchange pattern affected farming fundamentally. By planting ground with vines and olive trees, and waiting a few years for them to mature, wine and oil could be produced and then exchanged for grain and other less highly valued commodities on very advantageous terms. That is, an acre of land put under vines or olives could in most seasons produce a quantity of wine or oil exchangeable for an amount of grain that needed far more land for its production.

The organization of "barbarian" societies to provide a steady surplus of grain and some other key supplies—metals, timber, slaves—was just as necessary for the emergence of Greek civilization as the Aegean venture toward more and more specialized production of wine and oil. How suitably large-scale grain production was managed escapes written record; but it is clear enough that as they became aware of the charms of wine and oil (and of a few other civilized products), chieftains and men of power located at diverse spots around the Mediterranean and Black Sea coastlands found it advantageous to collect grain and other commodities from their subordinates in order to be able to barter what they had collected for the goods of civilization, brought from afar by Greek ships.

In such a relationship, the grain growers of remote coastlands played the role that Middle Eastern, Chinese, and Indian peasantries were long accustomed to play in their respective societies: they fed the city folk and got nothing tangible in return. The geographical separation that the Mediterranean system permitted did make a difference: citizens of the Greek world were pretty much insulated from the "barbarians" who fed them. Most Greeks experienced a world knit together economically by buying and selling among free citizens, and sustained politically by transactions that were no less free. Most significant of all: in the urban centers themselves the local farming population was part and parcel of the political community—buying and selling, participating in war and public deliberation as equals of anyone else.

Macroparasitism in Mediterranean lands thus took new forms. It became corporate, and the role of excluded and oppressed peasantries was consigned to distant barbarians. For many centuries this exchange pattern was not encapsulated within an imperial command structure. In other civilized lands, long-distance trade remained the affair of only a small urban element, and remained closely tied to the needs of political lordship. It was, therefore, closely regulated by rulers and their courts. The more open Mediterranean pattern of trade, in which most ranks of society participated, allowed multiple urban centers to form, wherever an exportable surplus of oil or wine or other valued commodity could be produced.

This led to prolonged political instability and recurrent local war, and for several centuries, spared the Mediterranean peasantries that produced the grain to feed distant cities at the command of local masters, the cost of also sustaining an imperial bureaucracy and army. For a long time, Mediterranean peasant populations thus escaped the Chinese and Middle Eastern fate of having to support two masters: local landlords plus an imperial officialdom.

Eventually (by 30 B.C.), empire prevailed in the Mediterranean also, but as compared with contemporary Chinese and older Middle Eastern patterns of political evolution, Rome's imperial consolidation came late. This reflected the difficulty inherent in bringing under one political roof a multiplicity of independent trade partners, each locally organized to defend its own interests, whether in war or in the market place. Shaped as they were by these circumstances, Greek and Roman political ideals actively opposed imperial subjection. Where wealth concentrated and predation was therefore most tempting, stalwart farmers, gathered as citizens and equipped as foot soldiers, were in a position to make their distaste for subjection to a distant imperial master effective in battle, as the Ionian revolt of 499 B.C. against Persia and the disruption of the Athenian empire in 404 B.C. both demonstrated.

It is a moot point whether organized fighting and the disruptions of market relations resulting from war were more costly to Mediterranean populations than imperial bureaucratic consolidation under the Romans turned out to be. One cannot therefore confidently argue that macroparasitic drain upon food providers in the Mediterranean coastlands before 30 B.C. was less than in contemporary China or the Middle East. Yet the prevalence of self-governing cities, in which a few thousand families managed their economic and political affairs as best they could, and as they themselves saw fit, certainly gave classical Mediterranean (and subsequent European) civilization a deep-seated preference for this sort of freedom. The price of such political fragmentation was frequent war, but this Europeans have long seemed willing to pay.

If we turn attention to the microparasitic side of the balance, it appears that Mediterranean coastlands offered a relatively disease-free environment into which populations could and did expand. The new patterns of cultivation did not of themselves invite new forms of microparasitism. Olive trees are believed to have been part of the wild flora of Greece before men did anything to alter it. Their cultivation, accordingly, involved relatively modest disruptions of pre-existing landscapes, particularly since olive trees will often flourish on rocky hillsides where little else will grow. Vines may have come into Greece from better-watered regions to the north. According to myth, Dionysos, the god of wine, hailed from Thrace, and this may preserve a memory of the importation of vines from that region. But even if they came from elsewhere, vines did not require alterations of pre-existing ecological balances nearly as drastic as those involved in rice paddy cultivation of the sort Chinese (and probably also Indian) farmers were experimenting with at the time vine cultivation reached Greece. The same may be said for the expansion of grain fields on the coastlands of the Black Sea and western Mediterranean. Wheat and barley were plants native to Near Eastern lands, and may also have belonged among the grasses of Mediterranean regions before men domesticated them. Thus, spread of grain farming also involved comparatively modest alterations of older biological balances.

There is, in short, no reason to think that the new cropping pattern brought with it any particular exposure to new diseases in Mediterranean coastlands. To be sure, as population became denser, various infections must have become commoner. The most important of these was surely malaria, although other and diverse parasites, often propagated via polluted water supplies, undoubtedly multiplied as people gathered into cities and became more numerous.

Hippocrates, the father of Greek medicine (traditional dates 460–377 B.C.), recorded case histories with enough precision and detail to prove the existence of diverse infections in ancient Greece, though in most cases we cannot determine from his words exactly which disease as recognized today may have been at work. He does unmistakably record an epidemic of mumps on the island of Thasos,[22] and the three- and four-day fevers he refers to frequently must be ancestral to modern tertian and quartan malaria.[23] With less certainty, modern medical experts may also identify diphtheria, tuberculosis and/or influenza from Hippocrates' accounts of his patients' symptoms, and the progress of their diseases. On the other hand, it is a striking and significant fact that no trace of smallpox or measles can be found in the Hippocratic writings. In view of the precision with which external symptoms were recorded, and the dramatic character of such diseases, it seems sure that Hippocrates and those of his followers responsible for creating the collection of writings that goes by Hippocrates' name never encountered these diseases. The same applies to bubonic plague, the other great epidemic killer of later European history.

As compared to the ecological circumstances confronting Chinese and Indian peasantries, therefore, the peoples of the ancient Mediterranean (always excepting Egypt, that ancient focus of intense disease parasitism) seem to have had an easy time. Intensified exposure to malaria may, in some Mediterranean locales, have set definite limits upon agricultural expansion. But in the Roman campagna and some other parts of Italy that later became malarial wastelands, dense farming populations existed between the sixth and third centuries B.C. Elaborate underground channels were dug to drain natural swamps and secure water for irrigation and drinking. Enormous labor went into these engineering works, and the effect of such water management probably was to prevent the malignant forms of malaria from gaining a foothold in regions near Rome that later suffered radical depopulation because of the disease.[24]

As is now known, local details of environment that affect the relative abundance of one variety of mosquito as against others, have much to do with making one Mediterranean region malarial and another relatively free from the disease. Critical variables include the availability of suitable water for hatching the eggs laid by different kinds of mosquitoes. Some species are adapted to spending their larval stage in moving as against still water, and in saline as against fresh. Presence and absence of minute trace elements in the water may also play a critical role in determining what sort of mosquito will prevail in a particular locality. In addition, such an unexpected item as the population ratio of human beings to cattle can make a difference. The mosquito species which is Europe's most efficient vector of malaria, for example, prefers to feed on cattle. If enough alternate sources of blood are available to them, these mosquitoes will eschew potential human hosts and thus interrupt the chain of infection, since cattle do not suffer from malaria.[25]

Delicate and seemingly minor details of this kind suffice in modern times to define areas of malarial infestation in Mediterranean lands, and no one would claim that all relevant variables are yet recognized or fully understood. Under the circumstances no one can expect to decipher the critical variables in ancient environments that defined where and how seriously malaria interfered with human activity. One can make this general observation, nonetheless: about 700 B.C., when the process of civilizational expansion throughout the Mediterranean coastlands began, the regions awaiting more intensive agricultural exploitation were either drier (as in North Africa) or cooler (as along the Black Sea coast and in parts of Italy and the western Mediterranean generally) than were the already developed Aegean and eastern Mediterranean (Syria, Palestine) regions. Both these circumstances tended to check intensification of disease even among increasingly dense human populations.

Malaria was undoubtedly destructive to humans in some places. Hippocrates' description of chronic sufferers makes that clear: "Those who drink it [stagnant water, which he thought responsible for malarial symptoms] have always large, stiff spleens and hard, thin, hot stomachs, while their shoulders, collar bones and faces are emaciated; the fact is that their flesh dissolves to feed the spleen. . . ."[26] Large cities, when they took form, also undoubtedly became seats of intensified disease circulation, and human life was significantly shortened there as a result.[27] But in spite of these facts, the Mediterranean landscape, as it evolved toward civilization, remained a relatively healthy place for human beings.

What little we know about ancient Greek, Roman, and Carthaginian social history suggests that up until the late third century B.C., when Rome and Carthage began to dispute imperial control of the western Mediterranean, the population of the classical world grew rather rapidly. Athens' brief but brilliant imperial career between 480 and 404 B.C. illustrates this unmistakably. Year after year, the Athenians sent out marauding fleets and armies; and sometimes their expeditions met with disaster. In 454 B.C., for example, all the crews manning a fleet of ninety to one hundred ships were lost in Egypt; yet only four years later a new Athenian fleet of two hundred vessels set out to attack Cyprus. War losses did not, in fact, suffice to keep the Athenian population in check. In the days of their imperial strength, the Athenians seized lands from weaker peoples overseas in order to settle poor citizens abroad in colonies where they could live the life of a good citizen, i.e., as a respectable landowner and farmer. At least nine such settlements had come into existence by the outbreak of the Peloponnesian War in 431 B.C.,[28] when Athenian imperial ambitions peaked and then collapsed in ruin.

In later centuries, a similar growth in the size of the Macedonian and of the Italian peasant populations underlay the imperial expansion of Macedon and then of Rome, just as surely as Athenian population growth sustained that city's period of greatness. The substantial emigration of Greeks to Asia, both before and after Alexander's meteoric career, and the long series of Roman colonies planted throughout Italy in course of that city's expansion, attest to similarly rapid demographic growth. The same pattern presumably underlay Carthaginian imperialism, though subsequent defeat by Rome meant the loss of almost all records that might show details of Carthage's population history.

To us, living also in an age of rapid population growth, this phenomenon may not seem particularly surprising nor need any special explanation. In the context of the entire human venture upon earth, however, persistent population expansion is exceptional. On a global time scale, in fact, population growth appears as a transient concomitant of some ecological upset permitting larger numbers of human beings to survive and multiply for a few generations until natural limits again assert themselves.

Among the most important factors in defining such natural limits are and always must be what I have called macro- and microparasitism. Changes in patterns of microparasitism affected Mediterranean populations profoundly, beginning in the second century A.D. This we will look into presently. But long before the ravages of new diseases began to cut into population, changes in macroparasitism incident to the rise of Roman imperial power had noticeably damaging effects. Wars and plunder worked vast and repeated destruction; enslavement and tax farming constituted almost as heavy a drain upon Mediterranean populations. After about 200 B.C. we begin to hear of abandoned villages and empty countrysides. Peasant populations all but disappeared from some landscapes where previously they had sustained the pattern of demographic growth mentioned above. But until after A.D. 150 such regions (concentrated, characteristically, in the older centers of urban and imperial development like southern Greece and Italy) were counterbalanced by population expansion in other parts of the Mediterranean coastlands, e.g., in Spain and southern France, and in more distant regions along the Rhine and Danube that lay outside the Mediterranean climate zone as well.[29]

The over-all picture that emerges from these considerations is that during the first millennium B.C. in three important centers of human population, the balances between macro- and microparasitism adjusted themselves in such a fashion as to allow persistent population growth and territorial expansion of civilized types of society. As a result, by the beginning of the Christian era, the civilizations of China, India, and the Mediterranean had attained a size and mass comparable to that of the more anciently civilized Middle East.

Definite population estimates are possible only for the Roman world and for Han China. Beloch's guess of 54 million for the Roman empire at the time of Augustus' death (A.D. 14) corresponds quite closely to the figure of 59.5 (or perhaps 57.6) million inhabitants of Han China, enumerated in an imperial census of A.D. 2.[30] Both of these global figures probably err on the downward side, since in the nature of things no official record intended for tax and corvée purposes can catch everybody,[31] but both are trustworthy indications of approximate magnitudes.

Populations attaining such massiveness, with appropriate concentrations in a few urban centers where tributes gathered from far and wide supported an imperial court, army, and administration, obviously could sustain our modern types of infectious childhood diseases. As we have seen, however, there is strong reason to believe that Mediterranean populations, at least, had not yet encountered such standbys as smallpox and measles in Hippocrates' time.

How vulnerable such populations could be to a sudden irruption of unfamiliar infection is vividly illustrated by what happened in Athens in 430–429 B.C. Thucydides' famous and detailed clinical description[32] of the disease that did so much to demoralize the Athenians and killed off about a quarter of the Athenian land army[33] cannot be firmly identified with any modern infection.[34] But if Thucydides is to be believed, the disease was new, and disappeared as mysteriously as it had come, afflicting only Athens and "the most populous of other towns." The infection "first began, it is said, in the parts of Ethiopia above Egypt, and thence descended into Egypt and Libya and into most of the king's country [i.e., Persia]. Suddenly falling upon Athens, it first attacked the population in Piraeus . . . and afterwards appeared in the upper city, when the deaths became much more frequent."[35] Since Piraeus was the port of Athens and in frequent touch with the entire eastern shoreline of the Mediterranean, there can be little doubt that the disease came by sea and burnt itself out within a single season by creating so many antibodies in Athenian bloodstreams that the chain of infection could no longer be sustained.[36]

Nevertheless, in that single season the disease inflicted a blow on Athenian society from which it never entirely recovered. This unforeseen and unforeseeable epidemiological accident, as Thucydides implies, may have had much to do with the failure of Athenian plans for the defeat of Sparta and the Peloponnesian League. Had Athens won that war, how different the subsequent political history of the Mediterranean would have been! But as things turned out, the Athenian empire, which lasted no more than three generations, was far more evanescent on a human time scale than the epidemic of 430–429 B.C. was on a time scale appropriate to the life span of infectious disease-causing organisms. When the mysterious epidemic had come and gone, it left no trace behind, and for a long time the Mediterranean did not witness anything comparable.

The epidemic experience of China cannot be reconstructed with so much detail, although mention of unusual outbreaks of disease abound in the Han dynastic history and other early texts. Phrases used to describe such episodes cannot be translated into modern medical terminology. All that can be concluded is that China too, like the Mediterranean, had a substantial acquaintance with disease in different forms, including some that acted in epidemic fashion from time to time.[37]

Texts from ancient India tell nothing about the antiquity of epidemic infection in that land. Surviving medical writings claim immemorial antiquity, but were subject to a lengthy process of amendment and interpolation via oral transmission.[38] Hence passages that have sometimes been cited as evidence for an enormous antiquity for smallpox and similar diseases in India do not prove any such thing. To be sure, on *a priori* grounds it is easy to believe that India offered particularly fertile soil for the development of civilized person to person diseases. Warm climatic conditions, such as prevail in India, are obviously more propitious for the survival of tiny infectious organisms (attuned to flourish at body temperature) in their moment of peril, when transfer from one host to another occurs. Hence it was undoubtedly easier in India than in colder climates for infections established among cattle and other herds to transfer to human hosts. In no other warm climate were there dense enough human settlements living in a close juxtaposition with suitable animal herds in those centuries when a disease such as smallpox must have first made good its transfer to humankind. The modern tradition that smallpox was indigenous to India[89] may therefore rest on a perfectly sound basis in fact. Bubonic plague and cholera, as we shall see, perhaps also began their careers as human diseases on Indian soil. But the universal human penchant for attributing the origin of an unfamiliar, nasty disease to foreigners[40] makes it impossible to trace the origins of any particular infection to India (or anywhere else) with any sort of historically convincing textual evidence.[41]

As for the Middle East, the biblical passages already cited show that epidemics were quite familiar there during the first millennium B.C. Clearly, the same infection could, on occasion, devastate both Middle Eastern and Mediterranean lands, as Thucydides declares to have been the case with the disease that attacked Athens in 430 B.C. Perhaps an epidemic might occasionally also leap across the thinly populated ground separating India from the Middle East and the Mediterranean. It is even conceivable that China, too, may sometimes have shared exposure to a contagious infection.[42] In general, however, any such sporadic bridging of epidemiological barriers separating the major centers of Eurasian population remained exceptional before the Christian era.

To be sure, within such well-traveled waters as the Mediterranean, movement by sea could, with favoring winds, attain an average of well over 100 miles per day.[43] Thus, all the coastal cities of the Mediterranean constituted a single disease pool. A person seemingly in good health at the time of embarcation might fall sick en route and communicate his illness to others on board. Shipboard travel could therefore easily carry an infection from one port to another, across hundreds or thousands of miles of water.

Overland travel, on the other hand, was slower, and persons falling ill could be left behind more easily en route. For both these reasons, disease traveled less easily overland than by sea. Nevertheless, long distance human travel, whether by land or sea, implied the possibility of bringing new infections to hitherto virgin host populations. Before the Christian era, however, regular movement between India, China, and western Eurasia did not attain any sort of stable organization. Opportunities for spreading infectious diseases from one part of the civilized world to another therefore remained exceptional and sporadic.

Under all ordinary circumstances thinly populated areas effectively insulated one center of dense human concentration in ancient Eurasia from others, since civilized person-to-person infections could not maintain themselves for any length of time amid a thinly scattered human host population. Indeed, even within what we are accustomed to think of as a single civilization, it is entirely probable that infections permanently residing in a large city or group of cities failed to establish themselves elsewhere on an endemic basis, but only invaded the less densely populated provinces sporadically, when a susceptible age group had become numerous enough to constitute a suitable field for infection.

We must therefore imagine that within each civilized region an ever-shifting microparasitic balance prevailed. Disease incidence must have altered as antibodies appeared and disappeared from human bloodstreams in response to individual encounters with infection. Simultaneously, genetic selection among both parasites and hosts operated to change disease behavior, and such factors as climate, human diet, human density, and patterns of movement all must have also impinged upon the sensitive and unstable equilibrium between disease organisms and their human hosts.

We may infer that by about the beginning of the Christian era, at least four divergent civilized disease pools had come into existence, each sustaining infections that could be lethal if let loose among populations lacking any prior exposure or accumulated immunity. All that was needed to provoke spillover from one pool to another was some accident of communication permitting a chain of infection to extend to new ground where populations were also sufficiently dense to sustain the infection either permanently, or at least for a season or two. The plague of Athens seems to have been such an episode; others undoubtedly occurred in India, China, and elsewhere without leaving any trace we can discover today.

When, however, travel across the breadth of the Old World from China and India to the Mediterranean became regularly organized on a routine basis, so that thousands of individuals began to make a living by traveling to and fro, both on shipboard and by caravan, then conditions for the diffusion of infections among the separate civilizations of the Old World altered profoundly. The possibility of homogenization of those infections, whose most critical limit was defined by the number of new human hosts available day in and day out, opened up. It is my contention that something approximating this condition did in fact occur, beginning in the first century A.D.

Unfortunately, most details of how communications among the separate civilizations of the Old World developed between 200 B.C. and A.D. 200 remain obscure. Only a few surprising events were recorded. We know, for instance, of a Chinese explorer who in 128 B.C. reached the fertile valley of Ferghana in what is now Afghanistan. He was followed by an army detachment to garrison that distant outpost of Chinese imperial power, beginning in 101 B.C. But a detachment of soldiers, each of whom had in all probability long since recovered from locally prevalent childhood diseases, were not very likely to be able to transfer an unfamiliar infection across the thousands of miles between China and the Middle East. For such an event to become probable, a far more variegated bridge of human travelers was needed so as to scatter susceptibles all across the intervening distances in sufficient number to permit an infectious chain to run all across Asia.

Only when caravan trade became well established could such conditions arise. Nearly two centuries elapsed before regular and relatively large-scale trade came to be organized between China and Syria, following the routes these Chinese imperial emissaries had traversed. Costs of such travel were large. Camels and caravan personnel had to be maintained throughout the months of plodding between northwestern China and western Asia. Protection from confiscation en route had to be arranged. This meant payments for protection that were large enough to maintain formidable bodies of professional military men along the way. Last but not least, large numbers of persons had to have adequate motivation for undertaking such arduous enterprise: profit, adventure, imperial command or some combination of these inducements had to exert a stable impulse upon suitable numbers of men before regular exploitation of the possibility of moving back and forth between eastern and western Asian centers of civilization became a reality. Of these, profit was the most pervasive and, for long-continued enterprise, probably the most dependable. Profitable trading in turn depended on the supply and demand for goods valued highly enough in each civilized community that they could command the prices needed to meet the risks and costs of such a long and dangerous journey.

There is some evidence in Chinese texts to suggest that the opening to the West was exploited from the Chinese side with some vigor for a brief time after 126 B.C., but soon broke down, when the impulse of imperial command slackened. Then during the first century A.D., movement picked up again. New and more stable political conditions established themselves throughout the length of what Romans soon began to call the Silk Road, since silk from China became the principal commodity carried westward in this manner. This trade reached a climax about A.D. 100, as the ladies of Rome and other Mediterranean cities began to dress themselves in semi-transparent silks. These were produced in Antioch by unraveling stout silk cloth imported from China and reweaving the thread into a loose web that achieved the desired transparency.[44]

The establishment of a regular caravan trade across Asia had important consequences for the continent's macroparasitic patterns. Traders accompanying their goods could be taxed, and taxed they were by local potentates along the way. Protection payments (whether in kind or in cash) hired guards; when such guards were not actually engaged in accompanying caravans, they were of course available for enforcing and extending their leader's sway at the expense of rivals. Trade thus sustained and provoked political consolidation of a string of states extending along the caravan route, all the way from Roman Syria to the northwestern border of China.

Successful rulers within this belt of semi-desert lands were either steppe nomads themselves or but recently descended from such folk. (Nomadry encouraged, indeed required, courage and other military virtues for defense of herds and pasturage, and their horses gave nomads a mobility superior to that which cultivators could attain, making concentration of superior force in course of a sudden raid relatively easy.) Interpenetration between nomad tribesmen of the steppelands and masters of the oases of central Asia became correspondingly intimate; state structures of hitherto unequaled extent and stability resulted.[45]

For a long time the resulting symbiosis was delicate and liable to frequent upset. By taking too much from caravan personnel, merchants' incentive to undertake the risks of travel could be snuffed out. Yet by not paying enough to support a superior military establishment along the trade route, merchants invited more distant nomad groups to push southward from the open steppe and try to seize as booty what they were not yet in a position to tax as rulers. The instability was not unlike the ecological instability characteristic of a new infection. And as is also the case with many new infections, fully stable trade and protection systems were never achieved. It is not therefore really surprising that the pace of trade seems to have slackened even before the middle of the second century A.D., owing to political (and perhaps epidemiological) difficulties along the way.[46]

Organization of sea contacts between Mediterranean, Indian, and Chinese peoples proceeded on almost the same temporal rhythm. A Greek explorer "discovered" the monsoons of the Indian Ocean some time before the Christian era. Thereafter, traders whom the Indians called "Yavanas," that is, "Ionians," continued to appear along Indian coasts, issuing from ports on the Red Sea, though it is impossible to estimate the number and frequency of such voyages. Other seafarers opened sea communications across the Bay of Bengal and throughout the South China Sea. Peoples of Indonesia and the southeastern Asian mainland took a leading part in this development, although seafarers living in India itself also participated.

One conspicuous result of the development of seafaring in the Indian Ocean and the South China Sea was the transplantation of Indian court culture to the river valleys and some of the islands of southeastern Asia, beginning not long before the Christian era. Broad new regions, climatically warmer and sometimes wetter, but otherwise quite similar to the Ganges Valley, thus opened up for civilized development. For many centuries the new states of southeastern Asia remained relatively isolated transplants, surrounded by untamed jungle whose slow retreat before agricultural settlement is still incomplete in our own time. The comparative slowness of civilized expansion in this environment is almost certainly connected with the health consequences of trying to concentrate dense human populations within a well-watered tropical landscape. Intensification of microparasitism—with malaria and dengue fever perhaps in the lead, water-borne infections of the alimentary tract close behind, and an extremely complex series of multicelled parasites available to batten upon what remained—presented formidable obstacles to the growth of population in southeastern Asia toward anything like the densities that sustained Chinese and Indian civilizations. Or so one may legitimately infer from the fact that strong and massive states equivalent to the Chinese or even Indian empires did not in fact arise in southeastern Asian river valleys at any time, despite the obvious fact that the geographical areas in question provided ample space for a powerful civilization to arise there.[47]

Nevertheless, the development of court life in southeastern Asia sustained trade in much the same way that the emergence of barbarian chieftains around the shores of the Mediterranean had sustained the trade patterns supporting urban civilization in that environment. There was one important difference, however. Food staples did not figure importantly in the trade of the southern seas, as was the case within the Mediterranean. Urban and court populations of southeastern Asia depended, as elsewhere in that continent, on food collected as rents and taxes from peasants living relatively close by, i.e., mainly upriver.

The development of this vast, if loosely reticulated, trade net across the southern seas was signalized by the arrival in China of "Roman" merchants in A.D. 166. They styled themselves ambassadors from Marcus Aurelius, and though their gifts were less impressive than the Chinese chronicler thought fitting, the event was nonetheless sufficiently out of the ordinary to have been officially recorded at the Han court.[48] An even more convincing demonstration of the scale of trade during the first two Christian centuries was the excavation in 1945–48 of a trading station on the coast of southern India near modern Pondicherry. Roman merchants established a trade base there in the age of Augustus (d. A.D. 14), and seem to have occupied the site until about A.D. 200.[49] This archaeological discovery backs up the remark of the geographer Strabo (ca. 63 B.C.–A.D. 24) to the effect that trade with India had assumed a much enlarged scale in his own time.[50]

During the two centuries that followed the beginning of the Christian era, therefore, it seems certain that trade between the eastern Mediterranean, India and China operated on a regular basis and attained a scale that dwarfed all earlier exchanges across such distances. Caravans passed overland across the oases and deserts of central Asia by regular stages, while ships traveled freely across the Indian Ocean and its adjacent waters.

Regular movement to and fro across such distances implied exchange of infections as well as of goods.[51] Chances of an unfamiliar infection spreading among susceptible populations certainly multiplied, and there is reason to suppose that before the end of second century A.D. epidemic disasters in fact struck severe blows to Mediterranean populations, and probably afflicted the population of China as well. In between, nearer the center of the web of civilized life in the Old World, signs of disastrous population decay arising from unaccustomed exposure to lethal epidemics do not seem to exist. Either the populations of Middle Eastern and Indian cities had little to fear from diseases previously established among the Chinese and Mediterranean populations, but did have diseases of their own to export with lethal effect; or surviving records are so imperfect that disease disasters in Middle Eastern and Indian landscapes cannot now be detected.

Indirect evidence suggests that exposure to new infections had little effect in either India or the Middle East. In Mesopotamia, for example, a survey of ancient canal systems concluded that population crested between A.D. 200 and 600, just in the age when epidemics were cutting deeply into Roman and Chinese populations.[52] In India, the political consolidation and cultural efflorescence of the Gupta age (A.D. 320–535) also suggests (though scarcely proves) that no particularly severe demographic disasters afflicted that country as a result of the merging of previously separate disease pools in the first Christian centuries.

It is easier to understand this seemingly contradictory situation if one remembers how little effect the disease circulation created by the opening of the oceans after A.D. 1500 had on Europe, where the ships and sailors responsible for the new patterns of disease circulation were at home. Lisbon and London became infamous for the fevers and fluxes ships occasionally brought back from foreign shores, but western Europe as a whole was scarcely affected, even though millions of Amerindians and other vulnerable peoples were suffering catastrophic die-offs. By the sixteenth century, clearly, Europe had much to give and little to receive in the way of new human infections. In the first Christian centuries, however, Europe and China, the two least disease-experienced civilizations of the Old World, were in an epidemiological position analogous to that of Amerindians in the later age: vulnerable to socially disruptive attack by new infectious diseases.

The Roman world assuredly met serious epidemiological disaster between the second and sixth centuries A.D. Roman data, however scant, are far better studied than is the case elsewhere, and it therefore seems best to survey the disease record of Europe in the centuries following the establishment of regular transport across Eurasia before considering what took place in other parts of the world.

Outbreaks of disease were, of course, nothing new in Roman history in the second century A.D. Livy records at least eleven cases of pestilential disaster in republican times, the earliest dated 387 B.C.[53] Another epidemic struck the city of Rome in A.D. 65,[54] but these experiences paled before the disease that began spreading through the Roman empire in A.D. 165. It was brought to the Mediterranean initially by troops that had been campaigning in Mesopotamia, and dispersed generally throughout the empire in the following years. As usual, it is not possible to identify this "plague" definitely with any modern disease, though smallpox (or a disease ancestral thereto) has often been suggested.[55] The disease remained epidemic for at least fifteen years, breaking out in different places from year to year and returning sometimes to cities previously affected.

Despite the scanty evidence, it is reasonable to conclude that the disease was new to Mediterranean populations, and behaved as infections are wont to do when they break in upon virgin populations that entirely lack inherited or acquired resistances. Mortality, in other words, was heavy. In affected places, probably as much as a quarter to a third of the entire population died.[56] Since such a disease is unlikely to reach every populated place, the population of the empire as a whole did not diminish so sharply; the over-all loss, however, was definitely noticeable. What mattered even more was the fact that this episode inaugurated a process of continued decay of the population of Mediterranean lands that lasted, despite some local recoveries, for more than half a millennium.[57]

One reason for the continued decay of population within Roman borders was that fresh ourbreaks of serious pestilence continued to occur. A new round of a magnitude fully comparable to the Antonine plague of 165–80 hit the Roman world in 251–66. This time reported mortality in the city of Rome was even greater: five thousand a day are said to have died at the height of the epidemic, and there is some reason to believe that rural populations were affected even more sharply than in the earlier epidemic years.[58]

As in the case of the Antonine plague, there is nothing in

existing records upon which to base an exact identification of the disease (or diseases) that ravaged Roman populations in the third century. Nevertheless, there are some suggestive circumstances that make it tempting to believe that these two demographic disasters may signalize the arrival among Mediterranean populations on an ongoing basis of the two most formidable of our familiar childhood diseases, i.e., measles and smallpox. As we have seen, the evidence of Hippocrates seems to show that no such diseases were known in his time. But by the ninth century A.D. when the Arabic physician al-Razi (850–923), who worked in Baghdad, gave the first unambiguous clinical description of these afflictions, epidemic diseases involving skin rashes were of immemorial familiarity in Near Eastern lands.[59]

If one looks for earlier mentions of fevers with skin eruptions, the most notable passage occurs in Gregory of Tours, who mentions an epidemic in southern France in the year 580 that involved skin rashes of some sort.[60] Before that, texts are vaguer, though various other references can be interpreted as referring to skin eruptions in connection with epidemic outbreaks. The great doctor and influential medical writer, Galen, actually lived through the Antonine "plague," but he is not very helpful. Galen classified the disease as an abscess of the lungs, because spitting blood seemed a far more important symptom to him than mere spots on the skin. Still, in several passages he refers incidentally to epidemic outbreaks of fever together with pustules, but his humoral theory of disease made such symptoms insignificant. His phrases therefore remain tantalizingly imprecise and resistant to conclusive modern diagnosis.[61]

By the sixteenth century, when European medical writers finally recognized that measles and smallpox were distinct diseases, there is no doubt that both had become standard childhood afflictions, familiar in all parts of the continent, and of considerable demographic significance, inasmuch as many children died of one or the other, with or without additional infectious complications. The literary record therefore points to the second to third centuries A.D. as the most probable time for these two diseases to have established themselves among Mediterranean populations. The sequence of two devastating pestilences, the first coming between A.D. 165 and 180, and the second raging from A.D. 251 to 266, is exactly what one would expect—indeed what was required—if, one after the other, these two highly infectious diseases broke in upon the comparatively massive but previously unexposed populations of the Mediterranean world.

No satisfactory estimate of over-all population loss can be made. It must have been very high, though, for disease was not the sole factor attacking Mediterranean populations. Beginning in 235, civil disorders and barbarian invasions spread destruction far and wide within Roman frontiers, and famine not infrequently followed. Agreements allowing barbarian tribesmen to settle within Roman frontiers in return for some sort of agreed military service began in the second century and multiplied in later times. This in itself is indication of empty or near-empty land that could be assigned to immigrants without displacing Roman taxpayers and potential recruits. Even more telling was the series of laws, beginning in the time of Diocletian (reigned 285–305), that prohibited cultivators from leaving the land and made a number of other occupations hereditary and obligatory. The object of such laws was to compel the population to provide services required for maintenance of the imperial administration. Obviously, the only reason for such legislation was persistent shortage of persons able to perform the required functions voluntarily.

One must, then, imagine prolonged population decay resulting from intensified micro- and macroparasitism within the Mediterranean lands. Even in the first century A.D. after the

Augustan peace had ended the destructive civil wars, there were some parts of the empire—Greece and Italy particularly—that failed to prosper. The Roman imperial system collected tax moneys from lands close to the sea and transferred spare cash to the armies stationed at the frontiers. This remained a viable arrangement (though Augustus and other emperors often found it difficult to meet the military payroll) until the heavy blow of unfamiliar disease seriously eroded the wealth of the Mediterranean heartlands between A.D. 165 and 266. Thereupon, rapid die-off of large proportions of the urban populations at the most active centers of Mediterranean commerce diminished the flow of cash to the imperial fisc. As a result, pay for the soldiers at accustomed rates could no longer be found, and mutinous troops turned upon civil society to extract what they could by main force from the undefended landscapes which the Roman peace had created throughout the empire's Mediterranean heartlands. Further economic decay, depopulation, and human disaster resulted.

Military uprisings and civil wars of the third century A.D. quickly destroyed one set of landlords—the *curiales*—whose rents had sustained the outward trappings of Greco-Roman high culture in the empire's provincial towns, but a new and more rural landlord class, often enjoying partial immunity from imperial taxes, arose almost at once. Insofar as this arrangement prevailed, the hard-pressed peasant population of the empire, by submitting to a local landlord's demands for goods and services, escaped the older jeopardy of owing rents and taxes to different authorities, but it is doubtful whether the over-all pressure upon cultivators was significantly reduced. Rather, by channeling more into the hands of local potentates, resources at the command of the central administration diminished, and the empire became more vulnerable to external attack. The upshot, as is well known, was the breakup of the imperial fabric in the western provinces and its precarious survival in the more populated east.

Historians have traditionally emphasized the macroparasitic side of this balance. This accords with the tenor of surviving sources, which allow a reasonably exact reconstruction of the wars, migrations and flights that resulted in the fall of the Roman empire in the west. Yet, the ravages of armies, and the ruthlessness of rent and tax collectors—great though these certainly were—probably did not damage Mediterranean populations as much as the recurrent outbreaks of disease, for, as usual, disease found fresh scope in the wake of marching armies and fleeing populations.

What seems to have occurred in the Mediterranean lands was that a tolerable macroparasitic system—the imperial armies and bureaucracy of the first century A.D. superimposed upon a diverse muster of local landlords who generally aspired to an urban, Greco-Roman style of life—became unbearably top-heavy after the first disastrous ravages of epidemic disease hit home in the second and third centuries. Thereafter the macroparasitic elements in Roman society became agents of further destruction to population and production, and the resultant disorders, famines, migrations, concentrations and dispersals of human flotsam and jetsam, in turn, created fresh opportunities for epidemic diseases to diminish population still more. A vicious circle thus arose that lasted throughout several centuries, despite some periods of partial stabilization and local population recovery.[62]

The importance of disease in the entire process has long been recognized by historians; but because they have not been aware of the unusual force of a fresh infection arriving amid a population lacking any sort of established immunities or resistances, they have systematically underestimated the significance of the two initial epidemics in triggering the entire devolution. There is, however, ample historical evidence of the catastrophic nature of epidemic invasions of virgin populations. In particular, as we shall see in Chapter V, the devastating effect of exposure to new infectious diseases was repeatedly demonstrated by what happened to islanded populations (Amerindians most conspicuously of all) when they encountered European diseases after 1500.

Political, economic, and cultural consequences of the intensification of micro- and macroparasitism in the Mediterranean lands are too familiar to need much emphasis here. Repeated waves of barbarian invasion accompanied by the decay of cities, migration of artisans to the countryside, loss of skills (including literacy) and the breakup of imperial administration are the familiar hallmarks of the so-called Dark Ages in the West.

Simultaneously, the rise and consolidation of Christianity altered older world views fundamentally. One advantage Christians had over their pagan contemporaries was that care of the sick, even in time of pestilence, was for them a recognized religious duty. When all normal services break down, quite elementary nursing will greatly reduce mortality. Simple provision of food and water, for instance, will allow persons who are temporarily too weak to cope for themselves to recover instead of perishing miserably. Moreover, those who survived with the help of such nursing were likely to feel gratitude and a warm sense of solidarity with those who had saved their lives. The effect of disastrous epidemic, therefore, was to strengthen Christian churches at a time when most other institutions were being discredited. Christian writers were well aware of this source of strength, and sometimes boasted of the way in which Christians offered each other mutual help in time of pestilence whereas pagans fled from the sick and heartlessly abandoned them.[63]

Another advantage Christians enjoyed over pagans was that the teachings of their faith made life meaningful even amid sudden and surprising death. Release from suffering was, after all, much to be desired, in principle if not always in practice. Moreover, even a shattered remnant of survivors who had somehow made it through war or pestilence or both could find warm, immediate and healing consolation in the vision of a heavenly existence for those missing relatives and friends who had died as good Christians. God's omnipotence made life meaningful in time of disaster as well as in time of prosperity; indeed untoward and unexpected disaster, shattering pagan pride and undermining secular institutions, made God's hand more evident than it was in quiet times. Christianity was, therefore, a system of thought and feeling thoroughly adapted to a time of troubles in which hardship, disease, and violent death commonly prevailed.

Christian writers recognized this fact too. Cyprian, bishop of Carthage in 251, wrote in a tract celebrating the plague that was raging at the time:

> Many of us are dying in this mortality, that is many of us are being freed from the world. This mortality is a bane to the Jews and pagans and enemies of Christ; to the servants of God it is a salutary departure. As to the fact that without any discrimination in the human race the just are dying with the unjust, it is not for you to think that the destruction is a common one for both the evil and the good. The just are called to refreshment, the unjust are carried off to torture; protection is more quickly given to the faithful; punishment to the faithless. . . . How suitable, how necessary it is that this plague and pestilence, which seems horrible and deadly, searches out the justice of each and every one and examines the minds of the human race. . . .[64]

Such sublime capacity to cope with the horrors and psychic shock of unexampled epidemic was a significant part of the attractiveness of Christian doctrine for the hard-pressed populations of the Roman empire. By comparison, Stoic and other systems of pagan philosophy, with their emphasis on impersonal process and natural law, were ineffectual in explaining the apparent randomness with which death descended suddenly on old and young, rich and poor, good and bad. In any case, it seems quite certain that the altered incidence of microparasitism upon the Roman populations after A.D. 165 had a good deal to do with the religious and cultural history of the empire as well as with its social and political development.

Such speculation cannot really be proven, even if it seems intrinsically persuasive. We move to firmer ground by returning to the history of disease in the Mediterranean coastlands, and noting that the next conspicuously significant pestilence arrived in A.D. 542 and raged intermittently until 750. On the strength of a lengthy and exact description by Procopius, the so-called plague of Justinian (542–43) can confidently be identified as bubonic,[65] although all of the subsequent infections that ricocheted through the Mediterranean coastlands in the following two centuries were not necessarily also bubonic.[66] The disease (or something very like it) had appeared previously in Egypt and Libya in the third century B.C., if a casual remark by a medical writer named Rufus of Ephesus (ca. 200 B.C.) is to be believed. Thereafter it disappeared until Justinian's time.[67]

In the case of bubonic plague the significance of extended contacts with distant lands is unusually clear, for the disease must have penetrated the Mediterranean from an original focus either in northeastern India or in central Africa. The plague spread within the Mediterranean by ship; the pattern of infection and details of its incidence as described by Procopius make this unmistakable. Presumably other ships, traversing the waterways of the Indian Ocean and Red Sea, allowed the infection to reach the Mediterranean in the first place.

A good reason for believing Procopius is that his account fits perfectly with modern patterns of bubonic plague dissemination among human populations. Medical research in the nineteenth and twentieth centuries proved that in some circumstances, the infection can pass directly from human host to human host when droplets put into the air by a sick person's coughing or sneezing enter another's lungs. In the absence of modern antibiotics, this pneumonic form of the plague is uniformly fatal; its extreme effects also mean that pneumonic outbreaks are short-lived. The more usual route of contagion is via the bite of an infected flea that acquires the disease from a sick rat (or some other rodent), and then, when the rat or other infected rodent dies, abandons its natural host in favor of a human being. In the absence of a reservoir of infected rats, the pneumonic form of the plague cannot long endure; hence human liability to plague is limited to regions where rats or some other rodent population also exists in sufficient numbers to act as carriers for the infection.

The species of "black rats" that carried the plague in Europe appear to have lived originally in India. Rats of this species survive in a wild state in parts of that subcontinent, and they probably existed there long before learning to live as a "weed species" in and around human houses. But as weeds, rats were able to enter a new ecological niche that permitted them to spread far beyond their original homeland.[68] The most convenient way to travel, for rats as much as for men, was by ship. The black rat is a skilled climber, and therefore found it easy to boards ships by ascending mooring ropes. Going ashore in a strange port was equally easy. In all probability, therefore, the arrival of black rats in the Mediterranean was an early result of the opening of sea communications between Egypt and India, and in subsequent centuries the invader presumably extended its range inland from the ports. But as late as the time of Justinian, the black rat had probably not reached northern Europe, thus confining the plague of that era to Mediterranean coastlands within relatively easy reach of navigation.[69]

The plague is, however, not a stable infection among black rats. Indeed their relation to the disease is precisely parallel to that of humankind, for it constitutes a lethal epidemic among rats as well as among humans. Rats pick up the infection not only by an exchange of fleas with one another but also from contacts with wild rodents whose burrows harbor the bacillus of plague, *Pasteurella pestis*, on a steady, ongoing basis. In modern times, all regions of the world where large populations of burrowing rodents live in underground "cities" are infected with *Pasteurella pestis*.[70] Most of these foci of infection are very recent—an affair of the twentieth century—but three of them are much older: one in the foothills of the Himalayas between India and China; one in central Africa in the region of the Great Lakes; and one scattered across the entire length of the Eurasian steppe from Manchuria to the Ukraine. As I will argue in the next chapter, it is highly unlikely that the steppe reservoir of this infection is older than the fourteenth century A.D. This means that either in central Africa or in northeastern India at some perhaps geologically ancient time, *Pasteurella pestis* and the community of ground-burrowing rodents set up housekeeping together in a fashion that has endured to the present.

There appears to be no basis for deciding which of these two natural reservoirs is the oldest. What matters, for human plague, was the development of a susceptible rodent population that could expose human beings to bubonic infection. This was the work of the black rat and that rat's fleas. Perhaps what happened was that as the Indian black rats began to expand their range by becoming dependent on food supplies concentrated for them by human activity, they somewhere encountered the plague bacillus (perhaps in Africa). Then, via a network of rats and ships that already extended around the shores of the Indian Ocean, they may in turn have transferred the infection to communities of burrowing rodents in the Himalayas, among whom it became a stable, ongoing form of infection. Alternatively, the accommodation between the plague bacillus and the community of ground-burrowing rodents may have evolved *in situ* in the Himalayan region. In that case, *Pasteurella pestis* presumably spread with the black rat, and at some time in the past found a new group of congenial hosts among the burrowing rodents of central Africa. The twentieth-century spread of the infection to communities of burrowing rodents in North and South America, Australia, and South Africa, proceeded in this fashion, as we will see in the next chapter.

Wherever *Pasteurella pestis* may have had its original home, the Himalayan (and probably also the central African) focus of the disease almost certainly date back at least to the beginning of the Christian era. This takes us back to a time before plague manifested itself in any part of the world where surviving records allow modern experts to identify the infection, though absence of records does not prove that bubonic infections did not occur among the human populations of India and Africa long before anything of the kind broke into the Mediterranean.

Learned discussion of plague has, unfortunately, been clouded by uncritical acceptance of biblical references to epidemics as cases of plague. The term "plague" came naturally to the translators of the King James Bible, since in their day the only epidemic disease that retained its terrors was bubonic plague. Thereafter, the word "plague" became enshrined in English sensibilities; and the same thing happend in other European lands. Hence Georg Sticker and other nineteenth-century scholars accepted the idea that the "plague of the Philistines" referred to in I Samuel 5:6–6:18 was bubonic, though the Hebrew word used to describe the affliction has no assignable meaning whatever. Yet the idea that bubonic plague was very ancient lingers on, despite scholarly efforts to challenge the biblical equivalency of epidemic with bubonic plague.[71]

The Egyptian land bridge, separating the Red Sea and southern oceans from Mediterranean waters, was obviously a significant barrier to the movement of ships' rats and their fleas. Hence an infection familiar enough for centuries among rats, fleas, and people of Indian Ocean ports could have dramatic and unparalleled effects when, by some accident, it surmounted the usual barrier and burst in upon virgin populations of the Mediterranean among whom acquired resistances to the disease and conventional means for coping with it were entirely lacking. A chronic risk to human life in India and Africa (for which in all likelihood suitable customary responses had been devised by folk wisdom and practical experience) could therefore manifest itself in Justinian's world as a lethal disease of catastrophic proportions.

Historic evidence, indeed, suggests that the plagues of the sixth and seventh centuries had an importance for Mediterranean peoples fully analogous to that of the more famous Black Death of the fourteenth century. The disease certainly provoked an initial die-off of a large proportion of the urban dwellers in affected regions, and the over-all diminution of population took centuries to repair. Precision is, of course, quite impossible; but Procopius reports that at the peak of its first visitation the plague killed 10,000 persons daily in Constantinople, where it raged for four months.[72]

As in the case of the earlier great pestilences of 165–180 and of 251–266, the political effects of this plague were far-reaching. Indeed, the failure of Justinian's efforts to restore imperial unity to the Mediterranean can be attributed in good part to the diminution of imperial resources stemming from the plague. Equally, the failure of Roman and Persian forces to offer more than token resistance to the Moslem armies that swarmed out of Arabia so suddenly in 634 becomes easier to understand in the light of the demographic disasters that repeatedly visited the Mediterranean coastlands from 542 onward, and accompanied the Moslems in the first critical stages of their imperial expansion.[73] More generally, the perceptible shift away from the Mediterranean as the pre-eminent center of European civilization and the increase in importance of more northerly lands—a shift Henri Pirenne noticed and made famous years ago—was powerfully assisted by the long series of plagues, which confined their ravages almost entirely to territories within easy reach of Mediterranean ports.[74]

To be sure, epidemics were not absent from northern Europe in these centuries. A severe disease raged in the British Isles after the Synod of Whitby (664) had brought together churchmen from Ireland, Wales, and England, for instance; though whether it was plague, smallpox, measles, influenza, or something else is hotly disputed.[75] This was the most important but by no means the only such visitation; indeed, Anglo-Saxon records mention no fewer than forty-nine outbreaks of epidemic between A.D. 526 and 1087.[76] Many of these were relatively minor; and indeed, a pattern of increasing frequency but declining virulence of infectious disease is exactly what a population learning to live with a new infection experiences as the accommodation between hosts and parasites moves toward a more stable, chronic state.

What is not clear is whether the ravages of disease were heavier in urbanized Mediterranean lands than in the rural Germanic and Slavic portions of Europe. Some diseases needed urban crowding (or equivalent military concentrations of personnel into armies and fleeing hordes) to attain epidemic intensity. This was generally the case for diseases communicated through drinking water—typhoid, dysentery, and the like. Some, like the plague, seem to have been confined to Mediterranean lands, simply because Indian black rats had not yet established themselves in Atlantic seaports. But other diseases, including both measles and smallpox, were capable of spreading far and wide amid rural communities; and previous isolation tended always to make the arrival of such an infection more lethal among rural folk than was likely in disease-experienced cities. Thus *a priori* considerations work in opposite directions, and one must remain content with uncertainty as to whether urbanized Mediterranean populations suffered more or less from epidemic diseases than rural northern peoples did.

What is certain is this: until after A.D. 900 the Germanic and Slavic peoples of Europe did not suffer anything like the macroparasitic drain on their resources that the continued existence of the Roman imperial state and of Mediterranean urban populations imposed on the peasantries of the South. Differential population growth, which does indeed seem to have favored the more northerly peoples, probably reflected this fact as much as any microparasitic advantage that may have arisen from the rural and dispersed patterns of settlement characteristic of the North. The chief evidence for population growth in the North between the fifth and eighth centuries A.D. is the colonization of the Balkan peninsula by Slavs and of Britain, together with the Rhine and Danube frontier lands, by Germanic settlers. Behind the Viking raids, 800–1000, must also lie a substantial swarming of population in remote Scandinavian fjords and coastlands.

To be sure, factors other than the balance between micro- and macroparasitism affected Europe's population. In particular, food production increased in northwestern Europe between the fifth and eleventh centuries, thanks to important improvements in agricultural methods resulting from the spread of moldboard plows. This in turn sustained the beginnings of what in some essentials was a new style of civilization in the North. But the outward manifestations of emerging civilization—organized states, hierarchical churches, and expanded movement of goods by sea and land, whether for raiding or trading—all brought about intensified contacts with the Mediterranean lands to the south. Within limits set by climatic gradients and population densities, therefore, the tendency clearly was for European populations as a whole to become sharers in a single disease pool, even in such formerly remote lands as Scandinavia and Ireland.

As this process worked itself out, diseases that on their initial appearance in Europe had been highly lethal, settled toward endemicity, at least in those places where sufficiently dense populations existed to sustain a chain of infection indefinitely. In fringe areas, where population was not dense enough to sustain a stable pattern of endemic infection, demographically costly epidemics continued to break out from time to time. Such pestilences sallied forth from regions of endemicity along the routes of trade and communication connecting scattered populations with the urban centers. This situation persisted in rural and remote parts, especially islands, until the nineteenth century.[77]

As encounters with such epidemics increased, however, death tolls decreased. Shortened periods of time between successive exposures meant an increase in the proportion of persons with effective immunities created by earlier disease invasions of the community in question. When a given disease returned at intervals of a decade or so, only those who had survived exposure to that particular infection could have children. This quickly created human populations with heightened resistances. The upshot, therefore, was relatively rapid evolution toward a fairly stable pattern of coexistence between host and parasite.

An infectious disease which immunizes those who survive, and which returns to a given community at intervals of five to ten years, automatically becomes a childhood disease. And since children, especially small children, are comparatively easy to replace, infectious disease that affects only the young has a much lighter demographic impact on exposed communities than is the case when a disease strikes a virgin community, so that old and young die indiscriminately. This process of epidemiological adjustment was energetically under way in Europe as a whole during the so-called Dark Ages. As a result, the crippling demographic consequences of exposure to unfamiliar diseases disappeared within a few centuries.

In western Europe adjustment to intensified microparasitism seems to have taken place long before containment of excessive macroparasitism proved feasible. It was only after about A.D. 950 that a class of knights, suitably armed and trained, and supported locally by peasant villages, became numerous enough on the ground and formidable enough in the field to repel Viking sea raiders from the most fertile regions of northwestern Europe. From that time forward, despite continued local disorders and sporadic renewal of depredation, the population of that part of the continent entered a new period of dramatic growth.

By that time, the biological as well as the political and psychological consequences of the interpenetration of civilized disease pools that commenced in the second century A.D. had been fully absorbed; and western Europe was in a position to cash in on technical and institutional innovations that had been propagated throughout Latin Christendom during the troubled centuries when that part of the earth came fully and finally into the circle of civilized lands.

No comparably circumstantial history of gradual accommodation to new diseases can be written for any other part of the world. It is probable that if scholars with appropriate linguistic skills were to comb Chinese sources for information about diseases in the Far East, similar patterns of initial disaster and subsequent epidemiological adjustment to new diseases would become apparent. Chinese medical literature is ancient and abundant; and references to unusual outbreaks of disease occur frequently in official dynastic histories, as well as in other sorts of records. But there are difficult problems of interpretation, and the scholars who have paid any attention at all to disease in ancient China and Japan approached the problem without asking the questions that are most important for this inquiry. Until expert and careful work has been done, therefore, answers which may be buried in the vast array of Chinese and Japanese texts remain inaccessible.

A few points do deserve our notice nonetheless. For China two compilations of recorded epidemics exist: one the work of a scholar of the Sung Dynasty (960–1279) named Ssu-ma Kuang, and a second compiled in 1726 as part of an imperial encyclopedia. The published versions of these two lists contain inaccuracies of transcription and calendrical translation; but it is possible to conflate the two and correct at least some of their errors by checking the sources they cite. The result is the list of recorded epidemics in China reproduced in the Appendix.[78]

By charting epidemic outbreaks thus recorded on a time line, two major clusters appear in the early Christian centuries, and two particularly severe die-offs stand out: one in A.D. 161–62, the second in 310–12. According to the list, in 162 a pestilence broke out in the Chinese army serving on the northwestern frontier against the nomads. Three or four out of ten men died. In 310–12, another great pestilence, preceded by locusts and famine, left only one or two out of a hundred persons alive in the northwestern provinces of China; and this was followed ten years later, in 322, by another epidemic in which two or three out of ten died over a wider region of the country.

Obviously, the first of these might and the second must—if the recorded statistics are even approximately correct—represent the arrival in China of some hitherto unknown infection, else such rates of mortality could not have occurred. In the second case, a disease involving rash and fever may well have been responsible, since the earliest description of such an illness traceable in Chinese medical writing comes from the hand of a doctor who lived A.D. 281–361, named Ko Hung. The relevant passage of his book has been translated as follows:

> Recently there have been persons suffering from epidemic sores which attack the head, face and trunk. In a short time, these sores spread all over the body. They have the appearance of hot boils containing some white matter. While some of these pustules are drying up a fresh crop appears. If not treated early the patients usually die. Those who recover are disfigured by purplish scars which do not fade until after a year.[79]

This seems like a clear description of smallpox (or measles), but there are difficulties, since the passage continues:

> The people say that in the fourth year of Yung-hui (A.D. 653) this pox spread from west to east and spread far into the seas. If the people boiled edible mallows, mixed them with garlic and ate the concoction, the epidemic would stop. If when first contracting the disease one ate the concoction with a small amount of rice to help it down, this too would effect a cure. Because the epidemic was introduced in the time of Chien-wu (A.D. 317 or, alternatively, A.D. 25–55), when Chinese armies attacked the barbarians at Nan-yang, it was given the name of "Barbarian pox."[80]

Reference to an event three hundred years after Ho Kung's lifetime certainly confuses the question of when this description of smallpox was first composed. Inasmuch as it was a common practice for Chinese scholars to attribute their own words to ancients, since antiquity made a text more respectable, one cannot be sure that Ho Kung wrote this part of the text ascribed to him, or that smallpox came into China in the early fourth century A.D. Nevertheless, the likelihood remains fairly high.

What one can conclude, even from this fragmentary and imperfect data, is that some time between A.D. 37 and A.D. 653 diseases like smallpox and measles arrived in China. Coming overland from the northwest, they acted like new infections, breaking in upon a virgin population. Demographic consequences must have been similar to those the Roman world was experiencing at the same time.

As for bubonic plague, the earliest Chinese description of this disease dates from A.D. 610. In 642 another writer again mentioned it and observed, significantly, that plague was common in Kwangtung (i.e., the province in which Canton is located) but rare in the interior provinces.[81] On the strength of these references it seems reasonable to believe that bubonic plague came to China via the seaways, arriving early in the seventh century, i.e., about two generations after the disease had penetrated the Mediterranean in 542.

In China as in the Mediterranean, outbreaks of bubonic plague must have depended on the prior dispersal of the black rat and its fleas. Rats may have taken a few centuries to work their way into the local life balances in sufficient numbers to create the conditions for really large-scale outbreaks of human plague. At any rate, a series of epidemics broke out in the coastal provinces of China, beginning in the year 762, when "more than half the population of Shantung province died," and recurred from time to time until 806, when the same high rate of mortality was reported for Chekiang province.[82]

On the basis of this imperfect evidence, then, the disease history of China in the early Christian centuries seems to have resembled that of the Mediterranean lands, inasmuch as new and lethal infections probably arrived in China, traveling both overland and across the sea. Moreover, there is sufficient reason to believe that Chinese population dropped sharply from the total of about 58.5 million recorded in A.D. 2. As in the Mediterranean lands, decay of population brought with it disruption of administration, and the records that survive are both fragmentary and unreliable. When another more or less dependable census becomes available for China, in A.D. 742, the number of hearths recorded was about 8.9 million, whereas in A.D. 2 a total of 12.3 million hearths had been registered. In between, various fragmentary statistical returns suggest far more drastic depopulation of certain parts of China, especially in the South where comparative security from raiding nomads was perhaps more than counterbalanced by the heavier disease risk to which peasants pursuing a Chinese style of cultivation were liable. By the middle of the fifth century, for instance, the region around Nanking on the middle Yangtze registered only one fifth as many hearths as in the year 140. Decay in the North, while substantial, was proportionately not so great.[83]

There are other and well-known parallels between Roman and Chinese history in these centuries. The fabric of imperial administration broke down in China with the end of the Han Dynasty in A.D. 220. Invasions from the steppes and political fragmentation ensued, and by the fourth century as many as sixteen rival states competed for control of China's northern provinces. Maximal political fragmentation coincided almost exactly with the putative arrival of smallpox and/or measles in China in A.D. 317, and if mortality was anything near the severity recorded by Ssu-ma Kuang ("one or two out of a hundred survived") it is easy to see why. The figure of 2.5 million hearths in A.D. 370 as against 4.9 million hearths for the same region of northern China in A.D. 140 may indeed be more credible than scholars who have not bethought themselves of the disease variable are inclined to believe.[84]

As of A.D. 589 China achieved political unification once again, whereas Justinian's parallel effort (reigned 518–65) to reestablish a Roman empire of the Mediterranean failed. One difference was that Justinian's empire was weakened by repeated exposure to plague from 542 onward, whereas comparably severe plague attacks do not seem to have occurred in China until after 762, and then they affected only coastal provinces. Nevertheless, the breakup of effective central authority in China subsequent to a great military revolt of A.D. 755 did coincide rather closely with these outbreaks of plague. Disease as crippling to a vulnerable population as bubonic plague normally is may well have made it impossible for the imperial authorities to gather sufficient resources from the coastal provinces (which were unaffected by the revolt) to be able to put down the rebellion. Instead, the emperor called upon the help of nomad Uighur armies. As victors, the Turkish-speaking Uighurs were in a position to dictate terms, and speedily siphoned off a considerable part of the imperial resources for their own uses.

Religious history also offers another striking parallel between Rome and China. The Buddhist faith began to penetrate the Han empire in the first century A.D., and soon won converts in high places. Its period of official dominance in court circles extended from the third to the ninth centuries A.D. This obviously parallels the successes that came to Christianity in the Roman empire during the same period. Like Christianity, Buddhism explained suffering. In the forms that established themselves in China, Buddhism offered the same sort of comfort to bereaved survivors and victims of violence or of disease as Christian faith did in the Roman world. Buddhism of course originated in India, where disease incidence was probably always very high as compared with civilizations based in cooler climates; Christianity, too, took shape in the urban environments of Jerusalem, Antioch, and Alexandria where the incidence of infectious disease was certainly very high as compared to conditions in cooler and less crowded places. From their inception, therefore, both faiths had to deal with sudden death by disease as one of the conspicuous facts of human life. Consequently, it is not altogether surprising that both religions taught that death was a release from pain, and a blessed avenue of entry upon a delightful afterlife where loved ones would be reunited, and earthly injustices and pains amply compensated for.

The rhythms of population recovery offer yet another parallel between East and West. By the latter part of the tenth century, Chinese populations, like those of northwestern Europe, seem to have achieved a successful biological accommodation to whatever new infections had assailed their forefathers in the preceding centuries. Human numbers began to grow at a pace to produce a population for the entire country of about 100 million by A.D. 1200.[85] To achieve such mass, two things were needed: a suitable microparasitic accommodation to the ecological conditions of the Yangtze Valley and regions farther south, and a regulated macroparasitism that left enough of their product with the Chinese peasants so that they could sustain a substantial rate of natural increase over several generations. Only then could the teeming millions of rice paddy farmers fill up the relatively vast spaces of central and southern China.

The biological adjustments required for survival in southern China probably took a long time. Signs of really dense populations in the Yangtze Valley and farther south do not become very noticeable until the eighth century; and only under the Sung Dynasty (960–1279) does anything like the population density familiar from ancient times in the Yellow River valley begin to exist in the Yangtze and other southern areas. As we saw in Chapter II, malaria, bilharzia, and dengue fever were probably among the major obstacles to Chinese penetration southward. Variations of inherited human resistance to these infections, together with very delicate balances between different species of mosquitoes, the prevalence of different kinds of warm-blooded animals (humanity being only one possible supplier of blood for mosquitoes, after all), and the virulence of the infectious organism itself, undoubtedly controlled the incidence and seriousness of these diseases. But we cannot expect to recover details of how Chinese peasants learned to survive and flourish in the South with the densities their style of rice paddy cultivation allowed. It is enough to realize that this adjustment was probably not perfected until after A.D. 700, and full occupancy was not attained until about 1100.

As for the macroparasitic side: with the establishment of the Sung Dynasty in A.D. 960 a relatively successful bureaucratic system spread throughout most of China (the northern tier of provinces remained under barbarian masters), and a remarkably rational pattern for training and selecting high officials became normal. While no one supposes that official oppression ceased, its scope may have been less under the Sung than in earlier times, since systematic supervision of the official class tended to check at least the more flamboyant form of corruption. The massive expansion of population into the South proves that traditional rents and taxes were set at a level that allowed the peasantry to thrive on hard work in the fields, at least as long as sufficient new land could be brought under cultivation to absorb surplus offspring.

Thus China apparently paralleled Europe's disease experience fairly closely in the centuries with which we are here concerned, arriving at a balance between micro- and macroparasitism that was, in the short run at least, more successful than that of the West. In Europe, after all, local self-defense by formidable arrays of knights did not guarantee peace, since knights and their feudal superiors frequently fell to fighting among themselves, thereby damaging peasant life and production. China's bureaucratic imperial administration was clearly superior from this point of view, as long as it continued to be able to ward off attack from the warlike barbarian peoples of the North and West. From the microparasitic side, too, one can rightfully say that the Chinese achievement was superior in the sense that Chinese populations moved up a disease gradient in learning to live successfully in warmer, wetter lands; whereas the shift of European populations toward the North was a movement down a disease gradient into lands where exposure to infestation was naturally less, thanks to cooler temperatures and longer periods of freezing winter weather.

China's superior success in accommodating to altered conditions of micro- and macroparasitism was reflected in the country's religious and cultural history. For after 845, Buddhism was replaced as a religion of state by a revived and elaborated Confucianism. It was as if Charlemagne, in reviving the title of Roman Emperor, had also restored paganism as the court religion. Buddhism, of course, continued to exist in China, appealing mainly to peasants and other uneducated classes. But victorious Confucianism absorbed and made its own some of the metaphysical doctrines that had helped to attract the court to Buddhism in the first place. Thus the antibodies that imported diseases provoked and sustained in Chinese bloodstreams had their anologues in the Buddhist themes engrafted into official Confucianism. For the new doctrines received into official Confucianism constituted moral and intellectual antibodies against the charms which Buddhist (and other alien) paths to salvation continued to exert among the lowly and uneducated classes.

Japan's geographical position obviously tended to insulate the archipelago from disease contacts with the world beyond. This was, however, a mixed blessing, for insulation allowed relatively dense populations to develop which were then vulnerable to unusually severe epidemic seizure when some new infection did succeed in leaping across the water barrier and penetrating the Japanese islands. Japanese rural populations remained much sparser than was the case in China, at least until rice paddy farming established itself also in Japan (a process still under way in the seventeenth century); and Japanese cities remained much smaller than those of China until quite recent times. This meant that a number of important and lethal diseases that became chronic in China could not establish themselves lastingly among the Japanese until about the thirteenth century. Consequently, for more than six hundred years, before Japan's population density surpassed the critical threshold that allowed these epidemics to subside into endemic infections, the islands suffered a long series of severe disease invasions.

The first recorded contacts with the mainland came in A.D. 552, when Buddhist missionaries from Korea first set foot on Japanese soil. The newcomers brought with them a new and lethal disease—perhaps smallpox.[86] A similar severe outbreak occurred again a generation later, in 585, by which time immunities arising from the epidemic of 552 would have worn themselves out. A far more sustained epidemic experience began in 698 and ricocheted through the islands during the following fifteen years; the disease returned again in 735–37; yet again in 763–64; and twenty-six years later, in 790, "all males and females under the age of thirty were afflicted." Periodic records of the return of this disease continue until the thirteenth century. Then it became a children's disease (first so described in 1243), having at last achieved permanent lodgment within the Japanese islands.[87]

Dates for the introduction and eventual lasting establishment of other infectious diseases in Japan are not so clear. A new disease from which "over half the population perished" arrived in 808. By analogy from the evidence of the probable spread of plague along the China coast between 762 and 806, it seems at least possible that this was an irruption of bubonic plague into Japan, although absence of clinical description makes the identification merely a guess. In 861–62 yet another new disease—the "coughing violence"—hit the islands, and recurred again in 872, and in 920–23, with heavy loss of life. Mumps (whose distinctive swelling makes it a disease easy to recognize in ancient texts) appeared in Japan in 959; and recurred in 1029. In 994–95 another disease struck in which "over half the population died." If such a statistic is anywhere near the truth, such a heavy mortality must also have been the result of an unfamiliar infection encountering a virgin population. The measles record is also of interest. The modern term used for measles appears for the first time in 756, but serious and repeated epidemics so named began only in the eleventh century (1025, 1077, 1093–94, 1113, 1127). It was first mentioned as a childhood disease in 1224—thus anticipating the date at which "smallpox" achieved a similar status by a mere nineteen years.

Such records show that the Japanese islands pretty well came abreast of the disease patterns of China (and the rest of the civilized world) during the thirteenth century. For more than six hundred years prior to that time, however, Japan probably suffered more from epidemics than other, more populous, and less remote parts of the civilized world. As long as the island populations were not sufficient to enable such formidable killers as smallpox and measles to become endemic childhood diseases, epidemics of these (and other similar) infections coming approximately a generation apart must have cut repeatedly and heavily into Japanese population, and held back the economic and cultural development of the islands in drastic fashion.

Precisely the same considerations apply also to the British Isles. The surprisingly low level of British population in medieval times as compared to that of France, Italy, or Germany, may owe far more to the vulnerability of an islanded population to epidemic attrition than to any other factors. Without a lifetime of research, however, it is unfortunately not possible to compare the epidemic experience of Britain with that of the continent of Europe, since there is no continental equivalent to Charles Creighton's classic, *A History of Epidemics in Britain.* Yet the very fact that Creighton could assemble so much data for the British Isles may itself reflect the fact that epidemics mattered more in Great Britain than on the mainland of Europe, where the shift to endemicity presumably occurred earlier because populations were larger and had more nearly uninterrupted contact with urban (initially, Mediterranean) sources of infection.

Moreover, in both Great Britain and Japan a critical threshold was eventually crossed when earlier vulnerability to epidemic disaster ceased to manifest itself. In Japan the transition took place in the thirteenth century; in Britain the catastrophic intervention of the Black Death in the mid-fourteenth century delayed matters, so that sustained population growth only set in after 1430. But once they had crossed the critcal epidemiological threshold, Japanese and British populations both exhibited more dynamic growth than occurred on the adjacent mainlands. The effect in Japan was dramatic. A plausible estimate of Japanese total population runs as follows[88]:

Period	Millions
ca. 823	3.69
859–922	3.76
990–1080	4.41
1185–1333	9.75

As for Great Britain, comparable estimates are only available for England[89]:

Period	Millions
1086	1.1
1348	3.7
1377	2.2
1430	2.1
1603	3.8
1690	4.1

Here the downturn resulting from the Black Death is dramatically apparent; and a doubling of population, such as probably occurred in Japan in the 250 years from 1080 to 1333, had its analogue in England only between 1430 and 1690, when population also almost doubled.

The laggard adjustment to infections that thus becomes evident in Britain and Japan can be clearly related to the political and military history of the two islanded peoples. England's record of moving into and subduing the Celtic fringe within the British Isles is well known; the further effort to conquer France, beginning in 1337, illustrates an even more ambitious scheme for utilizing the strength inherent in a growing population. Once the Black Death struck, of course, the force went out of both movements. English expansion was resumed only under Elizabeth in the second half of the sixteenth century. In Japan's case the pace of expansion within the archipelago itself (at the expense of the Ainu) and overseas (at the expense of Koreans and Chinese) also assumed noticeably greater speed and force from the thirteenth century onward. A big factor in this phenomenon must surely have been the achievement of a new disease balance within Japanese society, as once damaging epidemics coming from outside transformed themselves into less costly endemic infections.

Unfortunately, nothing in available scholarly writing allows any similar reconstruction of the disease history of the rest of the world. Very possibly, most of the new diseases to which European and Far Eastern populations had to accustom themselves in the centuries between A.D. 1 and A.D. 1200 had evolved previously in India and the Middle East. Plague, at any rate, seems pretty surely to have diffused east and west via the shipping lanes of the Indian Ocean; and the rash and fever afflictions that visited both the Roman and the Chinese worlds arrived by land routes, i.e., proximately, if not necessarily ultimately, from Middle Eastern lands.

Plague, when it came to Rome, came also to Mesopotamia and Iran,[90] and may have been quite as devastating in those re-

gions as it was in the Mediterranean. Since maintenance of canals required massive annual effort, any decay of population in
Mesopotamia was sensitively registered by the abandonment of
canals formerly in use. Modern surveys discover such a retreat
in generations just before the Arab conquest in 651. Decay continued after the conquest as well.[91] There is no reason to suppose that the Moslem newcomers wreaked any very significant
damage to the irrigation system, since the Arabs were already
familiar with irrigation and had no interest in destroying potential taxpayers. It therefore seems probable that something else
upset the population balance of Mesopotamia. Although salting and other technical difficulties may have already made the
irrigation system precarious, recurrent exposure to plague offers
a plausible explanation of the precipitous decay of Mesopotamian population that accompanied and followed the Arab
conquests of the seventh century A.D.

As for India, the existence of temples for worship of a deity
of smallpox shows that the disease (or something closely akin
thereto) was of considerable significance in Hindu India from
time immemorial—however long that may be historically. Unfortunately, absence of records permits no account whatever of
Indian encounters with infectious disease before 1200.

Because smallpox and measles are especially spectacular
when they attack virgin populations, and because plague
remained spectacular in its incidence always, these diseases almost monopolize literary references in those cases when it is
possible to surmise what infection caused some sudden and
large-scale die-off. But the same changes in human patterns of
communication that propagated these infections in new regions
obviously allowed other diseases also to circulate beyond earlier
limits. This seems to have been the case with the disease modern doctors call leprosy, for a special study of more than 18,000
skeletons showed no signs of the disease until the sixth century

A.D., when it appeared in Egypt, France, and Britain.[92] On the other hand, skin ailments that fell under the Old Testament ban on leprosy must have been much older. The establishment of special houses for lepers is attested in Europe as early as the fourth century A.D.,[93] but this should not be interpreted as evidence of the arrival of a new disease. Rather, it was probably the result of the Roman government becoming Christian and taking seriously biblical injunctions about how to treat persons with disfiguring skin diseases.

Other diseases must also have found new geographic range in the early Christian centuries. Some of them, tuberculosis, for example, or diphtheria and influenza, together with various forms of dysentery, may have exerted demographic effects comparable to the effects of smallpox, measles, and plague. Moreover, formerly formidable local diseases may have disappeared when forced to compete with some invading infection; at least, as we shall see in the next chapter, there is some reason to think that this happened in later times when new and drastic epidemics afflicted Europeans.

Uniformity of infectious patterns was never attained; but despite innumerable local variations, defined by climatic and other ecological factors, it seems reasonable to conclude that within the circle of Old World civilizations, a far more nearly uniform disease pool was created as a by-product of the opening of regular trade contacts in the first century A.D. By the tenth century, the biological adjustments provoked by this reshuffle of infectious patterns had had time to work themselves out both in Europe and in China, with the result that population began again to rise in each of these civilized areas. Correspondingly, the relative weight and mass of China and of Europe vis-à-vis the Middle East and India began to grow. Subsequent world history could in fact be written around this fact.

In addition, we may reasonably believe that a fringe of peoples all across Asia, and extending into both eastern and western Africa, entered at least marginally into the disease circulation centering in the older civilized lands. Moslem and Christian traders and missionaries penetrated far into the Eurasian steppe and northern forest lands; other pioneers of civilization infiltrated Africa. Everywhere they must have carried with them the possibility of exposure to civilized diseases, at least on a sporadic, occasional, once-a-generation or once-a-century basis.

Occasional heavy die-offs of some hitherto isolated population must often have occurred. Among the survivors, however, adjustment to the new epidemiological patterns of the Old World seems to have proceeded among the steppe peoples about as rapidly as it did in northwestern Europe. The reason for saying this is that Turks and other nomads, when they penetrated civilized landscapes, whether in Asia or in Europe, do not seem to have suffered any very sharp disease consequences. If they had been completely inexperienced with civilized diseases in their steppe homelands, these nomad invaders would have died off very quickly.

The conquests and ethnic encroachments which Turks and Mongols achieved before, and more spectacularly after, A.D. 1000 simply could not have occurred had these peoples not achieved and maintained a level of immunity to civilized diseases almost equivalent to that prevailing in the major civilized centers themselves. Everything known of the trade patterns and political structures of the steppe make this seem likely, indeed all but certain. Frequent movement across long distances, and occasional assembly into large gatherings for raids or (with the Mongols) for a great annual hunt, provided ample opportunity for infectious diseases to be exchanged and propagated among the nomads, and even, as Chinese records attest, to be sometimes communicated to less mobile civilized populations.

Trade and Islamic missionaries penetrated much of Africa in exactly the same way as other Moslem traders and missionaries roamed the Eurasian steppe; and presumably with almost the same epidemiological effect, although in many African landscapes diseases peculiar to that continent presented barriers to alien intrusion more formidable than anything present in other parts of the earth. Hence civilized encroachment was restricted and, mayhap, African exposure to civilized diseases may have been less thoroughgoing than was true in the Asian steppes. On the other hand, when African slaves began to come to the New World after 1500, they suffered no spectacular die-off from contact with European diseases, which is sufficient demonstration that in their African habitat some exposure to the standard childhood diseases of civilization must have occurred, if not before, then soon after 1200.

In the New World, on the contrary, the Eurasian epidemiological experience of the first Christian millennium had no echoes whatever. As population thickened and civilized centers arose in Mexico and Peru, comparatively vast human communities came into being that were highly vulnerable to Old World infections. Civilized Amerindians after 1200 were therefore like Mediterranean and Far Eastern peoples at the beginning of the Christian era: populations dense enough for epidemic decimation. But before exploring the fateful implications of this circumstance, we must first consider a second great Eurasian epidemiological upheaval, centering on the Black Death of the fourteenth century.

IV

The Impact of the Mongol Empire on Shifting Disease Balances, 1200–1500

If the disease history of the Old World as reconstructed in Chapter III is correct, at least in its main lines, one may conclude that epidemiological adjustments arising from the establishment of regular communication across the spaces separating one civilized community of Eurasia from another had worked themselves out by about A.D. 900 into a relatively stable pattern. That is to say, by that time human populations had adjusted to the confluence of the various infectious diseases that in earlier times had developed differently in different parts of Eurasia and Africa. In all probability, no considerable population within the ecumene remained altogether inexperienced with any of the major person-to-person epidemic infections, although in many places such diseases appeared only at intervals when an accumulation of susceptible age classes provided the tinder needed to sustain an epidemic conflagration.

Two systematic instabilities remained. One was the persistent and cumulatively massive growth of human population in the Far East and Far West, resulting from the way in which the Chinese and Europeans had broken through older epidemiological and technological barriers shortly before A.D.

900. Eventually this development affected the macro-balances of the Old World in emphatic fashion, making first China and then western Europe critically influential in military, economic, and cultural matters. The other source of systematic instability within the Eurasian world balance, as defined between 900 and 1200, was the possibility of further altering communications patterns, both by sea and land.

The first such change that affected both macro- and microparasitic patterns in far-reaching ways was the intensification of overland caravan movement across Asia that reached its climax under the Mongol empires founded by Genghis Khan (1162–1227). At the height of their power (1279–1350), the Mongol empires embraced all of China and nearly all of Russia (the distant Novgorod alone remained independent), as well as central Asia, Iran, and Iraq. A communications network comprising post messengers capable of traveling one hundred miles a day for weeks on end, and slower commercial caravans and armies, marching to and fro across vast distances, knitted these empires together until the 1350s, when rebellion flared within China, leading by 1368 to the complete expulsion of the Mongols from their richest conquest.

Before that upheaval, however, literally thousands of persons moved to and fro across Eurasia, often leaving scant trace in written records. Marco Polo's famous account of his travels, for instance, came into existence merely by accident. Captured in war and imprisoned in a Genoese jail, a fellow prisoner thought it worthwhile to write down Marco's stories. Otherwise, there would be absolutely no surviving record of the Polos' existence. Other records casually reveal how permeable the Eurasian continent became under the Mongols. When, for instance, the Flemish friar William of Rubruck, arrived as the French king's emissary in the Mongol capital of Karakorum in 1254, he met a woman, native to a village near his own birthplace, who had been captured fourteen years before in the course of a Mongol raid into central Europe.[1]

Mongol communications had another important effect. Not only did large numbers of persons travel very long distances across cultural and epidemiological frontiers; they also traversed a more northerly route than had ever been intensively traveled before. The ancient Silk Road between China and Syria crossed the deserts of central Asia, passing from oasis to oasis. Now, in addition to this old route, caravans, soldiers and postal riders rode across the open grasslands. They created a territorially vast human web that linked the Mongol headquarters at Karakorum with Kazan and Astrakhan on the Volga, with Caffa in the Crimea, with Khanbaliq in China and with innumerable other caravanserais in between.

From an epidemiological point of view, this northward extension of the caravan trade net had one very significant consequence. Wild rodents of the steppe lands came into touch with carriers of new diseases, among them, in all probability, bubonic plague. In later centuries, some of these rodents became chronically infected with *Pasteurella pestis*. Their burrows provided a microclimate suited to the survival of the plague bacillus winter and summer, despite the severities of the Siberian and Manchurian winters. As a result, the animals and insects inhabiting such burrows came to constitute a complex community among which the plague infection could and did survive indefinitely.

No one knows for sure when the burrowing rodents of the Eurasian steppe first became carriers of plague. Their role in sheltering bubonic infection was discovered in 1921–24 by an international team of epidemiologists dispatched to investigate an outbreak of human plague in Manchuria. That investigation, in turn, built upon work in the Don-Volga regions of southern Russia, dating back to the 1890s, which indicated that various rodent species were plague carriers. By then, the pattern of infection was age-old and local human customs for coping with the risk of infection were immemorial. Yet it does not follow, as Russian writers have assumed, that the infection did not establish itself in historic times.[2] Quite the contrary: I contend that Mongol movements across previously isolating distances in all probability brought the bacillus *Pasteurella pestis* to the rodents of the Eurasian steppe for the first time.

In order to evaluate such an hypothesis, it is helpful to step outside the chronological frame of this chapter to consider more closely the nineteenth- and twentieth-century plague epidemic whose containment by international teams of doctors constitutes one of the most dramatic triumphs of modern medicine.

The story begins deep in the interior of China, where, as we saw in the preceding chapter, plague had probably been endemic in Himalayan borderlands between China and India by a few centuries after the Christian era and perhaps long before that. Early in the nineteenth century, the upper reaches of the Salween River constituted the boundary between infected and uninfected areas. Then in 1855 a military revolt broke out in Yunnan. Chinese troops were sent across the Salween to suppress the rebels, and, being unfamiliar with the risks of bubonic infection, contracted the disease and carried it back with them across the river into the rest of China. Thereafter, outbreaks of plague continued to occur in various parts of the Chinese interior without attracting much attention from the outside world, until in 1894 the disease reached Canton and Hong Kong and sent a chill of fright through the European settlements in those ports.[3]

Techniques of bacteriology were still in their infancy in 1894, so news of the recurrence of a disease that still loomed large in European folk memory set disciples of Pasteur and Koch eagerly to work to unravel the mystery of its propagation. International teams were therefore dispatched to the scene, and within a matter of weeks of their arrival in Hong Kong a Japanese and a French bacteriologist independently discovered *Pasteurella pestis*, the bacillus of plague (1894). During the following decade most of the details of how the bacillus was transmitted by fleas from rodents to men became firmly established through the work of a series of international task forces operating in such diverse places as Hong Kong, Bombay, Sydney, San Francisco, and Buenos Aires.

International interest in the plague was intensified by the fact that within a decade of its arrival in Hong Kong, all the important seaports of the world experienced outbreaks of the dread disease. In most places, the infection was quickly contained; in India, however, plague broke through into the interior, and within a decade of its arrival in Bombay (1898) some six million persons had died of it.[4] Recurrent minor outbreaks and the obvious risk of a major disaster if the infection really got going among human populations in Europe, America, and Africa spurred research in every threatened area.

One of the most significant discoveries was this: in California, South Africa, and Argentina, burrowing communities of wild rodents picked up the plague bacillus even more readily than people. California ground squirrels were first discovered to be infected with plague in 1900, in the same year that a minor outbreak of the disease occurred among the Chinese population of San Francisco. The plague quickly disappeared among humans; but the bacillus throve among the ground squirrels, and continues to do so until the present day. Within less than a decade, similar infections were discovered among burrowing rodent communities of South Africa outside Durban, and in Argentina outside Buenos Aires soon after human plague episodes had occurred in those ports.

The fact that the species of rodents were different in each region, and differed from burrowing rodent communities in Asia, did not make much difference. The rodent burrows, whatever the exact mix of native inhabitants, proved very hospitable to the bacillus; and in fact, each year since the infection was first observed outside San Francisco, the infected region of North America has increased. As a result, by 1975 a reservoir of infection had come into existence throughout most of the western United States and extended into both Canada and Mexico. Such a vast area of infection, in fact, is equivalent to any of the long-standing plague foci of the Old World.[5]

The geographic spread of plague infection in North America occurred naturally in the sense that the life patterns of ground-burrowing rodents create conditions for the communication of the infection from one underground "city" to another. When the rodent young have attained a certain maturity, they are evicted from the familial burrow and mill around seeking a new home. Some of the young abandon the community entirely and wander across country, traveling as much as several miles. Such wanderers will readily attempt to join a new rodent community if they find one. This life pattern provides a very effectual way of exchanging genes, with the well-known evolutionary benefits such an exchange imparts; it also allows for the propagation of infection from one rodent community to another across as much as ten to twenty miles per annum. Plague propagation among North American rodents was also accelerated by human agency. Ranchers actually transported sick rodents in trucks, sometimes across hundreds of miles, with the intention of infecting local communities of prairie dogs and reducing their numbers, thus allowing cattle to find more grass. But the spread of plague in North America, while affected by such acts, did not depend on human intervention. The upshot was that by 1940 no fewer than thirty-four species of burrowing rodents were carrying plague bacilli in the United States, and thirty-five different species of fleas were also infected.[6]

After 1900, human plague continued to occur sporadically in North America as well as in Argentina and South Africa. Mortality held steady at about 60 per cent for those who contracted the infection until the discovery of antibiotics in the 1940s made cure easy and sure, so long as an appropriate diagnosis was made in time. But habits of life among ranchers and other twentieth-century human occupants of the semi-arid plains of America and South Africa were such as to create effectual barriers between themselves and the rodent-flea communities in which the bubonic bacillus flourished. Hence the occurrences of human plague in the newly infected regions of the world remained few in number and attracted little attention, especially since local authorities were often anxious to hush up the existence of so dread a disease within their zones of jurisdiction.

In 1911, however, a new and large-scale outbreak of human plague occurred in Manchuria and again in 1921. Fresh international efforts were speedily organized to contain these epidemics. Investigators soon discovered that the human plague had been contracted from marmots. These are large burrowing rodents, whose skins commanded a good price on the international fur market. But, like the recently infected ground squirrels and other rodents of North America, marmot burrows sometimes housed *Pasteurella pestis*.

Nomad tribesmen of the steppe region, where these animals lived, had mythic explanations to justify epidemiologically sound rules for dealing with the risk of bubonic infection from marmots. Trapping was taboo; a marmot could only be shot. An animal that moved sluggishly was untouchable, and if a marmot colony showed signs of sickness, custom required the human community to strike its tents and move away to avoid bad luck. Such customary prescriptions presumably reduced the possibility of human infection with plague to minor proportions.

But in 1911, as the Manchu Dynasty tottered toward its final collapse, long-standing government regulations prohibiting the Chinese from moving into Manchuria broke down. As a result, swarms of inexpert Chinese emigrants went after marmot furs. Knowing nothing of local traditions, the Chinese trapped sick and healthy animals indiscriminately—with the result that plague broke out among them and then spread along the newly constructed railroad lines of Manchuria from what speedily became its urban focal center at Harbin.[7]

This entire sequence of events from 1894 to 1921 occurred under the eyes of professionally sensitized medical teams whose job was to find out how best to control plague. In some instances researchers went to considerable pains to reconstruct the pattern of diffusion whereby the plague had penetrated new regions and populations. Without such study and the prophylactic measures that followed, the twentieth century might well have been inaugurated by a series of plagues reaching completely around the earth, with death tolls dwarfing those recorded from the age of Justinian and the fourteenth century, when the Black Death ravaged Europe and much of the rest of the Old World.

Three points seem worth making on the basis of what is known of mankind's nineteenth- and twentieth-century brush with bubonic plague.

First, the steamship network that arose in the 1870s was the vehicle that dispersed the infection around the globe, and did so, once the epidemic broke out in Canton and Hong Kong, with a speed that was limited only by the speed with which a ship could carry its colony of infected rats and fleas to a new port. Speed was obviously decisive in allowing a chain of infection to remain unbroken from port to port. Since it creates immunities among survivors, *Pasteurella pestis* was, after all, certain to run out of susceptible hosts among a ship's company of rats, fleas, and men within a few weeks. In the days of sail, the oceans had simply been too wide for the disease to survive on shipboard long enough to make a lodgment in the seaports and waiting rodent communities of America and South Africa. But when steamships began to travel faster and, being bigger, perhaps also carried larger populations of rats among whom the infection could circulate longer, the oceans suddenly became permeable as never before.

Second, infected ships' rats and their fleas not only conveyed plague bacilli to human hosts in diverse seaports, but also managed to infect their wild cousins in several semi-arid regions of the earth. Apparently in California, Argentina, and South Africa, potential wild reservoirs for bubonic infection had existed for incalculable ages. All that was needed to create new natural plague foci was a means to convey the bacillus across intervening barriers (in this case, oceans) to new regions where suitably massive populations of burrowing rodents were already in the ground. Such rodent populations proved both susceptible to the disease and capable of sustaining an unbroken chain of infection indefinitely, despite wide local differences of habitat and speciation.

No comparable unintended geographical transfer of an infection of importance to humanity has occurred since medical men became capable of observing such phenomena; but this does not mean that similar sudden shifts did not occur in earlier times. On the contrary, the history of the plague bacillus in the nineteenth and twentieth centuries offers a model and pattern for such transfers: not least, in the suddenness with which the infection occupied new ground when older barriers to its diffusion had been breached. The fact is that however sudden and surprising they may seem, these recent triumphs for *Pasteurella pestis* constitute a normal biological phenomenon. For a new ecological niche, wherever presented, tends to be occupied quickly by whatever organism—human or non-human—thereby multiplies its kind.

Thirdly: long-standing local customs among natives of Yunnan and Manchuria alike seem to have inhibited the transfer of bubonic infection to human beings quite effectually, despite the endemic presence of *Pasteurella pestis* in rodent burrows of those regions. Only when newcomers failed to observe local "superstitions" did plague become a human problem. Moreover, in both regions the irruption of epidemiologically uninformed strangers was associated with military-political upheavals of the sort that have often provoked disease disasters in times past.

In view of the apparent effectiveness of traditional customary safeguards against plague in Yunnan and Manchuria, one may recognize that the medical prophylaxis developed so successfully between 1894 and 1924 was a quite normal, though unusually speedy and effective, human response to epidemiological emergency. Instead of allowing myth and custom, through a process of trial and error, to define an acceptable style of human behavior that would keep disease within tolerable limits, as men had always done before, scientific medicine arrived at new rules of conduct and employed a world-wide political frame—international quarantine regulations—to compel general acquiescence in newly prescribed behaviors. In such a perspective the brilliant triumphs of twentieth-century medical science and public health administration do not seem quite so novel as they otherwise might; though the fact remains that the medical discoveries of this century with respect to bubonic plague far surpass the efficiency of earlier behavior patterns for containing the ravages of the disease. Doctors and public health officers, in fact, probably forestalled epidemics that might have checked or even reversed the massive world-wide growth of human population that distinguishes our age from all that have gone before.[8]

With this modern and carefully observed example in mind, let us return to the thirteenth century, and consider what probably happened to the distribution of *Pasteurella pestis* in Eurasia as a consequence of the new patterns of human movement that the Mongols inaugurated. We must assume that prior to the Mongol conquests the plague was endemic in one or more natural foci among communities of burrowing rodents. In such regions human populations had presumably arrived at a customary pattern of behavior that minimized chances of infection. As we saw in the preceding chapter, one such natural focus was probably located in the borderland between India, China, and Burma in the Himalayan foothills; another probably existed in central Africa in the region of the Great Lakes. The Eurasian steppelands between Manchuria and the Ukraine, however, were almost certainly not yet a focus of plague.

This becomes evident if one compares the history of plague after its first devastating appearance in Europe during the age of Justinian with what happened after 1346 when the Black Death arrived. In the first instance, plague eventually disappeared entirely from Christian Europe. The last mention of the disease in Christian sources dates from 767.[9] Arab writers, likewise, make no mention of plague for at least 150 years before the 1340s.[10] One must therefore assume that after a series of precarious transfers from city to city within the Mediterranean region, the chain of infection among rats, fleas, and humans broke off because *Pasteurella pestis* had failed to find a stable, ongoing ecological niche within which it could abide lastingly.

By contrast, ever since 1346 plague has remained chronic in Europe and the Middle East, right down to the present.[11] Even when northwestern Europe ceased to suffer from the plague in the seventeenth century, eastern Europe continued to be exposed. Moreover, in the eighteenth century, when consular reports allow a quite exact reconstruction of the plague history of the busy port of Smyrna in Asia Minor, it is clear that the disease came via caravan from the interior (i.e., from the

Anatolian plateau or steppelands beyond) and spread from Smyrna by sea to other ports. The continued seriousness of the infection can be surmised from the fact that between 1713 and 1792 only twenty years were entirely plague-free in Smyrna, and in the nine periods of epidemic, death tolls ranged up to 35 per cent of the entire population of the city.[12]

The contrast between Europe's recurrent experience of the plague after 1346 and the apparent absence of the disease from European soil for more than five and a half centuries before 1346 indicates that something drastic had happened to enhance Europe's exposure to the infection. In view of what is known of how the plague bacillus seized the opportunities that nineteenth-century steamships offered for expanding its radius of action, it seems probable that in the fourteenth century *Pasteurella pestis* somehow did likewise and penetrated the rodent populations of the Eurasion steppe for the first time, thereby inaugurating the endemic infections medical men in the 1920s discovered to exist in Manchurian and Ukrainian rodent burrows.

Nor is it hard to find circumstances that might have permitted the transfer of *Pasteurella pestis* from its earlier endemic focus in the Himalayan foothills to the broad northern grasslands of Eurasia. For in the second half of the thirteenth century, Mongol horsemen penetrated Yunnan and Burma (beginning 1252–53) and thereby entered the regions where wild rodents today play host to the plague bacillus on a chronic basis, and where similar infection had probably existed for many centuries before the Mongols arrived. As in 1855, when unusual military movement allowed *Pasteurella pestis* to cross the Salween and begin its nineteenth-century peregrination around the world, so also in the thirteenth century, it is entirely probable that the Mongol invaders disregarded whatever local rules and customs had arisen to insulate human populations from bubonic infection. Like Chinese marmot trappers of the twentieth century, they therefore presumably infected themselves and thus inadvertently allowed the disease to break through former geographic limits.

The superior speed mounted horsemen commanded meant that the infection was able to extend its range of action in the thirteenth century just as it later did in the nineteenth and twentieth centuries. Infected rats and fleas could, at least occasionally, hitch a ride in a saddlebag stuffed with grain or some other form of booty, and the rapidity with which Mongol military detachments habitually moved meant that rivers and similar barriers to the slow diffusion of the infection could now be crossed as easily as oceans later were to be. It does not require a very great leap of the imagination, therefore, to believe that some time after 1252, when the Mongols first invaded Yunnan-Burma, they inadvertently transferred the plague bacillus to the rodent population of their own steppe homeland and thereby inaugurated the chronic pattern of infection which medical researchers discovered in Manchuria in our own time.

Exactly when and how this geographic transfer occurred cannot, of course, be exactly discerned, any more than the paths by which bubonic infection reached the wild rodents of California or Argentina can be precisely described. On the analogy of events in the nineteenth and twentieth centuries we might suppose that infection of rodent underground cities in the steppelands began soon after the time when Mongol conquerors first erected a bridge of moving horsemen between Yunnan-Burma and Mongolia in the mid-thirteenth century. To be sure, infection in Mongolia was not equivalent to infection of the entire steppe. That would take time. We might, thus, imagine that for nearly a hundred years *Pasteurella pestis* moved across the Eurasian steppelands from one rodent community to another in the same fashion as occurred in North America after 1900.

One hypothesis, therefore, is that soon after 1253, when

Mongol armies returned from their raid into Yunnan and Burma, *Pasteurella pestis* invaded the wild rodent communities of Mongolia and became endemic there. In succeeding years the infection would then spread westward along the steppe, perhaps sporadically assisted by human movement, as infected rats, fleas, and men inadvertently transferred the bacillus to new rodent communities. Then, shortly before 1346, the pool of endemic rodent infection perhaps began to reach its natural limits.[13]

On the whole, however, this reconstruction of events seems improbable. The trouble is that Chinese records do not show anything unusual before 1331, when an epidemic in the province of Hopei is said to have killed nine tenths of the population. Not until 1353–54 do available records indicate a more widespread disaster. In those years epidemic disease raged in eight different and widely scattered parts of China, and chroniclers reported that up to "two thirds of the population" died.[14] Even allowing for interruptions of record keeping resulting from local disorder and the breakdown of administrative routines during the prolonged Mongol conquest of China (1213–79), it seems hard to believe that any really massive disease die-off would have escaped the antiquarian compilers, whose lists of disasters provide the basis for the only available information about Chinese epidemics.

Perhaps a careful and epidemiologically informed study of all surviving Chinese texts—and they are extraordinarily voluminous—will cast more light on the question some day. But until such a search has been carried out, one must, I think, assume that the plague that burst so lethally upon Europe in 1346 manifested itself in China no earlier than 1331. And if this is so, one cannot easily believe that *Pasteurella pestis* had found a new lodgment in steppe burrows as early as the 1250s. If that had happened, China's encounter with plague would have begun long before 1331, and the vast cities and dazzling splendor of Kublai Khan's court (reigned 1257–94), as reported to us by Marco Polo, could scarcely have flourished as they did.

By contrast, after 1331, and more particularly after 1353, China entered upon a disastrous period of its history. Plague coincided with civil war as a native Chinese reaction against the Mongol domination gathered headway, climaxing in the overthrow of the alien rulers and the establishment of a new Ming Dynasty in 1368. The combination of war and pestilence wreaked havoc on China's population. The best estimates show a decrease from 123 million about 1200 (before the Mongol invasions began) to a mere 65 million in 1393, a generation after the final expulsion of the Mongols from China.[15] Even Mongol ferocity cannot account for such a drastic decrease. Disease assuredly played a big part in cutting Chinese numbers in half; and bubonic plague, recurring after its initial ravages at relatively frequent intervals, just as in Europe, is by all odds the most likely candidate for such a role.

This interpretation of Chinese records fits well with what the best-informed contemporary observers in Europe and the Near East were able to find out about the origins of the plague. A Moslem writer, Ibn al-Wardi, who lived through the initial onslaught of the plague in Aleppo, remarked that the disease originated in the "Land of Darkness" and spread through northern Asia before invading the civilized world, starting with China, and proceeding thence to India and the realm of Islam.[16] Aleppo, being a caravan city itself, and a key point in the complicated network of trade that ran across the grasslands of Asia in the fourteenth century, was a particularly good place from which to get an accurate account of the spread of the plague. A Christian inquiry into the pre-history of the Black Death arrived at the conclusion that the plague had first appeared in China (the second station in al-Wardi's account of the peregrinations of the disease) and had spread thence across Asia to the Crimea.[17]

What seems most likely, therefore, is that *Pasteurella pestis* invaded China in 1331, either spreading from the old natural focus in Yunnan-Burma, or perhaps welling up from a newly established focus of infection among the burrowing rodents of the Manchurian-Mongolian steppe. The infection must then have traveled the caravan routes of Asia during the next fifteen years before reaching the Crimea in 1346; whereupon the bacillus took ship and proceeded to penetrate almost all of Europe and the Near East along routes radiating inland from seaports.

Assuredly, the far-flung network of caravanserais extending throughout central Asia and eastern Europe offered a ready-made pathway for the propagation of *Pasteurella pestis* across thinly inhabited regions. Each regular resting place for caravans must have supported a complement of rats and fleas, attracted there by the relatively massive amount of foodstuff necessary to keep scores or even hundreds of traveling men and beasts going. Such populations of rats and fleas stood ready, like similar concentrations of rats at gristmills in the interior parts of western Europe, to receive and propagate *Pasteurella pestis* whenever it might appear, whether introduced initially by rat, flea, or human carrier. Then, when the humanly lethal consequences of the local propagation of the infection became apparent, one can be certain that everyone able to flee would do so, thus transferring the bacillus to some new, similar locus for still further propagation.[18]

On this assumption, the spread of *Pasteurella pestis* to underground rodent "cities" of the Eurasian steppe, where the infection was to find lasting, stable hospitality, occurred in a much shorter period of time than would have been needed if the bacillus had spread as it did in the United States from one rodent community to another without significant human involvement. An isolated bit of evidence supports the hypothesis of a rapid diffusion across Eurasia, for in 1338–39 an epidemic broke out in a Nestorian community of traders in central Asia near Issyk Kul. A Russian archaeologist dug up their bones and, relying on a statistical analysis of burials and some ancient texts, concluded that bubonic plague had been responsible for the deaths.[19]

What probably happened between 1331 and 1346, therefore, was that as plague spread from caravanserai to caravanserai across Asia and eastern Europe, and moved thence into adjacent human cities wherever they existed, a parallel movement into underground rodent "cities" of the grasslands also occurred. In human-rat-flea communities above ground, *Pasteurella pestis* remained an unwelcome and lethal visitor, unable to establish permanent lodgment because of the immunity reactions and heavy die-off it provoked among its hosts. In the rodent burrows of the steppe, however, the bacillus found a permanent home, just as it was later to do among the burrowing rodent communities of North America, South Africa,[20] and South America in our own time.

Yet epidemiological upheavals on the Eurasian steppe, whatever they may have been, were not the only factors in Europe's disaster. Before the Black Death could strike as it did, two more conditions had to be fulfilled. First of all, populations of black rats of the kind whose fleas were liable to carry bubonic plague to humans had to spread throughout the European continent. Secondly, a network of shipping had to connect the Mediterranean with northern Europe, so as to be able to carry infected rats and fleas to all the ports of the Continent. Very likely the spread of black rats into northern Europe was itself a result of the intensification of shipping contacts between the Mediterranean and northern ports. These date, on a regular basis, from 1291, when a Genoese admiral opened the Strait of Gibraltar to Christian shipping for the first time by defeating Moroccan forces that had hitherto prevented free passage.[21] Improvements in ship design occurring in the thirteenth century made year-round sailing normal for the first time, and rendered the stormy Atlantic safe enough for European navigators to traverse even in winter months. Among other things, ships constantly afloat offered securer and more far-ranging vehicles for rats. Consequently rat populations could and did spread far beyond the Mediterranean limits that seem to have prevailed in Justinian's time.

Finally, many parts of northwestern Europe had achieved a kind of saturation with humankind by the fourteenth century. The great frontier boom that began about 900 led to a replication of manors and fields across the face of the land until, at least in the most densely inhabited regions, scant forest remained. Since woodlands were vital for fuel and as a source of building materials, mounting shortages created severe problems for human occupancy. In Tuscany, collision between an expanding peasant population and the agricultural resources of the land seems to have occurred even earlier, so that a full century before the Black Death struck, depopulation had begun.[22] On top of this, the climate worsened in the fourteenth century, so that crop failures and partial failures became commoner, especially in northerly lands, as the length and severity of winters increased.[23]

All these circumstances converged at the middle of the fourteenth century to lay the basis for the shattering experience of the Black Death. The disease broke out in 1346 among the armies of a Mongol prince who laid siege to the trading city of Caffa in the Crimea. This compelled his withdrawal, but not before the infection had entered Caffa itself, whence it spread by ship throughout the Mediterranean and ere long to northern and western Europe as well. (See map.)

The initial shock, 1346–50, was severe. Die-offs varied widely. Some small communities experienced total extinction; others, e.g., Milan, seem to have escaped entirely. The lethal effect of the plague may have been enhanced by the fact that it was propagated not solely by flea bites, but also person to person, as

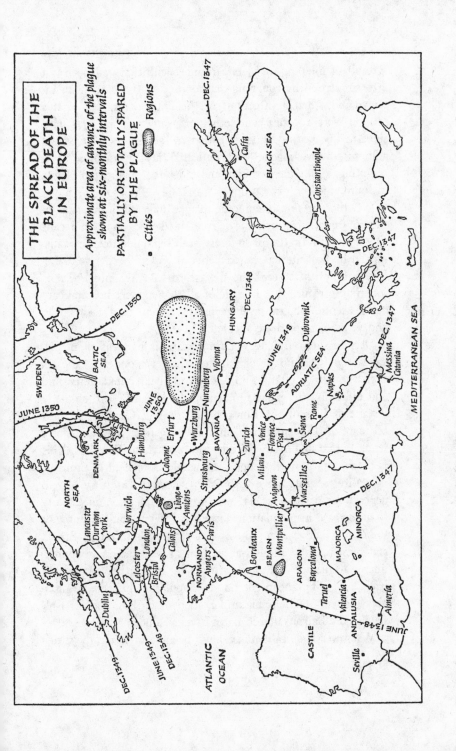

THE SPREAD OF THE
BLACK DEATH
IN EUROPE

—— Approximate area of advance of the plague
shown at six-monthly intervals

PARTIALLY OR TOTALLY SPARED
BY THE PLAGUE

Regions

• Cities

a result of inhaling droplets carrying bacilli that had been put into circulation by coughing or sneezing on the part of an infected individual.[24] Infections of the lungs contracted in this fashion were 100 per cent lethal in Manchuria in 1921, and since this is the only time that modern medical men have been able to observe plague communicated in this manner, it is tempting to assume a similar mortality for pneumonic plague in fourteenth-century Europe.

Whether or not pneumonic plague affected Europeans in the fourteenth century, die-off remained very high. In recent times, mortality rates for sufferers from bubonic infection transmitted by flea bite has varied between 30 and 90 per cent. Before antibiotics reduced the disease to triviality in 1943, it is sobering to realize that in spite of all that modern hospital care could accomplish, the average mortality remained between 60 and 70 per cent of those affected.[25]

Despite such virulence, communications patterns of medieval Europe were not so closely knit that everyone was exposed, even though an errant ship and infected rat population could and did bring the plague to remote Greenland[26] and similarly distant outliers of the European heartlands. Overall, the best estimate of plague-provoked mortality, 1346–50, in Europe as a whole is that about one third of the total population died. This is based on a projection upon the whole Continent of probable mortality rates in the British Isles, where the industry of two generations of scholars has narrowed the range of uncertainty to a decrease in population during the plague's initial onset of something between 20 and 45 per cent.[27] Transferring British statistics to the Continent as a whole at best defines an approximate magnitude for guess-estimation. In northern Italy and French Mediterranean coastlands, population losses were probably higher[28]; in Bohemia and Poland much less; and for Russia and the Balkans no estimates have even been attempted.[29]

Whatever the reality may have been—and it clearly varied

sharply from community to community and in ways no one could in the least comprehend—we can be sure that the shock to accustomed ways and expectations was severe. Moreover, the plague did not disappear from Europe after its first massive attack. Instead, recurrent plagues followed at irregular intervals, and with varying patterns of incidence, sometimes rising to a new severity, and then again receding. Places that had escaped the first onset commonly experienced severe die-off in later epidemics. When the disease returned to places where it had raged before, those who had recovered from a previous attack were, of course, immune, so that death tolls tended to concentrate among those born since the previous plague year.

In most parts of Europe, even the loss of as much as a quarter of the population did not, at first, make very lasting differences. Rather heavy population pressure on available resources before 1346 meant that eager candidates were at hand for most of the vacated places.) Only positions requiring relatively high skills—farm managers or teachers of Latin, for instance—were likely to be in short supply. But the recurrences of plague in the 1360s and 1370s altered this situation. Manpower shortages came to be widely felt in agriculture and other humble occupations; the socio-economic pyramid was altered, in different ways in different parts of Europe, and darker climates of opinion and feeling became as chronic and inescapable as the plague itself. Europe, in short, entered upon a new era of its history, embracing as much diversity as ever, since reactions and readjustments followed differing paths in different regions of the Continent, but everywhere nonetheless different from the patterns that had prevailed before 1346.[30]

In England, where scholarly study of the plague has achieved by far its greatest elaboration, population declined irregularly but persistently for more than a century, and reached a low point some time between 1440 and 1480.[31] Nothing comparably definite can be said about other parts of Europe, though there is no doubt whatever that plague losses continued to be a significant element in the Continent's demography until the eighteenth century.[32] If one assumes that population decay lasted about as long on the Continent as in England—an assumption liable to innumerable local exceptions but plausible overall[33]—the period required for medieval European populations to absorb the shock of renewed exposure to plague seems to have been between 100 and 133 years, i.e., about five to six human generations. This closely parallels the time Amerindian and Pacific island populations later needed to make an even more drastic adjustment to altered epidemiological conditions and suggests that, as in the case of Australian rabbits exposed to myxomatosis, 1950–53,[34] there are natural rhythms at work that limit and define the demographic consequences of sudden exposure to initially very lethal infections.

Parallel to this biological process, however, was a cultural one, whereby men (and perhaps rats, too) learned how to minimize risks of infection. The idea of quarantine had been present even in 1346. This stemmed from biblical passages prescribing the ostracism of lepers; and by treating plague sufferers as though they were temporary lepers[35]—forty days quarantine eventually became standard—those who remained in good health found a public and approved way to express their fear and loathing of the disease. Since everyone remained ignorant of the roles of fleas and rats in the propagation of the disease until the very end of the nineteenth century, quarantine measures were not always effectual.

Nevertheless, since doing something was psychologically preferable to apathetic despair, quarantine regulations became institutionalized, first at Ragusa (1465), then at Venice (1485); and the example of these two Adriatic trading ports was widely imitated elsewhere in the Mediterranean thereafter.[36] The requirement that any ship arriving from a port suspected of plague had to anchor in a secluded place and remain for forty days without communication with the land was not always enforced, and even when enforced, rats and fleas could sometimes come ashore while human beings were prevented from doing so. All the same, in many cases such precautions must have checked the spread of plague, since, if isolation could be achieved, forty days was quite enough to allow a chain of infection to burn itself out within any ship's company. The quarantine rules which became general in Christian ports of the Mediterranean in the sixteenth century were therefore well founded.

Yet plague continued to filter past such barriers, and continued to constitute a significant demographic factor in late medieval and early modern times in all parts of Europe. In the Mediterranean, access to the enduring reservoir of rodent infection was especially easy via Black Sea and Asia Minor ports.[37] Outbreaks of plague were therefore frequent enough to keep the quarantine administrations of all major ports continuously alive until, in the nineteenth century, new ideas about contagion led to relaxation of old rules.[38] The last important plague outbreak in the western Mediterranean occurred in and around Marseilles, 1720–21[39]; but until the seventeenth century occasional plague outbreaks, carrying off anything up to a third or a half of a city's population in a single year, were normal.[40] Venetian statistics, for instance, which became fully reliable by the second half of the sixteenth century, show that in 1575–77 and again in 1630–31, a third or more of the city's population died of plague.[41]

Outside the Mediterranean, European exposure to plague was less frequent and public administration in late medieval and early modern times was less expert. The result was to make visitations of plague rarer and, at least sometimes, also more catastrophic. A particularly interesting case was the outbreak of plague in northern Spain, 1596–1602. One calculation holds that half a million died in this epidemic alone. Subsequent outbreaks in 1648–52 and 1677–85 more than doubled the number of Spaniards who died of plague in the seventeenth century. *Pasteurella pestis* must thus be considered as one of the significant factors in Spain's decline as an economic and political power.[42]

In northern Europe the absence of well-defined public quarantine regulations and administrative routines—religious as well as medical—with which to deal with plague and rumors of plague, gave scope for violent expression of popular hates and fears provoked by the disease. In particular, long-standing grievances of poor against rich often boiled to the surface.[43] Local riots and plundering of private houses sometimes put the social fabric to a severe test.

After the Great Plague of London, 1665,[44] *Pasteurella pestis* withdrew from northwestern Europe, though it remained active in the eastern Mediterranean and in Russia throughout the eighteenth and nineteenth centuries. Quarantine and other public health measures probably had less decisive over-all effect in limiting the outbreaks of plague, whether before or after 1665, than other unintended changes in the manner in which European populations co-existed with fleas and rodents. For instance, in much of western Europe, wood shortages led to stone and brick house construction, and this tended to increase the distance between rodent and human occupants of the dwelling, making it far more difficult for a flea to transfer from a dying rat to a susceptible human. Thatch roofs, in particular, offered ready refuge for rats; and it was easy for a flea to fall from such a roof onto someone beneath. When thatch roofs were replaced by tiles, as happened generally in London after the Great Fire of 1666, opportunities for this kind of transfer of infection drastically diminished. Hence the popular notion that the Great Fire somehow drove the plague from the city probably had a basis in fact.

The spread of a new species of house rat through most of

Europe in the eighteenth century is also believed to have increased the distance between rats and humans, since the invading gray rat was a wilder, warier animal, and preferred to burrow in the ground instead of infesting roofs and house walls as the black rat—a better climber—was wont to do. There is, however, no ground for the common assertion that the invading gray rat was not susceptible to the plague bacillus; hence the argument that attributes the disappearance of plague to the supplanting of black by gray rats in most of Europe is epidemiologically faulty—as well as anachronistic, since the new rat species only reached western Europe toward the close of the eighteenth century.[45]

Perhaps more important but far more obscure were changes in infectious patterns among the populations of northwestern Europe. There is a possibility, for example, that a mutant form of *Pasteurella pestis* known as *Pasteurella pseudo-tuberculosis* may have established itself as a common person-to-person infection in the cooler, moister parts of Europe where conditions for droplet infection were better than in drier climates. "Pseudo-tuberculosis" was seldom fatal. Symptoms resembled typhoid; but the disease does confer at least a partial immunity to plague. Unfortunately, since its symptoms are readily confused with other fevers arising from infections of the digestive tract, there is no possibility of disentangling its history as a human disease from other afflictions. In addition, there are uncertainties as to the correct way to describe the relationship between the plague bacillus and *Pasteurella pseudo-tuberculosis*. Some bacteriologists claim to have observed mutation of *Pasteurella pestis* into pseudo-tuberculosis; others doubt their results.

Until these matters achieve better definition, it is therefore premature to jump to the conclusion that a mutation from *Pasteurella pestis* to *Pasteurella pseudo-tuberculosis* did in fact establish itself in Europe. One can, however, recognize that this is exactly the sort of adjustment that is to be expected when an initially very lethal infection has time to achieve a more stable relationship with its hosts. And it is clear that the pneumonic form of the plague, dispensing as it did with any intermediate host, and achieving 100 per cent lethal consequences for those affected within little more than a single day, could only survive as a human infection by undergoing such a mutation.[46]

Whatever combination of factors may have been responsible, the upshot for western Europe is not in doubt: the disappearance in the latter part of the seventeenth century of a disease which had haunted the European imagination for three centuries. This geographically modest retreat of *Pasteurella pestis'* range later provoked a grand theory to the effect that plague has appeared among humankind in three great pandemics: in the sixth century, in the fourteenth century, and, abortively, in the twentieth century. This idea developed among the medical teams concerned with plague control in the twentieth century—understandably enough since it gave their work special significance.[47] Yet the fact is that plague did not disappear among populations living closer to the Eurasian steppe reservoir, nor did it diminish in virulence, as the pandemic theory assumes, in those regions where it continued to manifest itself. It seems more likely therefore that changes in housing, shipping, sanitary practices, and similar factors affecting the way rats, fleas, and humans encountered one another were the decisive regulators, both in the advance and in the retreat of plague. The effort to structure scanty available evidence into three global pandemics seems to be a mistaken attempt to project the plague experience of western Europe onto the whole of Eurasia.[48]

Other significant changes in disease patterns also occurred in Europe, either as a result of the heavy incidence of the plague after 1346 or because other new infections besides the bubonic bacillus flooded westward with the altered pattern of human movement that the Mongol empire established within Eurasia.

The most notable phenomenon was the decline in the incidence of leprosy, which had been a significant disease in medieval Europe up to the time of the Black Death. Leprosy, of course, was a generic term used to describe a number of different infections that affected the skin in conspicuous and horrible ways. The specific disease known by that name today arises from a bacterial infection that was first identified in 1873 by a Norwegian medical man, Armauer Hansen; and to distinguish this infection from others formerly termed "leprosy," the term "Hansen's disease" is sometimes used.

Hansen's disease appears to have established itself in Europe and the Mediterranean coastlands in the sixth century A.D.[49] Thereafter, together with other infections classified as leprous, it remained of major importance until the fourteenth century. Leprosaria were established outside thousands of medieval towns. By the thirteenth century one estimate puts their number in all of Christendom at 19,000.[50]

The die-off incident to the Black Death certainly depopulated many leprosaria, but the notion that all infected individuals died, so that the disease therefore disappeared, is clearly wrong. Hansen's disease did continue to exist, on a significant scale, in Scandinavia and more sparsely in other parts of Europe as well. The fundamental fact, nevertheless, was that the number of lepers never again became anything like what it had been before 1346, and leprosaria had to be put to other uses—often converted into hospitals for the sick or, as in Venice, assigned as a quarantine station for suspected plague carriers.

Needless to say, the ecological circumstances that led to the remarkable decrease of leprosy in Europe cannot be reconstructed. Recent medical research suggests that the amount of vitamin C in the diet might be of importance, since that vitamin has the power to repress one of the chemical processes whereby the bacillus of leprosy feeds on human tissues.[51] But changes, if any, in European diets after the ravages of the Black Death seem totally inadequate to explain the widespread and abrupt decrease in leprosy that occurred.

A more likely hypothesis looks at changing patterns of disease competition. More specifically, leprosy may have retreated because of a rising incidence of pulmonary tuberculosis among Europeans. The reason for thinking this might explain what happened is as follows: immunity reactions provoked by the bacillus of tuberculosis, at least under some conditions, seem to overlap with immunity reactions provoked by Hansen's bacillus in such a way that exposure to the one infection increases the host's resistance to the other. In such a competitive situation, tuberculosis had a clear advantage. Moving from host to host via droplets put into the air by the sneezing and coughing of already infected persons, tuberculosis bacilli were far more mobile than their rivals. Exactly how Hansen's disease passes from host to host remains unsure even today; but it is clear that the disease is not very contagious. The bacillus seems to establish itself in a new host only after prolonged contact.

It is easy to imagine, therefore, that if pulmonary tuberculosis did in fact become more prevalent in Europe after 1346, it could have interrupted the infectious chain of Hansen's disease, provoking a higher level of resistance in European bloodstreams simply by getting there first and calling forth antibodies that made things more difficult for the slower-moving bacillus of leprosy.[52]

Such a hypothesis at once raises the question whether and why tuberculosis attained greater frequency in Europe after the plague years. Tuberculosis bacilli are among the oldest and most widespread on earth; and liability to tubercular infection long antedated the emergence of humanity itself. Stone Age and Egyptian Old Kingdom skeletons have been diagnosed as exhibiting signs of tubercular damage, although evidence for pulmonary tuberculosis remains, in the nature of the case, exiguous.[53]

Under modern conditions, pulmonary tuberculosis propagates itself best in urban settings, where strangers frequently come into close proximity so that coughing or sneezing may transmit the infection from one person to another.[54] Towns had of course become increasingly important in western Europe since about A.D. 1000; but townsmen remained a small minority of the entire population in every part of the continent until long after the fourteenth century. The rise of medieval towns therefore seems in and of itself entirely inadequate to account for a presumed shift away from Hansen's disease and toward pulmonary tuberculosis.

A plausible solution to this puzzle suggests itself if we make a detour to consider another disease change that also may have played a part in emptying Europe's leprosaria after 1346. Yaws is a disease which medieval doctors would have classed as leprosy. It results from infection by a spirochete which is indistinguishable from the organism that causes syphilis. Entering through the skin as a result of direct contact with an already infected person, the disease manifests itself in the form of deep, open sores. Whether yaws existed at all in medieval Europe and how prevalent it may have been if it did exist, cannot be known, since its nastier manifestations fell within the range of what was recognized as leprosy. There is, however, some reason to believe that Europeans were not unfamiliar with spirochetic infection before the time of Columbus; and a body of expert opinion holds that such infections were, like tuberculosis, among the oldest known to man, carried to all parts of the earth by hunters and gatherers in the course of their initial dispersal around the globe.[55]

If we accept the proposition that yaws was one of the infections classed as leprosy in Europe before 1346, it seems clear that the infection decayed thereafter, for when syphilis broke out so virulently at the end of the fifteenth century, it acted like a new disease among Europeans, exhibiting unusually florid symptoms and meeting minimal systematic resistance from the human bodies it invaded. Yet the spirochete causing yaws and that causing syphilis appear to be the same. The difference, it seems, is in how the infection transfers itself from host to host, and in the paths of infection within the body that result from different ports of entry.

Not one but two diseases may have thus altered their paths of infection among Europeans in the aftermath of the Black Death. If so, why? Obviously, the extent of skin-to-skin contact depended, among other things, on the adequacy of clothing and fuel available to the population at large, and particularly to the poor. In the absence of warm clothing and of enough fuel to warm living space in winter, the only way to conserve body heat was to huddle close together, especially at night, and in wintertime. In the thirteenth century, when wood became scarce in many parts of western Europe, very likely this was the only ordinary way peasants could survive the rigors of cold winter nights. The die-off of the fourteenth century, however, meant that by 1400 something like 40 per cent fewer persons had to find means of supporting life in the same geographic space as had done so in 1300. On the average this obviously meant more fuel, and more wool, to go around. The further fact that winters became distinctly colder in the fourteenth century as the climate worsened may also have meant that huddling no longer sufficed to maintain body heat without more adequate clothing than had been necessary in the warmer winters of the thirteenth century.

It is, of course, a well-known fact that western Europe expanded woolen textile production markedly between the fourteenth and seventeenth centuries. Export of high-quality cloth to Levantine and Asian markets figures more prominently in available records than does the local, shoddy manufacture of woolen cloth for peasant wear. Yet it would be very surprising if the increasing prevalence of sheep, especially in England and Spain, together with the onset of colder temperatures, had not combined to put more cloth on European backs than ever before. Insofar as wages rose, consequent upon manpower shortages arising from plague losses, a rise of real income allowed wage earners to buy better clothing; and even though a rise of real wages was not a uniform nor uninterrupted phenomenon, the basic fact of fewer human bodies in juxtaposition to an increased number of sheep fleeces in western Europe remains incontrovertible. It therefore seems probable that even the poor were able to cover their bodies more completely than before, and in so doing Europeans may very well have interrupted the older patterns of skin to skin dissemination used by Hansen's disease and by yaws. If so, the emptying out of Europe's leprosaria becomes readily understandable.

Increasing supplies of woolen textiles, however, would have benefited lice and bedbugs, and thus facilitated the spread of such a disease as typhus, which seems first to have manifested itself as a notable destroyer of European armies in 1490.[56] Still another by-product would be a new notion of decency, requiring everyone to cover most of the body most of the time. As is well known, puritanical drives in both Protestant and Catholic countries in the sixteenth and seventeenth centuries aimed at hiding sex, as well as other bodily functions. This in turn presupposed that enough cloth was available to cover human nakedness, even among the poor. The importance of these movements is indeed powerful, though indirect, evidence for the reality of my initial assumption that cloth did in fact become more abundant in Europe after 1346.

Cold weather and increasing supplies of woolen textiles in Europe may therefore have confronted the bacillus of Hansen's disease and the spirochete of yaws with a crisis of survival. The latter eventually hit upon a substitute method of passing from one host to another by infecting the mucous membranes of the sex organs. In doing so, symptomatic expressions of the disease altered and European doctors early in the sixteenth century gave it a new name—syphilis.[57] Instead of being (as yaws may have previously been, at least among the poor) a widespread infection, common among children and normally incapable of developing crippling sores except when resistance was somehow reduced, the spirochetes now usually invaded only adult bodies. At least initially, they there provoked far more dramatic symptoms, just as our still familiar childhood diseases, e.g., measles, will provoke far more serious symptoms in a young adult than commonly occur among children.[58]

The bacillus of Hansen's disease, however, failed to find a new route of infection and remained prevalent only in Scandinavia, where intenser cold—and perhaps an absence of any increase in availability of wool—maintained older customs and thereby presumably allowed the bacillus to sustain its old pattern of propagation. Whether an increased exposure to pulmonary tuberculosis in other parts of western Europe also contributed to the decay of Hansen's disease must be left open. It remains a possibility, if it was true that a brush with tuberculosis did, in fact, under medieval conditions, confer partial immunity against leprosy.

The hypothetical character of these notions is obvious and needs no emphasis. Other factors in the situation—change of diet, change of temperature, change of the way public bathing was conducted—may have been more important than the increasing prevalence of clothing. Nonetheless, certain hard facts remain: the repeated appearance of plague, the diminution of European population, the increase of wool production and the emptying out of leprosaria.

Regardless of how these and other factors may have interacted to achieve the result, by the last decades of the fifteenth century the shock to older microparasitic balances, registered so dramatically between 1346 and about 1420, had been successfully absorbed. A new era, in which European population again tended to increase, slowly asserted itself.

In this development, changes in macroparasitic patterns must also have played a part, but the varied political and military experiences of Europe between 1346 and 1500 defy generalization. Perhaps there was a slow drift toward diminution of local violence. After the end of the Hundred Years' War in 1453 this surely was true in France. If the phenomenon was more general, it must be attributed to creeping centralization of taxation, and corresponding monopolization of organized military force at fewer and fewer centers. But it is far from clear that this was happening everywhere. In Poland, for instance, development ran the other way. And even in France, England, and Spain, where monarchial centralization advanced most successfully, sporadic outbreaks of armed violence remained common and were sometimes locally destructive until after the middle of the seventeenth century.

Rents took varying proportions of peasant resources, as did taxes. Productivity was a third critical variable in defining Europe's macroparasitic balances, for peasants and artisans producing more could also part with more and still survive, or even improve their standards of living. Local variation in rents, taxes, and productivity do not seem to conform to any over-all pattern—at least none that I can discern. Only on the microparasitic side do changes clearly occur, and it seems reasonable, therefore, to think that these were the factors most active in reversing Europe's population trends toward the end of the fifteenth century.

To be sure, nothing resembling a lasting stabilization ensued. Not long after European peoples had effectually recovered from the shocks of the plague and its various epidemiological consequences and side effects, the spectacular opening of the oceans of the world by European explorers, 1492–1521, administered a new series of disease shocks to humanity, this time with consequences that affected the entire globe.

Before pursuing this theme, however, it seems worth venturing a few remarks about the psychological, economic, and cultural consequences of Europe's encounter with the plague in the fourteenth and succeeding centuries; and then we must survey as best we can the disease consequences for Asia and Africa of the Mongol opening of the steppelands to regular transit.

At the psychological and cultural level European reactions were obvious and varied. In face of intense and immediate crisis, when an outbreak of plague implanted fear of imminent death in an entire community, ordinary routines and customary restraints regularly broke down. In time, rituals arose to discharge anxiety in socially acceptable ways; but in the fourteenth century itself, local panic often provoked bizarre behavior. The first important effort at ritualizing responses to the plague took extreme and ugly forms. In Germany and some adjacent parts of Europe companies of Flagellants aimed at propitiating God's wrath by beating each other bloody and attacking Jews, who were commonly accused of spreading the pestilence. The Flagellants disdained all established authorities of church and state and, if accounts are to be believed, their rituals were well-nigh suicidal for the participants.[59]

Attacks on German-Jewish communities inspired by Flagellants and others probably accelerated an eastward shift of centers of Jewish population in Europe. Poland escaped the first round of plague almost entirely, and though popular rioting against Jews occurred there too, royal authorities welcomed German Jews for the urban skills they brought into the country. The subsequent development of east European Jewry was therefore significantly affected (and the rise in the Vistula and Nieman valleys of a market-oriented agriculture, largely under Jewish management, was probably accelerated) by the fourteenth-century pattern of popular reaction to plague.

These and other violent episodes attest the initial impact of the plague on European consciousness. In time, the fear and horror of the first onset relaxed. Writers as diverse as Boccaccio, Chaucer, and William Langland all treated the plague as a routine crisis of human life—an act of God, like the weather. Perhaps the plague had other, more lasting, consequences for literature: scholars have suggested, for instance, that the rise of vernacular tongues as a medium for serious writing and the decay of Latin as a *lingua franca* among the educated men of western Europe was hastened by the die-off of clerics and teachers who knew enough Latin to keep that ancient tongue alive.[60] Painting also responded to the plague-darkened vision of the human condition provoked by repeated exposure to sudden, inexplicable death. Tuscan painters, for instance, reacted against Giotto's serenity, preferring sterner, hieratic portrayals of religious scenes and figures. The "Dance of Death" became a common theme for art; and several other macabre motifs entered the European repertory.[61] The buoyancy and self-confidence, so characteristic of the thirteenth century, when Europe's great cathedrals were abuilding, gave way to a more troubled age. Acute social tensions between economic classes and intimate acquaintance with sudden death assumed far greater importance for almost everyone than had been true previously.

The economic impact of the Black Death was enormous, though local differences were greater than an earlier generation of scholars assumed. In highly developed regions like northern Italy and Flanders, harsh collisions between social classes manifested themselves as the boom times of the thirteenth century faded into the past. The plague, by disrupting wage and price patterns sharply, exacerbated these conflicts, at least in the short run. Some ninety years ago Thorold Rogers argued that the Black Death had improved the lot of the lower classes and advanced freedom by destroying serfdom.[62] His idea was that labor shortage caused by plague deaths allowed wage earners to bargain among rival would-be employers and thus improve their real wages. This view is no longer widely believed. Local circumstances differed widely. Employers died as well as laborers; and manpower shortages proved evanescent in those towns where a vigorous market economy did effect a short-term rise in real wages.[63]

In time, of course, the initial perturbations created by the plague tended to diminish. All the same, two general displacements of European culture and society can be discerned in the latter fourteenth and fifteenth centuries that seem plausibly related to the terrifying, constantly renewed experience of plague.

When the plague was raging, a person might be in full health one day and die miserably within twenty-four hours. This utterly discredited any merely human effort to explain the mysteries of the world. The confidence in rational theology, which characterized the age of Aquinas (d. 1274), could not survive such experiences. A world view allowing ample scope to arbitrary, inexplicable catastrophe alone was compatible with the grim reality of plague. Hedonism and revival of one or another form of fatalistic pagan philosophy were possible reactions, though confined always to a few. Far more popular and respectable was an upsurge of mysticism, aimed at achieving encounter with God in inexplicable, unpredictable, intense, and purely personal ways. Hesychasm among the Orthodox, and more variegated movements among Latin Christians—e.g., the practices of the so-called Rhineland mystics, of the Brethren of the Common Life, and of heretical groups like the Lollards of England—all gave expression to the need for a more personal, antinomian access to God than had been offered by Thomist theology and the previously recognized forms of piety.[64] Recurrence of plague refreshed this psychological need until the mid-seventeenth century; hence it is no accident that all branches of organized Christianity—Orthodox, Catholic, and Protestant—made more room for personal mysticism and other forms of communion with God, even though ecclesiastical authorities always remained uncomfortable when confronting too much private zeal.

Secondly, the inadequacy of established ecclesiastical rituals and administrative measures to cope with the unexampled emergency of plague had pervasively unsettling effects. In the fourteenth century, many priests and monks died; often their successors were less well trained and faced more quizzical if not openly antagonistic flocks. God's justice seemed far to seek in the way plague spared some, killed others; and the regular administration of God's grace through the sacraments (even when consecrated priests remained available) was an entirely inadequate psychological counterpoise to the statistical vagaries of lethal infection and sudden death. Anti-clericalism was of course not new in Christian Europe; after 1346, however, it became more open and widespread, and provided one of the elements contributing to Luther's later success.

Because sacred rituals remained vigorously conservative, it took centuries for the Roman Church to adjust to the recurrent crises created by outbreaks of plague. Hence it was mainly in the period of the Counter-Reformation that psychologically adequate ceremonies and symbols for coping with recurrent lethal epidemics defined themselves. Invocation of St. Sebastian, who in early Christian centuries had already attracted to himself many of the attributes once assigned to Apollo, became central in Catholic rituals of prophylaxis against the plague. The suffering saint, whose death by arrows was symbolic of deaths dealt by the unseen arrows of pestilential infection, began to figure largely in religious art as well. A second important figure was St. Roch. He had a different character, being an exemplar and patron of the acts of public charity and nursing that softened the impact of plague in those cities of Mediterranean Europe that were most exposed to the infection.[65]

Protestant Europe never developed much in the way of special rituals for meeting epidemic emergencies. The Bible had little to say about how to cope with massive outbreaks of infectious disease, and since plague seldom affected the North (though when it came it was sometimes exceptionally severe), Protestants lacked sufficient stimulus to such a development.

In contrast to the rigidities that beset the church, city governments, especially in Italy, responded rather quickly to the challenges presented by devastating disease. Magistrates learned how to cope at the practical level, organizing burials, safeguarding food deliveries, setting up quarantines, hiring doctors, and establishing other regulations for public and private behavior in time of plague. The ability of city authorities to react in these more or less effective ways was symptomatic of their general vigor—a vigor that made the centuries between 1350 and 1550 a sort of golden age for European city-states, especially Germany and Italy, where competition with any superior secular government was minimal.[66]

Italian and German city governments and businessmen not only managed their own local affairs with general success, but also pioneered the development of a far more closely integrated inter-regional market economy that ran throughout all of Europe. Ere long these same cities also defined a more secularized style of life and thought that by 1500 attracted the liveliest attention throughout the continent. The shift from medieval to renaissance cultural values, needless to say, did not depend on the plague alone; yet the plague, and the generally successful way city authorities managed to react to its ravages, surely contributed something to the general transformation of European sensibility.

When we turn attention from Europe and ask what the new plague pattern may have meant elsewhere in the Old World, a troublesome void presents itself. Scholarly discussion of the Black Death in Europe, its course and consequences, is more than a century old; nothing remotely comparable exists for other regions of the earth. Yet it is impossible to believe that the plague did not affect China, India, and the Middle East; and it is even more implausible to think that human life on the steppe was not also brought under new and unexampled stress by the establishment of a persistent reservoir of bubonic infection among the rodents of the Eurasian grasslands all the way from Manchuria to the Ukraine.

To be sure, there is ample evidence that plague became and remained, as in Europe, a dreaded recurrent affliction throughout the Islamic world. Egypt and Syria shared the plague experience of other parts of the Mediterranean coastlands with which they remained always in close contact. About a third of Egypt's population seems to have died in the first attack, 1347–49,[67] and the plague returned to the Nile Valley at frequent intervals thereafter, appearing there most recently in the 1940s.

This is not surprising, for Egypt developed special ties with the steppelands of eastern Europe. From 1382 until 1798 the Nile Valley was governed by a corporation of warriors, the so-called Mamelukes, who were recruited from the Caucasus region. They maintained constant communication with Black Sea ports, for only so could suitable reinforcement to their numbers be assured.

The disease consequences for Egypt were probably severe. A simple count of epidemic disasters mentioned by Arabic writers shows a sudden and dramatic upsurge in the frequency with which Egypt suffered from pestilence in the fifteenth century as compared to other parts of the Mediterranean and Moslem worlds.[68] Depopulation and impoverishment were a result, enhanced no doubt by Mameluke oppression and misgovernment. But since disease has always been a more efficient killer than human muscles, the decay of Egyptian wealth and numbers was probably due more to the microparasitic risks inherent in Egypt's special link with the western steppelands than to anything the Mamelukes did deliberately. Certainly, as long as their rule endured, Egypt maintained a sinister reputation among Europeans, who could often trace a new outbreak of plague affecting the rest of the Mediterranean either to Alexandria or Cairo. Although Egypt's ill repute among Christians was undoubtedly enhanced by religious xenophobia, it remains true that after Napoleon overthrew Mameluke rule in 1798, thus severing Egypt's long-standing tie with the coastlands of the Black Sea, outbreaks of plague diminished and even disappeared for a number of decades after 1844.[69]

In other parts of the Islamic world, major bouts of bubonic plague often lasted for several years, shifting from town to town or region to region with the seasons, but persisting as an unbroken chain of infection until susceptible human hosts ran out and the pestilence disappeared for a while. As in Europe, such visitations of plague tended to affect any given region at irregular intervals of twenty to fifty years, i.e., after a new human generation had arisen to replace those who had been exposed to the infection before.[70]

Moslem response to plague was (or became) passive. Epidemic disease had been known in Arabia in Muhammad's time, and among the traditions that Islamic men of learning treasured as guides to life were various injunctions from the Prophet's own mouth about how to react to pestilential outbreaks. The key sentences may be translated as follows:

> When you learn that epidemic disease exists in a country, do not go there; but if it breaks out in the country where you are, do not leave.

And again:

> He who dies of epidemic disease is a martyr.

And still again:

> It is a punishment that God inflicts on whom he wills, but He has granted a modicum of clemency with respect to Believers.[71]

The effect of such traditions was to inhibit organized efforts to cope with plague, though the word here translated as "epidemic disease" presumably applied to other forms of pestilential disease in Muhammad's own time—smallpox, perhaps, in particular, outbreaks of which seem to have preceded and accompanied the first Moslem conquests of Byzantine and Sassanian territories.[72]

By the sixteenth century, when Christian rules of quarantine and other prophylactic measures against plague had attained firm definition, Moslem views hardened against efforts to escape the will of Allah. This is well illustrated by the Ottoman Sultan's response to a request from the imperial ambassador to Constantinople for permission to change his residence because plague had broken out in the house assigned to him: "Is not the plague in my own palace, yet I do not think of moving?"[73] Moslems regarded Christian health measures with amused disdain, and thereby exposed themselves to heavier losses from plague than prevailed among their Christian neighbors.

In the Balkans and nearly all of India, where Moslems constituted a ruling class and lived by preference in towns, this turned into a demographic handicap. After all, exposure to most infectious diseases was intensified in towns. Only a steady stream of converts from the subject populations could countervail Moslem losses from plague and other infections. When in the Balkans (though not in India) conversion slowed almost to a halt in the eighteenth century, the human basis for Moslem dominion speedily began to wear thin in regions where the rural, peasant population remained of a different faith. National liberation movements among Balkan Christian peoples could not have succeeded as they did in the nineteenth century without this underlying demographic impetus.

As for China, from the fourteenth century onward that vast country possessed two frontiers vulnerable to plague: one to the northwest, abutting on the steppe reservoir, and one to the southwest, abutting on the Himalayan reservoir. Available records, however, do not make it possible to distinguish bubonic plague from other lethal epidemic diseases until the nineteenth century, when outbreaks in Yunnan, connected with the Himalayan reservoir, eventually broke through to the coast in 1894, with world-wide consequences already described. Before 1855, lethal infections were common enough in China; and many outbreaks were probably bubonic. But available information does not allow more definite statement. All the same, the halving of China's population between 1200 and 1393 is better explained by plague than by Mongol barbarity, even though traditional Chinese historiography preferred to emphasize the latter.[74]

Nor can China have been the only part of Asia to suffer from plague losses. Throughout the lands north of the Himalayas, it is reasonable to suppose that significant population decay occurred in the fourteenth century, when the steppe exposure to bubonic infection was still new, and local human adjustments to the risk of mortal infection had not yet had time to work themselves out. But information is almost wholly lacking, save for a very few scattered, casual remarks that modern scholars happen to have picked up. Thus, for example, an Arabic writer reported that before the plague reached Crimea in 1346 and began its devastating career in Mediterranean lands, Uzbek villages of the western steppe had been completely emptied by the disease.[75]

If we think instead of the eastern portions of the steppe, the fact that the decay of the Mongols' power, signalized by their retreat from China in 1368, followed rather closely on the presumed spread of *Pasteurella pestis* throughout the steppe is very striking. One may, surely, wonder whether intensified exposure to disease, and especially to bubonic plague, was not a real factor in undermining Mongol military might. If the hypothesis presented here is correct, it is hard to doubt that steppe nomad populations, all the way from the mouth of the Amur to the mouth of the Danube, suffered population decay as a consequence of their new exposure to highly lethal infection. If so, one can see why replenishment of military manpower needed to sustain the Mongol hegemony over settled populations—whether in China, Persia, or Russia—faltered, and how the processes accelerated whereby nomad overlords were overthrown and/or absorbed by their erstwhile agricultural subject populations across all of Asia and eastern Europe.

Such a demographic disaster—if such it was—also would account for the decay of urban centers on the steppe, where trading cities had assumed considerable significance in the early part of the fourteenth century. The destruction of cities on the Volga has usually been attributed to the ruthlessness of Timur the Lame (campaigned 1369–1405). Timur assuredly did transfer artisans en masse to his capital at Samarcand; and he plundered, killed, and burned far and wide in India, Asia Minor, and across the western half of the Eurasian steppe. But the ravages of such a conqueror were nothing new; and devastated cities recovered quickly, if a suitably populous rural base from which to attract new inhabitants lay at hand. This appears to have occurred in Asia Minor and in India in Timur's wake; it did not happen in the western steppe.

The intrinsic fragility of caravan linkages upon which the prosperity of these cities depended may explain this failure: successful organization of long-distance trade, after all, required favorable conditions across broad territories, and excessive macroparasitism or any other serious malfunction at any point in the system could quickly disrupt costly caravan movement of goods. This may adequately explain why recovery from Timur's ravages in the grasslands of western Asia was so slow as to be imperceptible. Yet altered patterns of microparasitism may have played the really critical role. In fact, political disorder in the steppe after 1346 may perhaps have been a violent and shortsighted response on the part of rulers accustomed to a higher level of income than could any longer be provided by plague-riddled merchants and artisans whose more numerous and prosperous predecessors had supported all earlier efforts at state-building in central Asia and eastern Europe by paying heavy taxes.

We may be sure that personnel who made a living by assembling goods, protecting them in transit, and buying and selling en route or at the caravan termini, were particularly vulnerable to plague. Especially in the decades when the disease was novel, so that tried-and-true rules for coping with it were lacking, heavy die-offs may have done much to destroy the caravan network that had sprung into existence throughout the Eurasian grasslands in the wake of Mongol conquests. It is ironical to reflect that if this reconstruction of events is well founded, the very success with which the Mongols exploited the military potentialities of steppe life exposed Eurasian nomadry to epidemiological disasters from which the nomad warriors, herdsmen, and traders of Eurasia were never to recover.[76]

This hypothesis of demographic disaster on the steppe is rendered more plausible by another obvious yet little considered change in the human ecology of Eurasia—a change that becomes unmistakable after the fourteenth century. Prior to that time, for more than three thousand years, steppe populations had persistently taken advantage of their superior mobility and military prowess to expand southward into agricultural, civilized regions. They came sometimes as conquerors, sometimes as slaves, sometimes as mercenaries; but the drift off the steppe and into the Eurasian agricultural world was unmistakable and persistent. From time to time it became massive enough to alter linguistic and ethnic boundaries in lasting ways. The distribution of Indo-European and of Turkish languages is testimony to the magnitude and persistency of this process. Moreover, in the centuries before 1300, movement from the steppe had attained a particularly massive scale, as Seljuk and Ottoman expansion, capped and climaxed by the Mongol storm itself, surely proves.

Yet after 1346 this pattern of migration disappeared and by the sixteenth century the drift of population on the western steppe had clearly reversed itself. Instead of nomads pressing outward from the grasslands and encroaching on cultivated ground, as had been happening for millennia, by 1550 at the latest, agricultural pioneers began to penetrate the western steppelands. They moved into what had, for the most part, become an uninhabited sea of grass.

The deserted condition of Europe's grasslands in late medieval and early modern times must be seen as a problem to be explained, though historians have usually been content to accept the situation of 1500 as "normal." But the Ukrainian steppe was excellent farmland, as Russian cultivators soon showed. It was equally promising as a habitat for nomads, offering the best pasture anywhere west of Mongolia. Why, then, was it almost devoid of human life in early modern times? Raiding, especially slave raiding, certainly served to diminish human numbers, once it assumed organized form in the late fifteenth century.

Ottoman slave markets were limitless. Tartar horsemen of the Crimea capitalized on this fact by attacking Russian villages, traversing miles of emptiness before they could find suitable human victims. But such slave raiding does not explain the emptiness of the steppe itself. Where had nomads and their herds gone?

Withdrawal to the Crimea, and partial urbanization in that specialized environment may represent a deliberate choice on the part of those who made such a withdrawal. It allowed closer contact with Ottoman civilization and all the delectations civilization involved. But it is impossible to believe that nomad inhabitants of the rich grasslands of the Ukraine could all have fitted within the narrow confines of the Crimea unless some prior, massive disaster had radically diminished their numbers and made the defensible bastion of the Crimean peninsula look especially attractive to the remnant.[77]

Inferential evidence from the eastern reaches of the steppe suggests that the peoples of Mongolia and Manchuria learned how to insulate themselves effectually against plague by the seventeenth century or earlier. Otherwise, the Manchu conquest of China in the 1640s, which matched older steppe invasions exactly, could not have taken place. Lasting success required a relatively numerous and disciplined military force of Manchu "banner men" to support the new dynasty.

Simultaneously, among Mongols and Tibetans, a vigorous religious and political movement manifested itself in the seventeenth century—the rise of the so-called "Yellow Church" of Lamaistic Buddhism. The resulting reorganization of nomad society was sufficiently formidable that the new Manchu rulers of China had to concern themselves with it from the 1650s. Eventually the Manchus used China's vast resources to sustain campaigns of conquest that added Tibet and Mongolia to their empire. This required substantial effort, however, and definitive success did not come to Chinese arms until 1757, when smallpox disrupted the last fighting confederacy of the steppe, led and organized by Kalmuks.

This military-political record implies that by the middle of the seventeenth century the peoples of the eastern steppe retained or regained numerical strength sufficient to sustain their traditional roles vis-à-vis settled Chinese society. How this occurred cannot, of course, be known. But, as we have seen already, by the time medically trained observers became aware of the ecology of *Pasteurella pestis* and could study its relationship with humans, marmots and the other burrowing rodents of Manchuria and Mongolia, effective folkways had indeed developed to make human infection unlikely. If we assume that these customs date back to the seventeenth century (or before), the revival of political-religious-military expansiveness among the peoples of the eastern steppe becomes intelligible.

By contrast, the nomads of the western steppelands, falling as they did under Moslem influence, may have accepted plague as irremediable. They also had to cope with a different rodent population than existed in the eastern steppe; and this may have made the development of suitably protective folkways more difficult. At any rate, it is clear that bubonic infections did continue to break out in eastern Europe at frequent intervals throughout modern times, down to and including the twentieth century. By way of contrast, the only recent plague outbreak in the Far East was, as we saw, the work of ignorant Chinese immigrants moving into an unfamiliar environment where they disregarded nomad customs that were quite adequate, if carefully observed, to protect the human populations from infection.

The disease disasters that probably decimated the people of the steppes in the thirteenth to fifteenth centuries were soon followed by two additional blows: first, the circumnavigation of Africa by European seamen (1499), followed by the systematic opening up of a sea route between Europe and the other major centers of civilized population. Thereafter the caravans of the steppelands were no longer the cheapest way to carry Chinese goods to Europe and vice versa. One of the sustaining impulses for overland movement of goods thenceforth disappeared, and the basis for any economic revival on the steppes diminished accordingly. This was in turn followed in the seventeenth century by the development of effective hand guns that made the traditional archery of steppe cavalry ineffective against well-trained infantry. Partitioning of the Eurasian steppelands between adjacent agricultural empires swiftly and ineluctably followed, with Russia and China the principal beneficiaries.[78]

It is therefore tempting to suppose that the major consequence of the changed distribution of bubonic infection in Eurasia was the disembowelment of steppe society. There is small likelihood of ever being able to find documentary support for such a view. On the other hand, Chinese, Islamic, and perhaps even Indian documents, if they were to be carefully perused by linguistically competent scholars sensitive to the question, probably would provide a basis for reconstructing population and disease history of those societies with approximately the same degree of precision that obtains today with respect to Europe. But since the necessary painstaking labor has not even begun, general statements about the population history of Asian societies other than China before the eighteenth century lack any satisfactory basis. Even for China, study of local records will be needed to assess the importance of disease in cutting back China's population by more than 50 per cent between 1200 and 1400.

Farther away from the new focus of infection in the steppes, human responses to the changed disease pattern probably weakened. In India, for instance, if that subcontinent was in fact one of the most ancient homes for chronic plague infection among communities of burrowing rodents, the changes wrought farther north by the Mongols would make little difference. The same is true of even more distant sub-Saharan Africa. Habits and customs that restricted human plague to bearable proportions had presumably defined themselves in both these regions in ancient times, when plague first went aboard ships and began to spread through the Indian Ocean and adjacent seas. Consequently, any additional exposure to *Pasteurella pestis* that may have filtered down from the North, across the Egyptian land bridge or by some other route, would make little difference to the plague-experienced peoples of Africa and India. The fact that there seem no special signs of any population crisis in India in the fourteenth century is not therefore surprising; though the almost total absence of documentation really makes this, and any alternative speculation, almost pointless. Plague did exist in India and east Africa between 1200 and 1700. How serious it may have been, no one can say.

What we see, then, as the over-all response to the changed communications pattern created in the thirteenth century by the Mongols is a recapitulation of what we saw happening in the first Christian centuries. That is to say, massive epidemics and attendant military and political upheavals in Europe and (less clearly) also in China led both in the early Christian centuries and in the fourteenth century to sharp diminution of population in the Far East and in the Far West; but in the regions between, both epidemic history and population history are difficult or impossible to discern. In the earlier instance, several diseases were probably at work, and it took a longer time for population to recover, especially in Europe. In the fourteenth century, on the contrary, a single infection was probably responsible for most of Europe's population decay, and recovery both in Europe and in China was swifter, so that by the second half of the fifteenth century unmistakable population growth again set in at each extreme of the Old World ecumene. Even in Muscovy and the Ottoman empire, lands lying close by the steppe focus of plague infection, population growth became unmistakable in the sixteenth century, perhaps beginning even earlier.[79]

Before the limits of that renewed growth had been attained, a fresh disturbance to ecological and epidemiological world balances set in as a result of the discovery of the New World by Europeans. Consideration of the drastic and dramatic epidemiological consequences of this event will be the theme of the next chapter.

V

Transoceanic Exchanges, 1500–1700

In the preceding chapters, little has been said about the New World and its disease experience. Absence of written records and the limited results attained by medical study of skeletal remains from Amerindian archaeological sites make such lopsidedness inevitable. Nevertheless, in view of what happened after the Spaniards inaugurated free exchange of infections between the Old World and the New, it seems certain that Amerindian encounters with disease before Columbus had been unimportant from an epidemiological point of view. The inhabitants of the New World were bearers of no serious new infection transferable to the European and African populations that intruded upon their territory—unless, as some still think, syphilis was of Amerindian origin—whereas the abrupt confrontation with the long array of infections that European and African populations had encountered piecemeal across some four thousand years of civilized history provoked massive demographic disaster among Amerindians.

Reasons for this disbalance are not far to seek. The New World was, by comparison with the mass and ecological complexity of the Old, no more than an enormous island. Forms of life were, in general, more highly evolved in Eurasia and Africa, having responded to a wider range of variability arising in the larger land mass. Consequently, plants and animals from the Old World introduced by Europeans to the Americas often displaced native American species, and disturbed pre-existing ecological balances in explosive and, at least initially, highly unstable ways. We seldom realize, for instance, that Kentucky blue grass, dandelions, and daisies, so familiar in contemporary North American landscapes, are all of Old World origin. Similarly, runaway swine, cattle, and horses developed into vast wild herds in the New World with results that were sometimes destructive to the vegetable cover and soon led to serious erosion of topsoil.[1] American food plants had far-reaching importance for the peoples of Europe, Asia, and Africa after 1500, but few organisms of American provenance were successful in competing in the wild with Old World life-forms—though some examples do exist, e.g., the spread of the plant louse, *phylloxera*, that nearly destroyed European vineyards in the 1880s.

The undeveloped level of Amerindian disease was, therefore, only one aspect of a more general biological vulnerability, but one that had peculiarly drastic consequences for human life. Precise information about disease in the Americas before Columbus is difficult to come by. Bone lesions can be found on pre-Columbian skeletons indicating some sort of infection. These have sometimes been interpreted as syphilitic by doctors seeking to confirm the American origins of that disease. But such identifications are controversial, since the way one microorganism attacks a bone is very similar to the way another is likely to do so; and tissue reactions to such invasions are also similar, no matter what the infectious agent may be.[2] Unambiguous proof of the presence of intestinal worms and protozoa has been discovered at pre-Columbian burial sites, but even so the array of parasitic worms fell considerably short of varieties abounding in the Old World.[3]

Indication of disease and epidemic death have been found in Aztec codices; but these seem related to famine and crop failure and may not have been the result of the sort of human-to-human infectious chain that existed in the Old World.

Moreover, disasters came far apart in time, only three being discernible in surviving texts.[4] After the Spanish conquest, old men even denied that disease had existed in any form in the days of their youth.[5] It looks, therefore, as though Amerindian communities suffered little from disease, even though in both Mexico and Peru, the size and density of settlement had reached far beyond the critical threshold at which contagious disease organisms could sustain a simple human-to-human chain of infection indefinitely. In this, as in some other respects, the Amerindian civilizations seem comparable to ancient Sumer and Egypt, rather than to the epidemiologically scarred and toughened communities of sixteenth-century Spain and Africa.

Several centuries—perhaps more than a thousand years—had passed since favored regions of Mexico and Peru had begun to carry human populations dense enough to sustain human-to-human disease chains indefinitely. Yet such infections do not seem to have established themselves. Presumably the reason was that the domesticable animals available to the Amerindians did not themselves carry herd infections of a sort that could transfer their parasitism to human populations when those populations became sufficiently large. This sort of transfer is what must have happened in the Old World, where massive herds of wild cattle and horses, dispersed across the steppe and forest lands of Eurasia, were sufficiently numerous and made close enough contact with one another in a wild state to be able to sustain infections that passed from animal to animal without any sort of intermediate host. By comparison, wild llamas and alpacas lived high in the Andes in small and dispersed groups. These were too few and too isolated to sustain such infections in the wild. There seems to be no plausible reconstruction of the style of life of the wild ancestors of the guinea pig—the other distinctive Amerindian domesticated animal. And as for dogs, mankind's oldest domesticated animal, though they today share many infections with humans, it is clear enough that in their wild state they, too, must have existed in relatively small and isolated packs. Thus with the possible exception of the guinea pig, the Amerindians' domesticated species, like the human hunting bands that had initially penetrated the Americas, were incapable of supporting infectious chains of the sort characteristic of civilized diseases. No wonder, then, that once contact had been established, Amerindian populations of Mexico and Peru became the victims, on a mass scale, of the common childhood diseases of Europe and Africa.[6]

The scope of the resultant disaster reflected the fact that both central Mexico and the heartlands of the Inca empire were very densely settled at the time of the European discovery of America. The two most important American food crops, maize and potatoes, were more productive of calories per acre than any Old World crops except rice. This allowed denser populations per square mile of cultivated ground in the Americas than was attainable anywhere in the Old World outside of the East Asian rice paddy region.

Moreover, Amerindian customary ways of preparing maize for food obviated some of the nutritional disadvantages of a diet in which that cereal plays the principal role. The kernels were soaked in a lime solution, which broke down some of the molecules of the maize in a way that allowed human digestion to synthesize needed vitamins that are absent from the maize itself. Without such treatment, a diet of maize leads to niacin deficiency. Symptoms of this deficiency, known as pellagra, were often seriously debilitating among European and African populations that took to maize cultivation. But Amerindians escaped pellagra by soaking maize to make "hominy grits," and by supplementing their diet with beans in those regions where hunting was no longer possible because human populations had become too dense.[7]

Ecological adjustment in Mexico and Peru showed signs of strain, even before the Spaniards arrived and upset everything so radically. In Mexico, erosion was already a serious problem; and in some irrigated coastal areas of Peru, salting of the soil seems to have led to population collapse not long before Pizzaro appeared.[8] Everything points to the conclusion that Amerindian populations were pressing hard against the limits set by available cultivable land in both Mexico and Peru when the Spaniards arrived. Moreover, the absence of any considerable number of domesticated animals meant that there was a smaller margin between the sum of agricultural productivity in the Americas and direct human consumption than was commonly the case in the Old World. In time of crop failure or other kind of food crisis, Eurasian flocks and herds constituted a sort of food bank. They could be slaughtered and eaten; and in times and places when overpopulation started to be felt, human beings always displace herds by turning pastureland into cropland—at least for a while. No such cushion existed in the Americas, where domesticated animals played a merely marginal part in human food patterns.

All these factors therefore conspired to make Amerindian populations radically vulnerable to the disease organisms Spaniards and, before long, also Africans, brought with them across the ocean. The magnitude of the resultant disaster has only recently become clear. Learned opinion before World War II systematically underestimated Amerindian populations, putting the total somewhere between eight and fourteen million at the time Columbus landed in Hispaniola.[9] Recent estimates, however, based on sampling of tribute lists, missionary reports and elaborate statistical arguments, have multiplied such earlier estimates tenfold and more, putting Amerindian population on the eve of the conquest at about one hundred million, with twenty-five to thirty million of this total assignable to the Mexican and an approximately equal number to the

Andean civilizations. Relatively dense populations also apparently existed in the connecting Central American lands.[10]

Starting from such levels, population decay was catastrophic. By 1568, less than fifty years from the time Cortez inaugurated epidemiological as well as other exchanges between Amerindian and European populations, the population of central Mexico had shrunk to about three million, i.e., to about one tenth of what had been there when Cortez landed.[11] Decay continued, though at a reduced rate, for another fifty years, reaching a low point of about 1.6 million by 1620. Recovery did not definitely set in for another thirty years or so and remained very slow until the eighteenth century.

Similarly drastic destruction of pre-existing Amerindian societies also occurred in other parts of the Americas, continuing even into the twentieth century. Disaster is to be expected whenever some previously remote and isolated tribe comes into contact with the outside world and there encounters a series of destructive and demoralizing epidemics. A relatively recent case history will illustrate how ruthless and seemingly irresistible such process can be. In 1903 a South American tribe, the Cayapo, accepted a missionary—a single priest—who bent every effort to safeguard his flock from the evils and dangers of civilization. When he arrived the tribe was between six thousand and eight thousand strong, yet only five hundred survived in 1918. By 1927 only twenty-seven were alive and in 1950 two or three individuals tracing descent to the Cayapo still existed, but the tribe had totally disappeared—and this despite the best intentions and a deliberate attempt to shield the Indians from disease as well as other risks of outside contacts.[12]

Other examples of swift and irretrievable disaster abound. In 1942–43, for instance, the opening of the Alcan highway exposed a remote Indian community in Alaska to measles, German measles, dysentery, whooping cough, mumps, tonsillitis, meningitis, and catarrhal jaundice in a single year! Yet thanks to airlift into modern hospitals, only 7 of 130 individuals actually died. A little more than a century before, in 1837, the Mandan tribe of the high plains found itself cooped up in two defended camps by their Sioux enemies when epidemic broke out. As a result their numbers were reduced from about 2,000 to a mere 30–40 survivors in a matter of weeks; and those survivors were promptly captured by enemies so that the Mandan tribe ceased to exist.[13]

In an age of almost world-wide population growth, it is hard for us to imagine such catastrophes. Even without total disruption of the sort that came to the Mandan and Cayapo, a 90 per cent drop in population within 120 years (i.e., across five to six human generations), as happened in Mexico and Peru, carries with it drastic psychological and cultural consequences. Faith in established institutions and beliefs cannot easily withstand such disaster; skills and knowledge disappear. This, indeed, was what allowed the Spaniards to go as far as they did in transferring their culture and language to the New World, making it normative even in regions where millions of Indians had previously lived according to standards and customs of their own.

Labor shortage and economic retrogression was another obvious concomitant. The development of forms of compulsory labor and dispersal from cities (where disease losses concentrate) to rural estates are necessary responses if social hierarchies are to survive at all. Late Roman institutions and those of seventeenth-century Mexico have an uncanny likeness in this respect, which Spain's heritage of the Roman law only partially explains. Landlords and tax collectors, facing a radically decaying population from which to derive support, can be counted on to react in parallel fashion; and this seems to be what happened in both the late Roman and the seventeenth-century Spanish empires.

It is not really surprising, therefore, to discover how much alike the late Roman system of compulsory labor and Mexican debt peonage were in practice, even though legal forms were different. The rise of haciendas in seventeenth-century Mexico exactly parallels the rise of villas in late Roman times. Both societies also saw a massive emptying out of older urban centers. To be sure, there were differences. Rome faced a serious problem of border defense, whereas the Spanish empire of the New World was threatened only by sea and was therefore spared the expense of trying to maintain any but the most sketchy sort of armed forces on its landward frontiers. On the other hand, Roman encounters with epidemic disease were undoubtedly less crippling than the concentrated exposure to the Old World's full repertory of infections proved to be for Amerindians. Consequently, Roman authorities had a less radically decaying population base upon which to draw than the labor force that remained available for the support of the Spanish imperial structure in the New World.

Wholesale demoralization and simple surrender of will to live certainly played a large part in the destruction of Amerindian communities. Numerous recorded instances of failure to tend newborn babies so that they died unnecessarily, as well as outright suicide, attest the intensity of Amerindian bewilderment and despair. European military action and harsh treatment of laborers gathered forcibly for some large-scale undertaking also had a role in uprooting and destroying old social structures. But human violence and disregard, however brutal, was not the major factor causing Amerindian populations to melt away as they did. After all, it was not in the interest of the Spaniards and other Europeans to allow potential taxpayers and the Indian work force to diminish. The main destructive role was certainly played by epidemic disease.

The first encounter came in 1518 when smallpox reached Hispaniola and attacked the Indian population so virulently that Bartoleme de Las Casas believed only a thousand survived.

From Hispaniola, smallpox traveled to Mexico, arriving with the relief expedition that joined Cortez in 1520. As a result, at the very crisis of the conquest, when Montezuma had been killed and the Aztecs were girding themselves for an attack on the Spaniards, smallpox raged in Tenochtitlán. The leader of the assault, along with innumerable followers, died within hours of compelling the Spaniards to retreat from their city. Instead of following up on the initial success and harrying the tiny band of Spaniards from the land, therefore, as might have been expected had the smallpox not paralyzed effective action, the Aztecs lapsed into a stunned inactivity. Cortez thus was able to rally his forces, gather allies from among the Aztecs' subject peoples, and return for the final siege and destruction of the capital.

Clearly, if smallpox had not come when it did, the Spanish victory could not have been achieved in Mexico. The same was true of Pizarro's filibuster into Peru. For the smallpox epidemic in Mexico did not confine its ravages to Aztec territory. Instead, it spread to Guatemala, where it appeared in 1520, and continued southward, penetrating the Inca domain in 1525 or 1526. Consequences there were just as drastic as among the Aztecs. The reigning Inca died of the disease while away from his capital on campaign in the North. His designated heir also died, leaving no legitimate successor. Civil war ensued, and it was amid this wreckage of the Inca political structure that Pizarro and his crew of roughnecks made their way to Cuzco and plundered its treasures. He met no serious military resistance at all.

Two points seem particularly worth emphasizing here. First, Spaniards and Indians readily agreed that epidemic disease was a particularly dreadful and unambiguous form of divine punishment. Interpretation of pestilence as a sign of God's displeasure was a part of the Spanish inheritance, enshrined in the Old Testament and in the whole Christian tradition. The Amerindians, lacking all experience of anything remotely like the initial series of lethal epidemics, concurred. Their religious doctrines recognized that superhuman power lodged in deities whose behavior toward men was often angry. It was natural, therefore, for them to assign an unexampled effect to a supernatural cause, quite apart from the Spanish missionary efforts that urged the same interpretation of the catastrophe upon dazed and demoralized converts.

Secondly, the Spaniards were nearly immune from the terrible disease that raged so mercilessly among the Indians. They had almost always been exposed in childhood and so developed effective immunity. Given the interpretation of the cause of pestilence accepted by both parties, such a manifestation of divine partiality for the invaders was conclusive. The gods of the Aztecs as much as the God of the Christians seemed to agree that the white newcomers had divine approval for all they did. And while God thus seemed to favor the whites, regardless of their mortality and piety or lack thereof, his wrath was visited upon the Indians with an unrelenting harshness that often puzzled and distressed the Christian missionaries who soon took charge of the moral and religious life of their converts along the frontiers of Spain's American dominions.

From the Amerindian point of view, stunned acquiescence in Spanish superiority was the only possible response. No matter how few their numbers or how brutal and squalid their behavior, the Spaniards prevailed. Native authority structures crumbled; the old gods seemed to have abdicated. The situation was ripe for the mass conversions recorded so proudly by Christian missionaries. Docility to the commands of priests, viceroys, landowners, mining entrepreneurs, tax collectors, and anyone else who spoke with a loud voice and had a white skin was another inevitable consequence. When the divine and natural orders were both unambiguous in declaring against native tradition and belief, what ground for resistance remained? The extraordinary ease of Spanish conquests and the success a few hundred men had in securing control of vast areas and millions of persons is unintelligible on any other basis.

Even after the initial ravages of smallpox had passed, having killed something like one third of the total population, nothing approaching epidemiological stability prevailed. Measles followed hard upon the heels of smallpox, spreading through Mexico and Peru in 1530–31. Deaths were frequent, as is to be expected when such a disease encounters a virgin population dense enough to keep the chain of infection going. Still another epidemic came fifteen years later, in 1546, whose character is unclear. Perhaps it was typhus.[14] Probably typhus was a new disease among Europeans, too; at least the medical men who first described it clearly enough to make diagnosis possible thought it was new when it broke out among troops fighting in Spain, in 1490.[15]

Hence if the pestilence of 1546 in the Americas was in fact typhus, the Amerindians were beginning to participate in epidemic diseases that also affected the populations of the Old World. This becomes unambiguous in course of the next American disease disaster: an influenza epidemic that raged in 1558–59. This epidemic, which broke out in Europe in 1556 and lasted on and off till 1560, had serious demographic consequences on both sides of the Atlantic. One estimate places die-off in England from the influenza at no less than 20 per cent of the entire population, for instance[16]; and comparable losses occurred elsewhere in Europe. Whether the influenza outbreak of the 1550s was a genuinely global phenomenon, like its more recent parallel, 1918–19, cannot be said for sure, but Japanese records also mention an outbreak of "coughing violence" in 1556 from which "very many died."[17]

The incorporation of Amerindian populations into the circle of epidemic disease that happened to be current in Eurasia in the sixteenth century did not relieve them of special exposure to still other infections coming across the ocean. Relatively trifling endemic afflictions of the Old World regularly became death-dealing epidemics among New World populations that were totally lacking in acquired resistances. Thus diphtheria, mumps, and recurrent outbreaks of the first two great killers, smallpox and measles, appeared at intervals throughout the sixteenth and seventeenth centuries. Whenever a new region or hitherto isolated Amerindian population came into regular contact with the outside world, the cycle of repeated infections picked up renewed force, mowing down the helpless inhabitants. The peninsula of Lower California, for instance, began to experience drastic depopulation at the very end of the seventeenth century, when a first recorded epidemic broke out there. Eighty years later the population had been reduced by more than 90 per cent, despite well-intentioned efforts by Spanish missionaries to protect and cherish the Indians assigned to their charge.[18]

Obviously, where European records are lacking, it is difficult to follow the course of disease and depopulation.[19] There is no doubt that epidemics often ran ahead of direct contact with Europeans, even in the thinly occupied lands north and south. Thus, because the French had already established a post at Port Royal in what is now Nova Scotia, we happen to know that in 1616–17 a great pestilence of some sort swept through the Massachusetts Bay Area. Thus God prepared the way, as Englishmen and Indians agreed, for the arrival of the Pilgrims just three years later. A subsequent outbreak of smallpox, starting in 1633, convinced the colonists (if they needed convincing) that Divine Providence was indeed on their side in conflicts with the Indians.[20]

Similar experiences abound in Jesuit missionary records from Canada and Paraguay. The smaller and more isolated populations of North and South America were just as vulnerable to European infections as the denser populations of Mexico and

Peru, even though their numbers were insufficient to maintain a chain of infection on the spot for very long at a time. The judgment a German missionary expressed in 1699 is worth repeating: "The Indians die so easily that the bare look and smell of a Spaniard causes them to give up the ghost."[21] If he had said "breath" instead of "smell" he would have been right.

The long and lethal series of European diseases was not all that Amerindians had to face. For in tropical regions of the New World climatic conditions were suitable for the establishment of at least some of the African infections that made that continent so dangerous to the health of strangers. The two most significant African diseases to establish themselves in the New World were malaria and yellow fever. Both of them became important in determining human patterns of settlement and survival in tropical and subtropical parts of the New World.

Fevers, leading to heavy die-off, often afflicted early European settlements in the New World. Columbus, for example, had to shift his headquarters in Hispaniola to a more healthful location in 1496. This and other disasters met by early expeditions of explorers and colonists have been adduced as proof that malarial fevers and/or yellow fever existed in the New World before European ships began crossing the ocean. But extremes of malnutrition arising from inadequate provisioning of expeditions that counted on somehow living off the land explain most such cases[22]; and there are a number of contrary evidences that make it practically certain that neither malaria nor yellow fever existed in the Americas before Columbus.

As far as malaria is concerned, the most telling argument rests on studies of the distribution of human genetic traits associated with tolerance of malarial infection. These appear to have been entirely absent from Amerindian populations. Similarly, malarial parasites that infect wild monkeys of the New World appear to be identical with those of the Old—

transfers, in fact, from human bloodstreams. Nothing like the extraordinary specialization of malarial parasites that occurs in Africa, whereby different forms of the plasmodium infect different host species and prefer different mosquitoes as alternate hosts, can be found in the Americas. Such facts make it almost certain that malaria is a newcomer to the American scene, and that neither man nor monkey harbored the parasites in pre-Columbian times.[23]

Literary evidence from the early years of Spanish invasion support this idea. Thus, for example, a Spanish expedition traveled down the Amazon in 1542, losing three men from Indian attack and seven from starvation; but the report makes no mention of fever. A century later another party ascended the Amazon and arrived at Quito on the other side of the Andes. The very detailed report of this voyage made no mention of fevers en route, and described the native populations along the river as vigorous, healthy, and numerous. No one today would describe the Amerindians of the Amazon basin as numerous, and those tribes that have entered into contact with outsiders are neither healthy nor vigorous either. Nor could any European expect to preserve his health during such a voyage today or at any time in the nineteenth century without a copious supply of anti-malarial drugs. The inference seems irresistible: malaria must have arrived in the Amazon some time after 1650.[24]

The establishment of malaria was not so long delayed in other, more traversed regions of the New World, although no clear time and place for the debut of the plasmodium in the New World can be discovered. Almost certainly, the infection was introduced many times, since Europeans as well as Africans suffered chronically from malaria. Before it could take root and spread in the American environment, suitable species of mosquitoes had to adjust to the plasmodium; and in some regions of the Americas this may have required the establishment of Old World types of mosquito on new terrain. The factors governing distribution of differing species of mosquitoes are not well understood, but studies in Europe show that small differences of widely discrepant factors affect the prevalence and absence of one as against another mosquito species.[25] Suitable anopheline species probably already existed in the New World, tinder for infection with the malarial plasmodium in much the same way that the burrowing rodent populations of North and South America were ready for infection with the plague bacillus in the twentieth century. Only so is the rapid development of malaria as a major disease factor in the New World credible. Yet malaria appears to have completed the destruction of Amerindians in the tropical lowlands, so as to empty formerly well-populated regions almost completely.[26]

Yellow fever announced its successful transfer from West Africa to the Caribbean for the first time in 1648, when epidemics broke out in both Yucatán and Havana. What delayed its establishment until this comparatively late date was probably the fact that before it could become epidemic in the New World, a specialized species of mosquito, known as *Aedes aegypti*, had to find and occupy a niche in the New World environment. This mosquito, in fact, is highly domesticated, preferring as its breeding places small bodies of still water. Indeed, it is said never to breed in water with a natural bottom of mud or sand, but to require a manufactured container—water cask, cistern, calabash, or the like, for laying its eggs.[27]

Until this specialized mosquito crossed the ocean aboard ship (riding, no doubt, in water casks) and established itself ashore in places where the temperature always stayed above 72 degrees Fahrenheit, yellow fever could not propagate itself in the New World. But when these conditions had been met, the situation became ripe for yellow fever to assume epidemic proportions among men and monkeys alike. Europeans were as vulnerable as Amerindians to this infection; and its sudden onset and frequently lethal outcome made it more feared among whites than malaria. Nonetheless, malaria was far more widespread and undoubtedly accounted for a larger number of deaths than its dreaded African cousin, whom English sailors nicknamed "Yellow Jack."

The peculiar affinity of *Aedes aegypti* for water casks meant that mosquitoes carrying yellow fever from sailor to sailor could remain on shipboard for weeks and months at a time. The disease could therefore keep on attacking the members of a crew throughout even the lengthiest voyages. This distinguished it from practically every other infectious disease, most of which, if they did break out on shipboard would speedily burn themselves out. Either almost everyone got sick and recovered simultaneously, as when influenza struck; or else only a few individuals, who happened to lack previously acquired immunities, fell ill. But since death from yellow fever was the usual outcome when a European met the infection as an adult, few sailors had any immunity to the disease. Consequently, a voyage lasting for months could be haunted by an unending chain of fatal attacks of yellow fever; and no one understood or could know who would get sick next and die in his turn. No wonder that the "Yellow Jack" was so dreaded by the sailors of the Caribbean and other tropical seas where the temperature-sensitive *Aedes aegypti* could flourish!

In regions of the New World where tropical infections from Africa could establish themselves freely—coming as they did on top of crushing exposure to European infections—the result was almost total destruction of the pre-existing Amerindian population. On the other hand, in regions where tropical infections could not penetrate, like the Mexican interior plateau and the Peruvian *altiplano*, the destruction of pre-Columbian populations was less complete, though drastic enough even there.[28]

African slaves took the place of the vanished Amerindians along the Caribbean coast and in most of the islands of the

Caribbean where plantation enterprises called for heavy input of human labor. Since many Africans were already attuned to survival in the presence of malaria and yellow fever, losses from these diseases were relatively small, although other unfamiliar infections—gastrointestinal in particular—led to a high mortality among the slaves. In addition, a heavy preponderance of males, unfavorable conditions for raising infants, and continual disturbance of local disease patterns as a result of the arrival of new human cargoes from Africa meant that the black population of the Caribbean area did not grow very rapidly until the nineteenth century. Then, when the flow of newcomers was cut off, and the noisome slave ships that for two and a half centuries had propagated disease on both sides of the ocean, ceased to ply the seas, black numbers began to surge upward in most of the Caribbean islands, whereas whites diminished proportionately and sometimes absolutely. Economic and social changes—the end of slavery and exhaustion of soils devoted single-mindedly to sugar cane—contributed to this result; but black epidemiological advantages in resisting malaria also helped.[29]

Overall, the disaster to Amerindian populations assumed a scale that is hard for us to imagine, living as we do in an age when epidemic disease hardly matters. Ratios of 20:1 or even 25:1 between pre-Columbian populations and the bottoming-out point in Amerindian population curves seem more or less correct, despite wide local variations.[30] Behind such chill statistics lurks enormous and repeated human anguish, as whole societies fell apart, values crumbled, and old ways of life lost all shred of meaning. A few voices recorded what it was like:

> Great was the stench of death. After our fathers and grandfathers succumbed, half the people fled to the fields. The dogs and vultures devoured the bodies. The mortality was terrible. Your grandfathers died, and with them died

the son of the king and his brothers and kinsmen. So it
was that we became orphans, oh, my sons! So we became
when we were young. All of us were thus. We were born
to die![31]

Though Amerindians were certainly the main victims of the
new disease regime, other populations also had to react to the
changed patterns of disease dissemination arising from transoceanic shipping, and the altered patterns of interior trade
routes that the rise of such shipping involved. Details are for
the most part irrecoverable, yet an over-all pattern is quite
clearly discernible.

First of all, previously isolated populations like the Amerindians, when brought into contact with European and other seafarers, regularly experienced a series of drastic die-offs, like that
which so massively altered American history. Which civilized
diseases wreaked the greatest damage differed from case to case,
depending partly on climate, partly on the mere chance of
what infection arrived when. But the vulnerability of isolated
populations to such diseases was an epidemiological fact of life
—and death. Locally disastrous die-offs therefore became recurrent phenomena of all the centuries after 1500.

Among civilized populations, however, the effect was just the
opposite. More frequent contacts across ocean distances tended
to homogenize infectious disease. As this took place, sporadic
and potentially lethal epidemics gave way to endemic patterns
of infection. To be sure, in the first centuries after ships began
to ply the oceans of the earth and united all the coastlines of
the world into a single intercommunicating network, the process of homogenization of disease distribution involved expansion of some diseases onto new ground. Such arrivals, at more
and more frequent intervals, could and did produce locally destructive epidemics. Cities like London and Lisbon became notorious in Europe as seats of disease, and deservedly so. By

about 1700, however, sailing ships had done what they could to spread new diseases to new lands. Thereafter, the demographic significance of epidemic outbreaks began to drop off. Where other factors did not supervene to mask the phenomenon, the result was to open the way for our modern experience of persistent, pervasive growth among the disease-exposed and disease-experienced populations of all the earth.

Such a contrast between radical decay of previously isolated communities on the one hand and a globally enhanced potential for population growth among disease-experienced peoples on the other, acted to tip the world balance sharply in favor of the civilized communities of Eurasia. The cultural and biological variety of humankind was reduced correspondingly, as the age-old process of epidemiological disruption and absorption of survivors into the expanding circle of civilized society accelerated everywhere on earth.

Details are only occasionally recoverable. Thus, although epidemiological disaster to previously isolated populations occurred in parts of Africa, e.g., among the Hottentots of the Far South, no one can say which disease caused the principal dieoffs or exactly when. In western and central Africa, the slave trade also led to mixing of populations, and movement from one to another natural disease environment on a scale far greater than had prevailed previously. The effect must surely have been to extend patterns of infection toward their natural limits, but it is impossible to tell whether any important changes for human life ensued. Clearly nothing demographically disastrous occurred on a mass scale, since the supply of slaves did not slacken, despite the undoubted damage raiding parties brought to innumerable inland villages.

But whatever demographic effects the brisker circulation of infections within sub-Saharan Africa may have had—and they must have been substantial[32]—any increased mortality from disease was masked and in most cases more than compensated

217

for by improved nutrition resulting from the rapid spread of maize and manioc among African farmers. Heightened caloric yields that these American imports made possible lifted older ceilings on population densities per cultivated acre; and while no statistics are available, it certainly seems not merely possible but probable that large regions of sub-Saharan Africa shared with other parts of the Old World in the population advance starting in the second half of the seventeenth century.[33]

As usual, we are far better informed about disease events in Europe. Three new infections assumed spectacular forms during the age of the oceanic explorations, 1450–1550; and each of them came to European attention as a by-product of wars. One, the so-called "English sweats," disappeared after a brief career; the other two, syphilis and typhus, have lasted to our time.

Both syphilis and typhus appeared in Europe during the long series of Italian wars, 1494–1559. The first of them broke out in epidemic fashion in the army that the French king, Charles VIII, led against Naples in 1494. When the French withdrew, King Charles discharged his soldiers, who thereupon spread the disease far and wide to all adjacent lands. Syphilis was regarded as a new disease not merely in Europe, but in India, where it appeared in 1498 with Da Gama's sailors, and in China and Japan as well, where it arrived in 1505, a full fifteen years before the first Portuguese reached Canton.[34] Symptoms were often peculiarly horrible so that the disease attracted a great deal of attention wherever it appeared.

Contemporary evidence therefore amply attests that syphilis was new in the Old World, at least in the sense that the venereal mode of transmission and the symptoms that resulted therefrom were new. But as we saw in the last chapter, this may have arisen independently of contacts with America, if a strain of the spirochete causing yaws found a means of short-circuiting the increasingly ineffective path of skin-to-skin infection by instead moving from host to host via the mucous membranes of the sex organs.

Yet medical opinion is not unanimous. Some competent experts continue to believe that syphilis came to Europe from America, and was therefore exactly what contemporaries thought it was—a new disease against which Eurasian populations had no established immunities. The timing of the first outbreak of syphilis in Europe and the place where it occurred certainly seems to fit what one would expect if the disease had been imported from America by Columbus' returning sailors. This theory, once it had been promulgated in 1539, became almost universally accepted among Europe's learned until very recently, when the inability to distinguish between the spirochete causing yaws and that of syphilis in laboratory tests led a school of medical historians to reject the Columbian theory entirely. Proof, one way or the other, awaits the development of precise and reliable methods whereby the organisms causing lesions in ancient bones can be identified. If this proves permanently beyond the reach of biochemical techniques, it seems unlikely that any adequate basis for choice between the rival theories as to the origin of syphilis will be attainable.[35]

However conspicuous and distressful syphilis may have been for those who contracted it, its demographic impact does not seem to have been very great. Royal houses often suffered and the political decline of Valois France (1559–1589) and of Ottoman Turkey (after 1566) may have been related to the prevalence of syphilis in the respective reigning families of the two states. Many aristocrats suffered similarly. But the inability of royal and aristocratic families to give birth to healthy children merely accelerated social mobility, making more room at the top of society than there would otherwise have been. Lower down the social scale syphilis had less devastating effects, for the fact seems to be that European populations continued to increase throughout the sixteenth century when the disease was at its height. By the end of the century, syphilis began to recede. The more fulminant forms of infection were dying out, as the normal sorts of adjustment between host and parasite asserted themselves, i.e., as milder strains of the spirochete displaced those that killed off their hosts too rapidly, and as the resistance of European populations to the organism increased. Even though data seem lacking, the same pattern of relatively speedy adjustment without significant demographic loss along the way presumably also prevailed in the other parts of the Old World.

The same must also be said of typhus. As a recognizable and distinct disease, typhus made its debut on European soil in 1490, when it was brought to Spain by soldiers who had been fighting in Cyprus. Thence it came into Italy with the wars between Spaniards and French for dominion over that peninsula. Typhus achieved a new notoriety in 1526 when a French army besieging Naples was compelled to withdraw in disarray due to the ravages of the disease. Thereafter, outbreaks of typhus continued to be sporadically important in disrupting armies and depopulating jails, poorhouses, and other—in the literal sense —lousy institutions, down to World War I, when two or three million died of this infection.[36]

Yet the occasional military and political importance of typhus fever was not matched by any notable demographic significance for the peoples of Europe or anywhere else, so far, at least, as the very sketchy indications of population trends allow one to judge. Typhus was, after all, a disease of crowding and of poverty. For most of the poor who died of typhus, statistical probability assures us that if infected lice had not assisted their demise, some other disease would soon have carried them off. Particularly in urban slums, or anywhere else that undernourished people huddled miserably together, there were plenty of other infections—tuberculosis, dysentery, pneumonia —competing for victims. The fact that typhus brought death quicker than most of the other infections therefore perhaps made less difference demographically than the number of typhus deaths might suggest at first glance.

The third new, or apparently new, infection, the "English sweats," is of interest on two counts. It exhibited an opposite social impact from typhus, preferring to attack the upper classes much as poliomyelitis did in more recent times. Secondly, it disappeared after 1551 as mysteriously as it had come in 1485. The disease broke out first in England as the name implies, soon after Henry VII had won his crown at the battle of Bosworth Field. Then it spread to the Continent and created considerable furor because of the high mortality it caused among upper classes. Symptoms resembled scarlet fever, but such an identification has not won general acceptance among medical historians. The fact that it was believed to be a new disease does not prove that it had not existed in some endemic form as a modest childhood affliction elsewhere, perhaps in France whence Henry VII recruited some of the soldiers who won him his crown.[37] But even more clearly than in the cases of syphilis and typhus, the sweats did not affect enough people to have any noticeable over-all demographic effect.

On the other hand, it is the case that an outbreak of the dreaded "sweats" in 1529 led Luther and Zwingli to break off their colloquy in Marburg, without achieving agreement on a definition of the eucharist.[38] Whether a longer conference would have led to agreement between these two headstrong paladins of ecclesiastical reformation may well be doubted. Nevertheless, the fact remains that it was their precipitate flight from risk of infection that sealed the split between Lutheran and Swiss (soon to become Calvinist) reform along lines that deeply affected subsequent European history, and have endured to the present.

Such events involve the interaction of sharply different determinants of human action: the one ideological and conscious, the other epidemiological and independent of human intention. Historians have never been comfortable when trying to deal with such "accidents," and it is partly for that reason that the history of disease had been so little attended to by my predecessors. Infection and fear of infection, indeed, as manifest at Marburg in 1529, resemble for us today the unpredictable and incomprehensible intervention of Divine Providence which our ancestors invoked to explain epidemics. Heirs as we are to the Enlightenment, which sought to banish the inexplicable, if necessary by neglecting it, historians of the twentieth century have also usually preferred to overlook such events. Anything else spoiled the web of interpretation and explanation through which their art sought to make human experience intelligible.

Though it is the aim of this book to correct such oversight and bring the role of infectious disease in shaping human history into a juster perspective than others have allowed, it remains the case that accidental events like this, however pervasive the results which may be thought to have flowed from them, seem somehow too trifling to be credited with vast consequences. There is, alas, simply no way to decide whether the division between the two main branches of the Protestant movement in Europe would have taken place anyway, or whether that important phenomenon did take a decisive turn when Luther and Zwingli bade one another a hasty adieu in 1529 in order to escape the "sweats."

It is, paradoxically, far easier for historians to talk about statistical results and longer-range demographic phenomena, even when hard data are absent and guesswork has to provide a substitute. Thus one may be comfortable in asserting that population in Europe, or those parts of it where reasonable estimates can be made, seems to have increased uninterruptedly and relatively rapidly from the mid-fifteenth century (when recovery from plague losses set in) until about 1600.[39] Yet it was during these decades that the oceanic discoveries took place, and European sailors had the opportunity to import new infections into their homelands from the ports of all the earth. Even so, the new disease risks such transport patterns permitted did not prove very serious for European populations, presumably because most infections that could flourish in the European climate and under the conditions then prevailing in European cities and villages had already penetrated the Continent as a result of older circulation of infections within the Old World.

For Europe, as for other civilized lands, infections by familiar epidemic disease surely became more frequent, at least in the major ports and at other foci of communication; but infections that returned at more and more frequent intervals became, by necessity, childhood diseases. Older persons would have acquired suitably high and repeatedly reinforced levels of immunity through prior exposures. Thus by a paradox that is only apparent, the more diseased a community, the less destructive its epidemics become. Even very high rates of infant mortality were relatively easily borne. The costs of giving birth and rearing another child to replace one that had died were slight compared to the losses involved in massive adult mortality of the sort that epidemics attacking a population at infrequent intervals inevitably produce.

Consequently, the tighter the communications net binding each part of Europe to the rest of the world, the smaller became the likelihood of really devastating disease encounter. Only genetic mutation of a disease-causing organism, or a new transfer of parasites from some other host to human beings offered the possibility of devastating epidemic when world transport and communications had attained a sufficient intimacy to assure frequent circulation of all established human diseases among the civilized populations of the world. Between 1500 and about 1700 this is what seems in fact to have occurred. Devastating epidemics of the sort that had raged so dramatically in Europe's cities between 1346 and the mid-seventeenth century tapered off toward the status of childhood diseases, or else, as in the case of both plague and malaria, notably reduced the geographic range of their incidence.[40]

The result of such systematic lightening of the microparasitic drain upon European populations (especially in northwestern Europe where both plague and malaria had about disappeared by the close of the seventeenth century) was, of course, to unleash the possibility of systematic growth. This was, however, only a possibility, since any substantial local growth quickly brought on new problems: in particular, problems of food supply, water supply, and intensification of other infections in cities that had outgrown older systems of waste disposal. After 1600 these factors began to affect European populations significantly, and their effective solution did not come before the eighteenth century—or later.

All the same, the changing pattern of epidemic infection was and remains a fundamental landmark in human ecology that deserves more attention than it has ordinarily received. On the time scale of world history, indeed we should view the "domestication" of epidemic disease that occurred between 1300 and 1700 as a fundamental breakthrough, directly resulting from the two great transportation revolutions of that age—one by land, initiated by the Mongols, and one by sea, initiated by Europeans.

Civilized forms of person-to-person infection had entered the scene with the rise of cities and the development of intercommunicating human herds of half a million or so. Initially this could only occur at selected spots on the globe, where agriculture was especially productive and local transport nets made concentration of resources into urban and imperial centers relatively easy. For millennia thereafter, these civilized infections played a double role. On the one hand, they cut down formerly isolated populations that came into contact with disease-bearers from one or another of the civilized centers, and thereby facilitated the process of "digestion" of small, primitive groups into the body politic of persistently expanding civilized communities. On the other hand, these same diseases enjoyed an imperfect circulation within civilized communities themselves, and could often therefore invade a particular city or rural community with almost the same lethal force they regularly exerted vis-à-vis isolated populations.

Particularly when it came to disease relations across civilizational boundaries, this possibility remained demographically important for civilized humankind, as the disease die-offs of early Christian centuries attest. After 1300, contacts between the major civilizations of the Old World became closer and closer. Disease exchanges intensified correspondingly, with frequent disastrous but never quite paralyzing consequences. In the sixteenth and seventeenth centuries, when the Amerindian die-off was at its peak, the homogenization of civilized infectious disease throughout the world gradually attained such a level that the old forms of sporadic epidemic that could carry off up to half the population of a particular community in a single season could no longer occur in those parts of the world where long exposure to the multiplicity of infectious organisms created suitably complex patterns of immunity among all but young children.

Thus there emerged a new relation between humankind and parasitic micro-organisms. It was a more stable pattern of parasitism, less destructive to human hosts, and correspondingly more secure for the parasites. The infectious organisms could count on a fresh supply of susceptible children, whose numbers and availability were subject to far smaller statistical variation than had been the case when epidemic patterns of disease produced alternate feast and famine for the organisms infecting humanity. Both sides were therefore more secure, and in that sense better off. As endemicity set in at one port city after another, filtering inland along main routes of movement and seeping more slowly into the countryside, a new ecological era dawned. Massive growth of civilized populations, and correspondingly accelerated destruction of the remaining isolated human groups was the first and most obvious consequence of the new disease regime, a disease regime we can appropriately call "modern." Imminent collision with limits on food supply, as well as other strains upon human adaptation to the environment, was the other side of this modern microparasitic regime.

The shift from epidemic to endemic forms of infection was, of course, not complete; the next chapter will have something to say about smallpox and cholera and some other notable encounters with epidemics that humanity has experienced in recent centuries. Nonetheless, the force of the modern pattern of infection was clearly evident by 1700, or by 1750 at the latest[41] —and not only in Europe, but throughout the world.

Before turning briefly to consider what little can be said of disease and population histories of Asia and Africa, however, another point about Europe's disease experience should be made. The fundamental character of the changing incidence of epidemic disease was obscured in early modern times by the onset of particularly severe weather conditions that created frequent crop failures and famines in northern Europe.[42] Simultaneously, the Mediterranean lands underwent a general crisis owing to mounting shortages of food and fuel.[43] Parts of Europe were also devastated by war—e.g., Italy between 1494 and 1559, and Germany between 1618 and 1648. These wars were waged with more than customary brutality, owing to difficulties regularly constituted governments faced in supplying mercenary troops. Armies tended, therefore, to plunder friend and foe almost indiscriminately.[44]

Moreover, urban growth in northern Europe often put strains on pre-existing sanitary arrangements, so that death rates in thriving cities like London or Amsterdam may well have edged upward.[45] Yet on the whole it seems safe to say that intensified efforts at public sanitation forestalled major disaster. These were largely initiated in times of plague, stimulated in the North by the example of Italian cities whose public sanitation and health services were more highly developed than elsewhere in Europe.[46] The result, therefore, was that the tendency toward systematic population growth inherent in the changing pattern of disease incidence was partially masked for two centuries by factors that acted in a contrary sense. Yet the fundamental fact remains: European population did continue a slight increase despite local setbacks and temporary crises; and did so despite adverse weather and war.

Europe's expansion is such a central fact of modern history that we are likely to take it almost for granted and fail to recognize the quite exceptional ecological circumstances that provided sufficient numbers of exportable (and often expendable) human beings needed to undertake such multifarious, risky, and demographically costly ventures. The fact was that Europe found itself in a position to capitalize handsomely on the new capacity for demographic growth which the altered disease pattern conferred on all civilized peoples of the Old World. Lands emptying of Amerindians[47] were supplemented by lands emptying of Pacific islanders and Australians,[48] of Siberian tribesmen,[49] and of Hottentots.[50] In all these disparate regions, Europeans were uniquely in a position to move in, thanks to their control of transoceanic shipping and other means of transport, and to the possession of other technological skills superior to those which disease-decimated local peoples could command. In all of this vast process, bacteriology was at least as important as technology. The decay of native numbers and the availability of European populations to occupy such vast and varied emptied spaces both derived from the distinctive modern pattern of epidemiology.

The key significance of the altered pattern of infectious disease in the complex of factors sustaining Europe's expansion is confirmed if we turn attention to what happened among other civilized peoples of the Old World. For there, too, the opening of the oceans to regular shipping and the intensification of contacts resulting from circulation of ships and crews had noticeable effects on populations and disease.

The only new disease known to have come to India, China, Japan, and the Middle East was syphilis; and its demographic impact in these lands seems no different from that in Europe. That is to say, initial dismay and extended comment ebbed away as the infection became less florid in its symptoms and subsided toward chronic endemicity.[51]

Familiar infections continued to manifest themselves as epidemics, in Asia as much as in Europe; and there is reason to think that the frequency of epidemics may have increased. Certainly, Chinese records show a sharp upsurge in epidemic outbreaks, as the following table, based on the researches of Dr. Joseph Cha, makes obvious[52]:

1300–1399	18 epidemics mentioned
1400–1499	19
1500–1599	41
1600–1699	37 (an age of political disorder)
1700–1799	38
1800–1899	40

Unfortunately one cannot conclude that the number of pestilences increased as suddenly as this table suggests, since records from the earlier times are more fragmentary than from recent centuries. All the same, the apparent doubling of recorded instances of epidemic disease in the sixteenth century probably corresponds to a real increase in the frequency with which epidemics arrived in China. China's political system was then in good order, so that wars and rebellions cannot account for the disease record. New contacts arising from European transoceanic voyaging seem a far more plausible cause. If so, we can safely assume that an epidemiological basis was being laid in China after 1500 for the pattern of population growth that became such a prominent feature of subsequent Chinese history. The best available estimates for China's total population are as follows[53]:

1400	65 million
1600	150 million
1700	150 million
1794	313 million

The setback to China's population growth apparent between 1600 and 1700 corresponds to the slowing of western Europe's population growth in the same period. Colder winters and shortened growing seasons probably played a part in keeping Chinese population almost steady during the seventeenth century. A graph of temperatures, based on the frequency with which the Yangtze lakes froze over in wintertime, shows the coldest time in all recorded history to have fallen in the middle decades of the seventeenth century,[54] precisely at the time when disorders incident to the displacement of the Ming by the Manchu Dynasty were at their peak. Such a coincidence of cold weather and civil disorder offers an obvious and adequate explanation for the cessation of China's population growth in the seventeenth century. But only a changing disease regime, reflecting the increasing homogenization of infections around the world, seems adequate to explain the systematic population growth before and after the seventeenth-century halt.

China's modern demography and disease experience therefore seems to correspond to that of Europe. Japan's population curve stands sharply in contrast. After rather rapid growth in the four centuries before 1726, when the first reasonably accurate census becomes available, Japanese population remained nearly constant until the middle of the 19th century. Estimates are as follows[55]:

1185–1333	9.75 million
1572–1591	18.0 million
1726	26.5 million
1852	27.2 million

Widespread infanticide is believed responsible for this stabilization of population. But disease may have played a part in what happened, for the number of recorded epidemics, as compiled by Fujikawa Yu, also showed a notable increase after 1700, when the leveling off of population growth occurred.[56]

No worthwhile estimates for Indian or Middle Eastern demographic history can be made on the basis of existing scholarship. Ottoman population history probably paralleled developments in other parts of the Mediterranean; and some bold demographers have suggested that the number of India's inhabitants increased with the establishment of a more perfect internal peace in the second half of the seventeenth century, following the Mughal conquest of most of the peninsula, 1526–1605.[57]

What exact course infectious disease may have followed in India and inner Asia remains unascertainable; but inasmuch as Indian ports shared on the intensified trade network that European ships extended across the world's oceans, an intensified disease circulation surely must have existed in India also. Thus, despite gross lacunae in the evidence, nothing obstructs the inference that the modern disease pattern also established itself among civilized populations of Asia, perhaps less uniformly and more slowly than in Europe; but in parallel, indeed identical, fashion all the same.

Diseases, however, were not the only biologically significant items that diffused more uniformly throughout the civilized world as a result of intensified transoceanic voyaging. Food crops did the same; and wherever a strange new plant offered some sort of value—including initially often merely the value of novelty—it was cherished and introduced into gardens and fields.

By far the most important new food crops came from the Americas. Maize, potatoes, tomatoes, chili peppers, peanuts, and manioc all became available in Eurasia and Africa only after Columbus' discovery of America. In many regions of the Old World, one or another of these crops was capable of producing far more calories per acre than anything known before. Older ceilings on population rose correspondingly wherever the new crops became generally cultivated. China, Africa, and Europe all were profoundly affected.[58]

American food crops were important not solely for the increased calorie production per cultivated acre they permitted. Chili peppers and tomatoes, for instance, supplied a rich vitamin source whose importance in the diets of Mediterranean and Indian populations in modern times is very great indeed. How rapidly these American novelties became commonly available to supplement earlier and sometimes vitamin-deficient diets is unclear, though the first introduction of the new plants dates to the sixteenth century. As these foods entered into widespread use among rich and poor alike, one can be sure that a more adequate diet became available to the Indian and Mediterranean peoples, and health levels presumably reflected this fact.[59] Oranges, originally cultivated in China, and other citrus fruits were also diffused widely by Europeans, even before the sovereign value of their juices against shipboard scurvy became widely known. But exactly when and where consumption of citrus fruits assumed dietary significance is impossible to say.

Obviously enough, without the capacity to produce additional quantities of food, the population growth that set in toward the end of the seventeenth century in so many parts of the civilized world could not have gone very far. The superior productivity and nutritiousness of American food crops was therefore of the greatest importance for human life in every part of the Old World.

Changes in disease patterns and the increase in productivity that the spread of American food crops permitted were probably the two most active factors in triggering civilized population growth in early modern times. They operated world-wide, and in parallel fashion to allow more human beings to survive and grow to maturity than had ever been possible before. There was, however, another significant change, this time on the macroparasitic side. Governments became fewer and more capable of maintaining domestic peace over broader regions of the earth, thanks to the global diffusion of a new weapon: the cannon. Cannon spread just as disease germs and plants did— along the world's seaways. Everywhere that the big guns established themselves, the effect was to concentrate overwhelming force in fewer hands. Cannon were expensive, requiring large amounts of metal for their manufacture and rare skills for their management. Yet when the technique was new, a single big gun brought into position against a defended place was capable within a few hours of blasting a hole even in the stoutest fortification.

Such sovereign power to penetrate otherwise redoubtable strongholds radically diminished the military power of local potentates. Whoever possessed a few of the new weapons or commanded the skills needed for manufacturing them on the spot, was in a position to enforce his will much more effectively and overpoweringly than ever before. The result, naturally, was the consolidation of a relatively small number of "gunpowder empires." Thus the late Ming and Manchu empires of China, together with the Mughal, Tokugawa, Safavid, Ottoman, Muscovite, Spanish, and Portuguese empires all may be classed as imperial states held together by a monopoly of decisive force exercised by a few cannoneers in the employ of the respective imperial governments. The territorial expansion of these states and the predictability with which imperial cannoneers could batter down the defending walls of local rivals meant that most of Asia and much of Europe began to enjoy a superior level of public peace from the latter part of the seventeenth century when these empires all came to be firmly established. War and plunder diminished their scope accordingly, being more and more brought under bureaucratic control, and directed toward distant and often thinly populated frontiers.[60]

Such a general change in macroparasitic patterns had not occurred in human history since the end of the second millennium B.C., when the dawn of the Iron Age made weapons (and tools) vastly cheaper than before, and thereby increased the devastation men could wreak upon their fellows. Some twenty-five hundred years later the invention of cannon made weaponry more expensive. The new technology therefore acted in the opposite way, directing organized violence into narrower channels so that fewer human beings died in war or from its consequences despite the enhanced killing power well-equipped armies could exert in battle and siege.

Taxes to support the new armament were heavy. Collection probably became more regular in parts of Asia and Europe, as bureaucratic structures of government consolidated their hold on supreme armed force thanks to the new power cannon could exert. But for peasants and artisans, regular taxation, even if hard to bear, was almost always less destructive than raiding and rapine of the sort that armed bands had resorted to for their support ever since barbarians carrying iron swords and shields had assaulted the citadels of Middle Eastern civilization after 1200 B.C. The symbiosis of cannon with a limited number of imperial bureaucracies must therefore be counted as a third global factor favoring the world-wide growth of civilized population from the late seventeenth century until the present day.

These three factors continue to affect the conditions of

human life in the twentieth century. Indeed the world's biosphere may be described as still reverberating to the series of shocks inaugurated by the new permeability of ocean barriers that resulted from the manifold movement of ships across the high seas after 1492. Yet almost as soon as the initial and most drastic readjustments of the new pattern of transoceanic movements had subsided, other factors—scientific and technological for the most part—inaugurated still further and almost equally drastic changes in the world's biological and human balance. To survey them will be the task of our next chapter.

VI

The Ecological Impact
of Medical Science
and Organization
since 1700

Hitherto in seeking to understand the changing patterns of disease and its importance for human history as a whole, there has been little occasion to mention the practice of medicine. Undoubtedly folkways that reduced exposure to disease were as old as human society and language; and various customs, justified on other grounds, also had important epidemiological consequences—often of a positive kind. Thus, as we saw in Chapter IV, nomads of Manchuria diminished their exposure to plague on the basis of a theory that departed ancestors might be reincarnated as marmots. As such, these animals, which sometimes harbored the plague bacillus, had to be treated with special care.[1] Another modern folk practice helped to protect the health of Tamil laborers brought from southern India to work on plantations in Malaya. They conformed to a custom that required them to bring water into their houses only once a day, and not to store it between times. This, of course, deprived mosquitoes of a breeding place indoors. As a result, Chinese as well as native Malays, who lived and worked under similar conditions but did not observe the Tamil custom, suffered distinctly higher rates of infection from dengue fever and malaria.[2]

In numberless circumstances, such beliefs and rules of behavior must have helped to insulate human communities from disease chains. On the other hand, hygienic rules, especially when promulgated on the authority of divine revelation presumed to be universally applicable, sometimes had unfortunate side effects, as in the instance of the mosque in Yemen whose ablution pool harbored bilharzia parasites.[3]

More generally, religious pilgrimages rivaled warfare in provoking epidemic infection. The doctrine that disease came from God could easily be interpreted to mean that it was impious to interfere with God's purposes by trying to take conscious precaution against disease, either in war or on pilgrimage. Part of the meaning of pilgrimage was the taking of risks in pursuit of holiness. To die en route was, for the pious, an act of God whereby He deliberately translated the pilgrim from the hardships of life on earth into His presence. Disease and pilgrimage were thus psychologically as well as epidemiologically complementary. The same may be said of war, where risk of sudden death—one's own or the enemy's—was at the very core of the enterprise.

Thus customs and beliefs tending to safeguard human communities from disease were matched by others that invited and provoked disease outbreaks. Until very recently, medical theories and treatments fitted into this tangle of contradictory practices smoothly enough. Some cures were helpful; some indifferent; some, like the practice of bleeding for fevers, must have been positively harmful to most patients. Like popular folkways, medical theories were crudely empirical and excessively dogmatic. Doctrines set forth in a few famous books were treated as authoritative: Galen and Avicenna for the European and Moslem world played this role, as Caraka did for the Indian; whereas in China, several authors shared canonical status. Experience was then interpreted in terms of theory, and cures inflicted accordingly.

Overall, it is very doubtful whether the physiological benefits of even the most expert medical attention outweighed the harm done by some of the common forms of treatment. The practical basis of the medical profession rested on psychology. Everyone felt better when self-confident, expensive experts could be called in to handle a vital emergency. Doctors relieved others of the responsibility for deciding what to do. As such their role was strictly comparable to that of the priesthood, whose ministrations to the soul relieved anxieties parallel to those relieved by medical ministrations to the body.

Yet there was a difference. Doctors dealt with things of this world, and as such their skills and ideas were more liable to empiric elaboration over time. Medical professionals in fact behaved in about the same way as humble folk did by cherishing responses to disease that by some happy chance seemed to achieve desired results. This relative openness to new departures was, perhaps, the most important quality of the medical professional prior to the spectacular breakthroughs of the past century or so. Even the august Galen was subject to emendation, though it was not before the seventeenth century that the theory of humors on which he had based his medical practice began to be widely questioned among European doctors. Among Asians, medical ideas and practices, once they achieved a classical definition, seem to have responded less coherently to novelty.[4]

The organization of the profession in Europe around medical schools and hospitals may have been decisive in producing more systematic responses to new disease experiences. Hospitals gave opportunity for repeated observation of the symptoms and course of a disease. A cure that worked once could be tried again on the next patient, and professional colleagues were on hand to observe the result. Such colleagues stood ready to accord admiration and respect to the man whose cures worked better than usual; and a reputation for skill above the ordinary also meant swiftly rising income for the successful innovator. Under such circumstances, everything pushed the ambitious medical man toward empiric adventure, trying out new cures and watching to see the result. Moreover, the ancient Hippocratic tradition, emphasizing careful observation of disease symptoms, made such conduct professionally respectable. It is not, therefore, surprising that European doctors reacted to the disease novelties of 1200–1700 by altering major elements of older theory and practice. By contrast, Asian medical experts, who did not operate in hospital environments, met the disease experiences of these centuries by holding fast to ancient authorities—or claiming to do so even when something new crept in.

To be sure, even in Europe almost a century passed before medical response to the emergency of plague achieved anything resembling a clear definition. But by the end of the fifteenth century, Italian doctors had worked out within the framework of city-state government a series of public health measures designed to quarantine plague, and if it came, to cope with the heavy die-offs such visitations regularly brought. In the course of the sixteenth century these measures became both more elaborate and better administered. Preventive quarantines probably began to intercept chains of plague infection more and more often. Theories of contagion were advanced to justify quarantine, and notions originating from practical folk experience such as the belief that wool and textiles could carry plague—a belief vindicated by the behavior of hungry fleas that, having taken refuge in a bale of wool after their rat host had died, were liable to discover a much-wanted next meal by biting the arm of the man who unpacked the bale—at least achieved the dignity of being discussed in print.[5]

European doctors reacted to the disease consequences of the

discovery of America in much the same way as their predecessors had to the plague. Learned discussion of syphilis was as florid as the symptoms of the disease itself when new. Other novelties excited no less attention, and none of them fitted smoothly with ancient learning. The blow to reverence for the ancients was fundamental, and one from which traditional medical practice and education could never completely recover. As more and more details about America became available, the inference that modern knowledge had, in some ways at least, surpassed the ancients became irresistible. Such views opened wider the door to medical innovation, and encouraged Paracelsus (1493–1541) to reject Galen's authority entirely. New diseases like syphilis seemed to call for new and "stronger" medicines; and this became one of the stock arguments for resort to the Paracelsian chemical pharmacopeia and mystical medical philosophy.[6] With every fundamental of medicine thus called into question, the only logical recourse was to observe results of cures administered in accordance with the old Galenic as against the new Paracelsian theories, and then to choose whichever worked better. The swift development of European medical practice to levels of skill exceeding all other civilized traditions resulted.

Nevertheless, before the eighteenth century the demographic impact of the profession of medicine remained negligible. Relatively few persons could afford to pay a doctor for his often very expensive services; and for every case in which the doctor's attendance really made a difference between life and death, there were other instances in which even the best available professional services made little difference to the course of the disease, or actually hindered recovery. For this reason, mention of medical practice and its history in the earlier chapters of this book seemed unnecessary. Only with the eighteenth century did the situation begin to change; and it was not really until after 1850 or so that the practice of medicine and the organization of medical services began to make large-scale differences in human survival rates and population growth.

Long before then, the new ecological balances among the world's continents and civilizations that had begun to define themselves in the latter half of the seventeenth century became spectacularly evident. In particular, massive population growth in China and Europe assumed unexampled scale, thanks to the fact that both regions started from a higher initial population level than similar growth spurts of times past had ever done. After about 1650 Amerindian population figures began to bottom out in those regions where exposure to European and African diseases was of longest standing, and by the mid-eighteenth century Old World emigrants to America began to demonstrate remarkable rates of natural increase. Die-offs among formerly islanded populations continued (e.g., among natives of Oceania); but this phenomenon affected smaller numbers,[7] since after the sixteenth century no really large human communities remained outside the disease-net European shipping had already woven across all the earth's oceans and coastlines.

To be sure, even in the most intensely studied regions, population estimates for the seventeenth century are unsatisfactory, so that statistical demographers now prefer to begin making generalizations about 1750, rather than, as an earlier generation of experts had tried to do, retrojecting their estimates to 1650.[8] But no one doubts that some time between 1650 and 1750 (and recent opinion inclines toward the latter rather than the earlier date), a "vital revolution" took place in parts (though not in all) of Europe, manifesting itself in a more massive population growth than that continent had ever known before. The same was true in China, where the pacification brought by the new Manchu Dynasty after 1683 inaugurated a century of population growth during which Chinese numbers more than doubled, rising from about 150 million in 1700 to about 313 million in 1794.[9]

By comparison, Europe's population seems puny, reaching only a total of about 152 million by 1800.[10] Moreover, the unparalleled spurt in Chinese population affected all parts of the country, whereas in Europe comparable growth rates were chiefly evident toward the margins—in the steppelands to the east and in Great Britain and America to the west. The core area of continental Europe continued to suffer periodic devastation by war and crop failure, so that any tendency toward massive population growth of the sort manifest in China was quite effectually masked until late in the eighteenth century.

The relation between population growth and the intensification of industrial production which we have learned to call the Industrial Revolution, is a much debated point among historians, and especially among historians of England.[11] That country witnessed extraordinary changes in both industry and population during the eighteenth century; and the two obviously supported each other, in the sense that new industry needed workers, and expanding population needed new means of livelihood. Minute study of English parish records has much to teach in these matters; but to understand the general process one must consider all of Europe and the transoceanic zones of colonization as an interacting whole. Such a perspective on European demography, 1650–1750, brackets the agricultural pioneering and population growth along the eastern frontier with the parallel process of pioneering taking place in colonial lands across the seas, above all in North America. The difference between migration overland and migration overseas was less significant than the basic identity of the process of opening up new agricultural land that was taking place simultaneously on both frontiers. The intensification of commercial industrial activity in the center, mainly in Great Britain, also requires this larger perspective, for it was as a focus of the enlarged Europe of the Old World and the New that the English Midlands and London developed the new commercial and industrial patterns—above all more extensive use of mechanically powered machinery—that we lump together as the industrial revolution. But even if one accepts this expanded definition and counts both wings of the colonial movement as part of Europe, it only adds about 8–10 million to the total for European populations in 1800.[12] Hence the increase of European numbers remains far less massive than the Chinese expansion of the same period, being only about one fifth as great.

Elsewhere in the civilized world there seems good reason to suppose that population changed little, one way or another, until after 1800. In India, extensive civil disorder broke out during the latter part of the reign of the Emperor Aurangzeb (1658–1707) and sporadic warfare continued thereafter until 1818. Indeed, in the Moslem world as a whole, none of the signs of an expanding population are discernible, and political disorder tended to increase as the morale and efficiency of both Ottoman and Safavid administrations, like that of the Mughals in India, diminished.

Hence it appears that the Chinese eighteenth-century response to the altered ecological balances of the world was atypical. Parallel potentialities elsewhere were masked by a variety of countervailing circumstances. Only in China did public peace prevail unbroken and conventional limitations upon taxes and rents remain well defined, so that damaging or destructive macroparasitism remained rare. Simultaneously, increasingly frequent epidemics worked less and less demographic damage, as one disease after another verged toward the relatively harmless status of becoming an endemic childhood affliction. This opened wide the gate toward all the familiar features of the vital revolution: lessened adult mortality sustaining more completed families, whereupon a numerically reinforced generation, confronting the same situation, expanded the numbers of its children even more, etc.

Snowballing population growth of course confronted the

farmers of China with the task of wresting more food from the same landscape, since political and ecological obstacles prevented any very notable geographical expansion across Chinese frontiers. The imperial government prohibited overseas ventures in the 1430s and subsequent rulers maintained the ban, thus choking off any possibility of large-scale Chinese settlement in the Pacific coastlands of America, or in nearer lands like the Philippines or Malaya. From the time of the Manchu conquest in the 1640s, Chinese settlement in Manchuria and Mongolia was also prohibited, for the new rulers of China wished to maintain their ancestral lands and nomadic way of life unchanged. Only in the South could expansion of Chinese area of settlement continue; and even there local political resistance organized by the kingdoms of Annam and Burma, together with the epidemiological perils of monsoon forest environments, slowed Chinese pioneering to quite modest proportions.

Nevertheless, within the broad circuit of lands already firmly incorporated into China's landscape, it proved possible in the eighteenth century to find food enough to more than double previous levels of population. Increasingly intensive application of labor to the land did the trick, together with massive reliance on new crops, mainly American in origin—sweet potatoes, maize, peanuts in particular—that could be cultivated on land too steep or too dry for rice paddies.

China's circumstances, in other words, gave full scope to the new possibilities inherent in the changed disease regime, crop distribution and military technology resulting from the opening of the oceans to human movement. China, in fact, anticipated by more than a century similar responses among peasant masses in other parts of the world, who reacted similarly to new ecological balances in the nineteenth and twentieth centuries, wherever political pacification and the possibility of expanding agricultural production simultaneously presented themselves.

China's precocity in this respect may have been due in large part to the cultural traditions of the Middle Kingdom. Political unity came easier to a land accustomed from antiquity to regard imperial centralization as the only rightful form of government. And Confucian principles put high value upon family continuity from father to son. Such attitudes must have contributed to the early and dramatic expansion of China's population; yet this does not mean that the altered role of diseases was not also of great importance in securing the actual result.

Elsewhere, the potential for enhanced population growth presumably also existed among all the disease-experienced civilized communities of the world, but difficulties with expanding the food supply and/or suppressing destructive patterns of macroparasitism masked overt manifestations of the new possibilities until the nineteenth century. Only along frontiers of colonization, where civilized agricultural techniques impinged upon land previously thinly inhabited, did the same combination of circumstances as prevailed in most of China also unleash extraordinary population expansion before 1800.

The two principal such regions were the Ukraine in Russia and the Atlantic coast of the Americas. In the Ukraine, and Russia generally, risk of bubonic infection from ground-burrowing rodents remained a significant demographic factor throughout the eighteenth century. In 1771, for instance, plague in Moscow killed 56,672 persons in a single season, according to official figures—a total not far short of that recorded in London during the famous plague years, 1664–66.[13] Nevertheless, with each acre of land broken to the plow, the natural habitat available to ground-burrowing rodent communities diminished, and thereby the possibilities for transfer of infection from rodent to human populations was restricted. The plow could never banish plague, but it did undoubtedly reduce its dangers by slow, almost imperceptible degrees. The remarkable growth of Russian population in the eighteenth century, estimated at 12.5

million in 1724 and 21 million by 1796,[14] attests the fact that an enlarged food supply quite overbalanced any disease losses incident to breaking in upon lands formerly occupied by infected rodents.

American settlers did not have to worry about bubonic infection. They did, however, confront special problems because of their semi-isolation from the main centers of European civilization and disease circulation. Smallpox, for instance, so destructive to Amerindians, often killed white settlers as well when they met infection only as adults because of their remoteness in childhood from a dependable focus of infection. For this reason, as we shall soon see, many Americans were willing to accept the risks inherent in deliberate inoculation with smallpox—a technique that became familiar to European doctors in the eighteenth century—whereas in the more thoroughly diseased communities of Europe, where only small children were likely to die of smallpox, such risks were unacceptable, and inoculation failed to win general acceptance until the nineteenth century, when better methods reduced the risk of mortal infection to negligible proportions.

Ireland offers an interesting, territorially less impressive but demographically more dramatic, case of frontier expansion in the eighteenth century. After years of brutal war, the country was effectively pacified in 1652. Three distinct national groups —English, Scots, and Irish—thereafter confronted an almost empty island with diverse agricultural methods and economic expectations. In most of Ireland, it was the latter nationality that prevailed, despite profound political disadvantages. What made their success possible was an early acceptance of the potato as a staple crop—an acceptance made easier by the fact that the Irish had previously practiced agriculture on only a limited scale, and did not, like the English, depend on expensive plows and plow teams for tillage. Cheap and abundant potatoes allowed the Irish to live for less, and thereby to undercut

English settlers systematically. Scots, whose techniques of cultivation and living standards were almost on a par with those of
the Irish, managed to survive in Ulster. They, too, took to the
potato as a staple after widespread failure of the grain crop
early in the eighteenth century proved how valuable that
previously despised root could be. Explosive Irish population
growth got into high gear only toward the end of the eighteenth century, when, ironically enough, rising prices for grain
in England made tillage profitable as never before for the
Anglo-Irish landlords who ruled the island. This required labor;
and the native Irish were available to provide it in return for an
acre or so of land for a potato patch upon which an entire family could live—in abjective poverty perhaps, but in a reasonably
good state of nutrition all the same.[15]

While such remarkable swarmings of peasant populations as
occurred in eighteenth-century Ireland and in China were, perhaps, symptomatic of things to come elsewhere in a later age,
the population and disease history of Great Britain also assumed a special significance as the industrial revolution
gathered headway in that island. Until the 1870s, when grain
and other food supplies began to flood in from across the
oceans, the growth of urban population in Britain required intensification of local food production. Improved farm machinery, fertilizers, crop rotations, seed selection, and methods of
food storage and preservation, all played a part in making this
possible. The most significant change was the abandonment of
fallowing as a method for keeping down weeds. Crops such as
turnips that required careful tillage during their growth seasons, allowed simultaneous destruction of weeds and production of a valuable crop. Agricultural productivity was thereby
enhanced by almost a third.

There was another unexpected consequence of this "new
husbandry" that began to spread from its original foci on either
side of the North Sea in the later seventeenth century. For tur-

nips and alfalfa (the other important crop that replaced fallow) provided feed for cattle on a scale hitherto impossible in European agriculture; and the presence of larger numbers of cattle both improved human diet by expanding meat and dairy production, and simultaneously provided malaria-carrying anopheles mosquitoes with a preferred source of blood. Since the malarial plasmodium does not find cattle suitable hosts, mosquito preference for the blood of cattle had the effect of interrupting the chain of malarial transmission in those parts of Europe where the number of cattle increased sufficiently. Malaria thus gradually withdrew to the Mediterranean lands, where the new fodder crops could not be produced because of summer drought. Consequently, what had been a chronic and important disease among northern Europeans for centuries ceased to afflict regions where the new husbandry prevailed.[16]

Other complex ecological results flowed from the spread of the new style of agriculture. More animals meant more meat and milk in human diet, and an enlarged supply of protein. This may well have increased human capacities to manufacture antibodies against infection of any and every kind, since such antibodies are themselves proteins and can only be produced from the chemical building blocks proteins supply. Generalized levels of resistance to infectious disease may therefore have risen significantly among wide segments of the population.

Another possibility: enclosure of wasteland and of open fields, which proceeded rapidly in Britain in the eighteenth century, had the side effect of removing the incentive to overstock pastures, and segregated sheep and cattle into relatively small, privately owned populations. This almost certainly led to notable improvement in the health of flocks and herds. First of all, the animal got a better diet than had been possible when overstocking the common pasturelands was the only way for an individual villager to take maximum advantage of his rights. Secondly, chains of infection among the flocks and herds could often be interrupted. Previously, animals ran freely throughout the village common land, and made occasional contacts with animals from adjacent villages as well, since no fences divided the pastureland belonging to one community from the lands of its neighbors. Hence an infection could easily affect every animal in the village and for miles around. Such epizootics were far less likely to occur when fences and enclosed fields broke up the animals even of a single village into separate and mutually isolated groups. Such a change was important for human health, too, since a good many animal infections—bovine tuberculosis and brucellosis, for instance—were readily transferable to humankind.[17]

Diminution of such infections and the parallel decay of malaria changed the disease experience of England in far-reaching ways between 1650 and 1750. In France, where enclosure did not occur and the new husbandry hardly got started in the eighteenth century, peasant health remained miserable. Epidemics and chronic infections ravaged whole provinces; malaria and tuberculosis remained serious health problems; and a vaguer battery of other lethal infections—grippe, dysentery, pneumonia, and "military sweats"—continued to kill off a significant number of French peasants after 1775, when careful administrative records first become available.[18] Inasmuch as English population growth far outstripped French in the eighteenth century, while both countries remained predominantly agricultural, there is little doubt that the health of the countryside in England became noticeably better than what prevailed in France. Unfortunately, the absence of administrative records of disease incidence from Britain comparable to those French officials began to compile after 1775 makes direct comparison impossible.

A major consequence of the improvement in rural health such as seems to have taken place in England in the century after 1650 was a notable increase in the efficiency of agricultural labor. Healthy people work better—and more regularly; and, as is obvious, losses to agricultural production resulting from inability to do necessary work at the right time of the year disappear in proportion as laborers cease to suffer from debilitating fevers and similar afflictions which tend to crest during the growing season. As health improved, fewer workers could therefore feed larger numbers of city folk. The urbanization of Great Britain, which was such a conspicuous feature of late eighteenth-century development, could not have taken the course it did under any other circumstances.

Another and very important change in disease incidence in eighteenth-century Britain, however, was not the result of this sort of unexpected and accidental ecological alteration, but was instead a result of deliberate resort to smallpox inoculation. The practice was introduced into England in 1721. In the next year the royal children were successfully immunized. The method was to transfer the infection by introducing matter from a smallpox pustule into a slight wound made in the patient's skin. Occasionally the patient developed a severe case of smallpox from such treatment, and some died. But usually the symptoms were slight—a few score of pox only; and immunity proved equivalent to that resulting from contracting the disease naturally.

The technique was simple, and mass inoculation proved easy to arrange when its effectiveness came generally to be recognized. Hence the practice became widespread in England during the 1740s, and, with improvements in technique that reduced the risk of serious infection to a very slight proportion, inoculation became general in rural communities and small towns from the 1770s.

Interestingly enough, the practice of smallpox inoculation did not "take" in London and other big cities. The unusual situation whereby an innovation spread first in rural and small-town environments and bypassed large urban centers can readily be understood if one remembers the different pattern of incidence that prevailed in the two environments. In big cities smallpox was already a childhood disease; in rural England it remained epidemic, and could therefore attack young adults and adolescents, whose deaths were far more noticed than the die-off of infants. Hence it was in small towns and villages that interest in inoculation centered: it could solve what had remained a serious problem for such communities. In London, however, where the poor were plagued by too many children anyhow, there was no comparable impulse to take deliberate steps against the disease.[19]

Deaths from smallpox therefore remained a very conspicuous feature of the London Bills of Mortality throughout the eighteenth century. There, the ravages of the disease only began to diminish in the 1840s, when the safer method of vaccination with cowpox had been introduced, and initial resistances to that procedure had been overcome.[20] In rural and small-town Britain, however, inoculation with the smallpox virus itself had become widespread seventy to one hundred years earlier. The result was to reinforce and expand the pattern of demographic growth that the health changes sketched above were bringing to rural England in the same period of time.

Public opposition to smallpox inoculation lasted much longer on the Continent. Opponents criticized the practice both as an interference with God's will and as wanton spreading of dangerous infection among healthy people. The latter argument was effectively countered in England by careful (and methodologically path-breaking) statistical studies conducted by the Royal Society between 1721 and 1740; but in France it was not until after the death of Louis XV from smallpox in 1774 that organized resistance to inoculation crumbled. And even then, deliberate immunization against smallpox did not become a widespread practice on the European continent until the nineteenth century.[21]

Interestingly enough, smallpox inoculation became significant in the English colonies of America early in the eighteenth
century. In America, the fearful power of the disease to kill
adults was frequently demonstrated by outbreaks among Indians; and the rural and small-town structure of colonial society, like its counterpart in England, was also very vulnerable
to sporadic epidemics.[22] The remarkable upthrust of colonial
population in the eighteenth century may have owed a good
deal to the reduced smallpox death rate that inoculation brought
about. White settlement along the frontier was assisted also
by the fact that destruction of Indian populations by infectious
diseases, of which smallpox remained the most formidable,
continued unabated. The ravages of smallpox among Indians
may in fact have been assisted by deliberate efforts at germ
warfare. In 1763, for instance, Lord Jeffrey Amherst ordered
that blankets infected with smallpox be distributed among
enemy tribes, and the order was acted on. Whether the result
was as expected seems not recorded.[23]

In Spanish America, on the other hand, official efforts to protect Indians against smallpox waited only until an approved
method of prophylaxis against the disease came to be recognized in Spain itself. This followed swiftly on the discovery of
vaccination by Edward Jenner, an alert English country doctor,
who published his results to the world in 1798. He had noticed
that milkmaids seemed never to suffer from smallpox and surmised that they instead contracted cowpox from the animals
they tended. Experiment with inoculation of human patients
with cowpox showed that immunity to human smallpox did indeed result; and the dangers from cowpox for humans was
negligible. Thus the main objection which had previously ham-
pered the acceptance of inoculation with the smallpox itself
was removed: and the value of the new method of "vaccination" came swiftly to be recognized in all of Europe.

As a result, in 1803, a mere five years after Jenner's book appeared, a medical mission from Spain arrived in Mexico to instruct local doctors in the new technique. By the time the mission departed for the Philippines (1807) to repeat the performance in that distant outpost of Spanish power, the practice of vaccination had been established among New World doctors. Thereafter, insofar as medical services reached the Indian communities the terrors of one of the principal killers that had so long ravaged Amerindian populations under Spanish rule must have diminished.[24]

Elsewhere in Christian Europe, control of smallpox through deliberate medical action seems to have conformed rather to the French than to the English pattern, i.e., it became effective only shortly before 1800. Thus Catherine the Great introduced inoculation into Russia in 1768 by importing an English doctor to immunize herself and the Crown Prince; but only the court benefited from the Englishman's expertise. In 1775, after Louis XV's death from the disease, Frederick II of Prussia introduced inoculation into his kingdom, and characteristically did so by having the technique taught to doctors in the provinces, not just at court. It was, however, only when entire armies began to be immunized by command from the top that the practice really penetrated the lower social orders of continental Europe. In 1776, George Washington ordered inoculation for all the soldiers of his army; in 1805 Napoleon commanded that the improved vaccination method be used by all under his command.[25] Effective prophylaxis against smallpox in Europe was thus a by-product of the Napoleonic wars; and the extraordinary population growth that set the nineteenth century apart from all its predecessors in Europe's history was in substantial part a consequence of the effective containment of this long-standing scourge of civilized human communities.

In Turkey, however, smallpox inoculation had been practiced, at least in some milieux, earlier than anywhere else in Europe. It was, in fact, from Turkey that smallpox inoculation reached England, having been introduced to London in 1721, along with other oriental exotica like bloomers and the fez, by Lady Mary Wortley Montagu, wife of a returned ambassador to the Porte.[26] A pair of Greek doctors in Constantinople, who had achieved familiarity with western medicine at the famous medical school of Padua, served as go-betweens. They transmitted information about the folk practice of Turkey to the learned community of Europe by writing a pair of pamphlets on the subject that were widely reproduced in England and elsewhere. According to their report, it was generally believed in Constantinople that the practice of inoculation had long been familiar among Greek peasant women of the Morea and Thessaly.

Indeed, smallpox inoculation seems to have been known and practiced at a folk level throughout Arabia, North Africa, Persia, and India.[27] Reports of a more elaborate Chinese method, involving the insertion of a suitable infected swab of cotton inside the patient's nostril, reached London in 1700.[28] Chinese texts assert that this practice had been introduced into China at the beginning of the eleventh century by a wandering wise man come from the Indian borderland. Subsequently it is said to have become very popular.[29] It therefore seems probable that deliberate inoculation of children with smallpox had been a folk practice in much of Asia for centuries, long before it came to the attention of European doctors and penetrated the repertory of their officially approved techniques in the course of the eighteenth century.[30]

Since the practice was so old and widespread at a folk level, why was it that the European medical profession and learned community picked up the practice of inoculation only in the eighteenth century, and why did this notable improvement in medical practice take place in England rather than elsewhere?

One factor, surely, was accidental. Mary Wortley Montagu's interest in inoculation was provoked by the fact that her own fair face had been scarred by smallpox that struck only after she had become an established hostess and lady of fashion. But London's alert response to her news from Turkey depended on the fact that smallpox deaths among the reigning families of Europe twice affected British public life in important ways during the first decades of the eighteenth century. In 1700 Queen Anne's son and sole surviving direct heir died of smallpox, thus opening afresh the question of succession to the English throne. Scarcely had the union of England and Scotland and the Hanoverian succession been agreed upon than another smallpox death in 1711, this time in the imperial Hapsburg house, disastrously disrupted plans agreed upon among the powers allied against France in the war of the Spanish succession. These two events, coming so close upon one another, and in both instances sharply altering the course of British political history, alerted the ruling classes of the British Isles to the dangers of smallpox. This set the stage for systematic inquiry by members of the Royal Society for ways of forestalling unexpected adult deaths from the disease, and prepared the ground for the positive and thoroughly scientific reaction to Lady Mary Wortley Montagu's initiative among London's medical and court circles.[31]

Personal and political accidents, scientific and professional organization, and a systematically expanded network of communication among men of learning all came together therefore in the course of the eighteenth century to bring a sharp reduction of smallpox death tolls within the power of European doctors. Organized medicine thereby began for the first time to contribute to population growth in a statistically significant fashion. Even if, as seems probable, smallpox inoculation had been demographically significant in China and other parts of Asia for centuries before 1700, it had been a matter of folk practice analogous to the innumerable other customs and rules of hygiene that human beings had everywhere worked out and justified to themselves by a variety of naive and ingenious myths.

Near Eastern folkways, as a matter of fact, had encrusted the simple practice of smallpox inoculation with a full complement of myth and ritual by the time learned Europeans first investigated the matter. The person to be inoculated was viewed as "buying" the disease, and to make the transaction effective, had to give ritual gifts to the person who performed the inoculation. The inoculation was made between thumb and forefinger so that the resulting pock mark showed quite conspicuously, and identified the receiver as a sort of initiate ever after. The entire ritual looked like an adaptation of commercial customs; and *a priori* one may believe that spread of inoculation at a folk level could most readily have occurred via caravan personnel, for whom protection against smallpox was an obvious advantage. Wherever the practice first developed, one may easily suppose that caravan traders heard of it, tried it, and thereafter propagated it as folk practice throughout the parts of Eurasia and Africa where caravan traffic constituted the main form of long-distance trade.[32]

As we saw in Chapter V, bubonic plague followed precisely the same routes in disseminating itself among human populations of Asia and eastern Europe in modern times. There may, in fact, have been a sort of demographic balancing act in the way plague exposure and an effective prophylaxis against smallpox spread along the same paths at nearly the same time. When, however, the technique of inoculation reached western Europe, where plague had already disappeared, the effect was obviously to reinforce possibilities of population growth as never before.

Only in Europe was the medical profession well enough organized to spread news of new methods rapidly among rank-and-file practitioners, who were then able to inoculate on a massive scale as soon as local demand for such protection developed. Hence, once the technique came to doctors' attention, inoculation against smallpox remained part of professional medical practice in Europe. This in turn meant that systematic efforts to discover and test improvements could and did take place from the start. The spectacular upshot was the discovery and acceptance of vaccination within less than a century.

Even more spectacular was the speed with which the technique of vaccination spread throughout the world on the strength of the existing European medical communications network. Thus, for example, a doctor in backwoods Kentucky had vaccinated some five hundred persons in the small town of Lexington by 1803[33]; Russian doctors began vaccinating natives in Khiatka, on the Chinese border, in 1805, and in the same year a Portuguese merchant in Macao brought vaccine from the Philippines to meet the crisis of a large-scale outbreak of smallpox in South China.[34] More remarkable still: in 1812 Tartar merchants in Bukhara and Samarcand (then still beyond Russia's borders) distributed pamphlets describing Jenner's method of vaccination which had been printed at Kazan in Arabic and Chagatay Turkish, presumably as part of the Russian government's systematic effort to spread the technique throughout their Asian territories.[35]

Two observations about the connection between disease history and the more general patterns of Europe's development seem appropriate at this point. First, the rise of Great Britain in comparison with France in the course of the eighteenth century depended, among other things, on the remarkable population growth that set in earlier and continued longer in Britain than it did in France. Political institutions, the distribution of coal and iron ore, social structures, values, and individual inventiveness all played a role in defining the over-all result: but in light of what can now be said about the retreat of plague, malaria, and other infectious diseases from the English countryside, together with England's head start in the deliberate control of smallpox, it seems clear enough that divergent disease experiences in the two countries had much to do with their divergent population histories. Shifting patterns of disease therefore take a place as one of the determinants of European and world history in the eighteenth century, for the rise of the British empire and the temporary eclipse of France overseas after 1763 must certainly rank as a critical turning point in the history of America, Africa, and Asia, as well as of Europe.

Secondly, although in the eighteenth century the major triumphs of scientific medicine lay still in the future, it does not seem absurd to suggest that decreasing significance of epidemic disease, partly due to medical advances but mostly due to ecological adjustments of which men were entirely unaware, constituted an essential background for the popularization of "enlightened" philosophical and social views. A world where sudden and unexpected death remains a real and dreaded possibility in everyone's life experience makes the idea that the universe is a great machine whose motions are regular, understandable and even predictable, seem grossly inadequate to account for observed reality. Epidemic disease, after all, strikes erratically as well as unpredictably, and can never be dismissed as insignificant by those exposed to it. Before the findings of the astronomers and mathematicians of the seventeenth century could become a basis for a popularized world view, therefore, epidemic disease had also to relax its dominion over human minds and bodies. The retreat of plague and malaria and the containment of smallpox were thus essential preparations for the propagation of deistic opinions of the kind that became fashionable in advanced circles in the eighteenth century.

A world in which lethal infectious disease seldom seized a person suddenly in the prime of life no longer stood so much in need of belief in Divine Providence to explain such deaths. Moreover, as in other orthogenetic evolutionary situations, newfangled mechanistic world views sustained the search for more effective methods for coping with disease, and made the medical profession increasingly systematic in testing new treatments empirically. Real improvements resulted; and the thought that human intelligence and skill could improve life not only in mechanical but also in health matters became increasingly plausible.

There seems therefore a clear correlation between Europe's shifting encounter with disease and the phases of that continent's cultural and political history. Between 1494 and 1648 the stresses upon older cultural traditions were especially acute because Europeans had to adjust to the initial impact of transoceanic movement of men, goods, ideas, and diseases—all at once. The political and ideological storms of the Reformation and wars of religion manifested these strains. Only as the first shocks wore off, including, significantly, the decay of epidemic disease and its replacement by more predictable, less damaging patterns of infection, was it possible for the relaxed political and cultural style of life we call the Old Regime to establish itself. Obviously, the changing incidence of disease was only one, and not the most conspicuous, factor in bringing about such changes. Yet because it has usually been completely overlooked by historians, the experience of disease and of shifting encounters with lethal infections, seems worth emphasizing here.

In all ecological relationships, a significant breakthrough for one organism or group of organisms quickly creates new stresses in the system. These stresses usually are such as first to diminish and then contain the original disturbance. So it was with Australian rabbits, 1856–1960, and so it was in northwestern Europe between 1750 and 1850, as the industrial revolution began to gather headway. Living conditions in new industrial towns were, and long remained, notoriously unhealthful. On the other hand, improvements in transportation allowed increasingly efficient patterns of food distribution to fend off local famines. Food preservation was almost equally important. Canning, for instance, was invented in 1809 in response to an offer of a handsome reward by the French government; and Napoleon's armies pioneered its large-scale use.[36]

The Napoleonic wars were, of course, among the most hard fought Europeans had experienced up to that time. Yet battle deaths were far less numerous than deaths from infectious diseases, especially typhus, that accompanied Napoleon's armies and those of his enemies as they marched and countermarched across Europe.[37] Nevertheless, population growth, which had gone into high gear all across Europe by 1800, quickly replaced such losses. By the 1840s limitations upon the availability of food became critical in many parts of the Continent. The "hungry forties" became disastrous for millions after 1845 when a parasitic fungus, native to Peru, succeeded in establishing itself in Europe's burgeoning potato fields.[38] The result was widespread failure of the potato crop upon which millions of poverty-stricken Irish, Belgians, and Germans had come to depend. Famine accompanied by typhus and other diseases resulted. Millions died, and the extraordinary multiplication of Irish rural population came abruptly and lastingly to a halt, while in the following decades a world-girdling Irish diaspora profoundly affected North America and Australia, as well as other parts of the British empire.

Apart from such acute but short-lived crises as that which struck the potato fields of Europe, 1845–49, the acceleration of movement resulting from application of mechanical power to transport both by land and sea introduced a long series of disease exposures to European and world populations in the nineteenth century. Simultaneously human migration into larger and more numerous urban centers had a parallel effect of intensifying encounters with old and familiar infections. The result was a sort of race between the development of medical skills among Europe's doctors and public administrators on the one hand and the intensification of infections together with chronic ills provoked by altered conditions of living.

Until near the end of the nineteenth century the race remained close in most of the world's great cities. Growing urban centers that lagged in implementing sanitary reforms, like New York and most other American cities, actually saw a sharp increase in mortality.[39] But from the 1880s onward, a series of dramatic triumphs accrued to medical reseachers who succeeded in isolating and studying the "germs" of one infectious disease after another. Careful study usually allowed experts to devise effective ways of checking infection, whether by synthesizing new drugs or devising immunizing injections, introducing new sanitary practices, altering older patterns of human encounter with insects, rodents, or other alternate hosts for the disease in question, or in some other fashion contriving to interrupt the established patterns of disease transmission. International organization supplemented urban and national measures aimed against infectious diseases, so that by the first decades of the twentieth century preventive medicine began to make a dent in the epidemiological experience of Asian and African as well as European and European-descended populations.

Success was sufficient so that by the second half of our century, professionals seriously proposed the global eradication of a number of mankind's most formidable infections, and thought it a feasible goal for the near future.[40] But as is their wont, such massive and fundamental successes in altering humanity's experience of disease carried within them a potential nemesis: population crises on a continent-wide scale seemed likely to supplant the localized population crises afflicting the new industrial cities with which nineteenth-century medical reformers had to cope. The race between skills and ills was thus by no means decisively won—or lost; and in the nature of ecological relationships is never likely to be.

The first and in many ways most significant manifestation of the altered disease relationships created by industrialization was the global peregrination of cholera. This disease had long been endemic in Bengal, and spread thence in epidemic fashion to other parts of India and adjacent regions from time to time. It was caused by a bacillus that could live as an independent organism in water for lengthy periods of time. Once swallowed, if the cholera bacillus survives the stomach juices, it is capable of swift multiplication in the human alimentary tract, and produces violent and dramatic symptoms—diarrhea, vomiting, fever, and death, often within a few hours of the first signs of illness. The speed with which cholera killed was profoundly alarming, since perfectly healthy people could never feel safe from sudden death when the infection was anywhere near. In addition, the symptoms were peculiarly horrible: radical dehydration meant that a victim shrank into a wizened caricature of his former self within a few hours, while ruptured capillaries discolored the skin, turning it black and blue. The effect was to make mortality uniquely visible: patterns of bodily decay were exacerbated and accelerated, as in a time-lapse motion picture, to remind all who saw it of death's ugly horror and utter inevitability.

The statistical impact of cholera was occasionally severe: in Cairo about 13 per cent of the total population succumbed in 1831 when the disease first affected that city.[41] But this was unusual, and in European cities losses were never anything like that great. But this did not diminish the unique psychological impact of the approach of such a killer. Cholera seemed capable of penetrating any quarantine, of bypassing any man-made obstacle: it chose its victims erratically, mainly but not exclusively from the lower classes in European towns. It was, in short, both uniquely dreadful in itself and unparalleled in recent European experience. Reaction was correspondingly frantic and far-reaching.

The disease first came acutely to European attention when an unusually severe outbreak of cholera developed in the hinterland of Calcutta in 1817. Thence it spread to other parts of India, and soon transgressed the boundaries that had previously confined it to the subcontinent and immediately adjacent regions. What seems to have happened is that an old and well-established pattern for spreading cholera across the Indian landscape intersected new, British-imposed patterns of trade and military movement. The result was that the cholera overleaped its familiar bounds and burst into new and unfamiliar territories, where human resistance and customary reactions to its presence were totally lacking.

From time immemorial, it appears, Hindu pilgrimages and times of festival had drawn great crowds to the lower Ganges, where cholera was endemic. Consequently, the celebrants had been liable to pick up cholera along with other infections. Those who did not succumb on the spot were liable in turn to carry the infection back home, where it ran an accustomed if nasty and sometimes demographically destructive course.[42] The association of cholera with pilgrimage and holy days in India continues to the present[43]; and prior to 1817 one may safely assume that well-defined custom pretty well confined the dissemination of the infection to the range of Hindu pilgrimage, i.e., to India proper. Nevertheless, from time to time cholera infection reached as far afield as China, traveling by ship. This is attested by the fact that when cholera penetrated China early in the nineteenth century, the Chinese did not regard it as a new disease, even though it had not been seen on the China coast for some time previously.[44]

In 1817, however, when an unusually severe cholera epidemic started to re-enact its familiar pattern, English ships and troops were also on the scene; and their presence and movement to and from the primary focus in and around Calcutta, carried the infection to completely unfamiliar ground.

The expansion followed two routes. One was overland, and of relatively limited range. British troops fighting a series of campaigns along India's northern frontiers between 1816 and 1818 carried the cholera with them from their headquarters in Bengal, and communicated the disease to their Nepalese and Afghan enemies. Far more dramatic were the movements by sea. Ships carried cholera to Ceylon, Indonesia, the southeastern Asian mainland, China, and Japan between 1820 and 1822. Muscat in southern Arabia encountered the disease when a British expeditionary force, intent on suppressing the slave trade, landed there in 1821; and from Muscat the cholera filtered south along the east coast of Africa, following the slave traders. The infection also entered the Persian Gulf, penetrated Mesopotamia and Iran, and continued north into Syria, Anatolia, and the Caspian shores. There it stopped short, more perhaps because the winter of 1823–24 was unusually severe than because of any action by either Russian, Turkish, or Persian authorities. It lingered longer in China and Japan; indeed it is not clear that the disease had disappeared from China before the second epidemic wave got going in 1826.[45]

The episode proved only a foretaste of the far more extensive wanderings of the cholera bacillus in the 1830s, making the disease genuinely global. A new cholera epidemic emerged from Bengal in 1826 and quickly retraced its previous path into southern Russia. Military movements connected with Russia's wars against Persia (1826–28) and Turkey (1828–29) and the Polish revolt of 1830–31, carried the cholera to the Baltic by 1831, whence it spread by ship to England. In the next year it invaded Ireland; and Irish emigrants carried the disease to Canada, whence it filtered southward into the United States (1832) and Mexico (1833).

More enduringly important than this first sally into the European heartlands was the fact that cholera established itself at Mecca in 1831 at the time of the Moslem pilgrimage.[46] The inevitable result was the re-enactment of the patterns of epidemic dispersion long familiar within India, but this time on a much expanded geographic scale as followers of Muhammad headed homeward, whether west to Morocco or east to Mindanao, or to points between. Thereafter until 1912, when cholera broke out in Mecca and Medina for the last time,[47] epidemics of this dread disease were a common accompaniment of the Moslem pilgrimage, appearing no fewer than forty times between 1831 and 1912, or every other year on the average.[48]

As cholera thus added the Moslem pilgrimage to its older Hindu pilgrimage dispersal routes, the exposure of peoples beyond India's borders to the new disease became chronic. On top of this, after mid-century the swifter movement of steamships and railroads became increasingly able to accelerate the global diffusion of cholera from any major world center. As a result, cholera deaths beyond India's borders certainly totaled millions in the nineteenth century, although no precise calculation seems feasible. In India itself the disease was and remains important, causing far more deaths than plague[49]; but cholera in India, being thoroughly familiar, excited no special alarm or surprise.

It was otherwise, however, beyond India's borders. Moslems had long been resigned to plague and found European quarantine efforts rather amusing. But the unfamiliar, dreadful, and sudden nature of cholera deaths created among the population of Egypt and other affected Moslem lands almost the same alarm that prevailed in Europe. Neither Moslem medical nor religious traditions were able to cope. The popular fright cholera aroused helped to discredit traditional leadership and authority within the Moslem world, and opened the way for reception of European medicine.[50]

In Europe, to be sure, there were a few localities where memories of former visitations by the plague remained sufficiently vivid that public and private responses to the emergency could find fitting if somewhat archaic expression. This was the case in much of Mediterranean Europe, where a combination of religious supplication and medical quarantine had been built into public law ever since the sixteenth century. Thus in Marseilles, where annual commemoration of the plague of 1721 had kept memories of that disaster very much alive, the cholera became an occasion for renewal of Christian piety.[51]

In northern Europe, however, traditional guidelines for behavior in time of epidemiological crisis were less well defined. To be sure, chronic tensions between social classes tended to find overt and even ritualized expression in places as diverse as St. Petersburg and Paris[52]; but such symptoms of social strain did not easily convert into concrete and definite programs of action. People had therefore to improvise, argue, and flee, as well as plead, threaten, and pray. In other words, there was a wide spectrum of behavior from which to choose the most effective way to cope with what everyone agreed was a real and present threat to life and society. From these perturbations, refreshed at frequent intervals during the rest of the nineteenth century, came the major impetus to improvements in urban sanitation and public health regulation.[53]

To begin with, cholera added new urgency to long-standing debates between rival schools of thought about epidemics. Since the days of Hippocrates, some European doctors had held that sudden outbreaks of disease were caused by a miasma, emerging perhaps from dead corpses or other rotting matter in the earth. When the miasma encountered appropriately weakened constitutions, these theorists believed, disease resulted. Wherever encounters with malaria and other insect-borne diseases remained important, the miasmatic theory had a firm and satisfactory empirical basis—or seemed to.

The rival germ theory of contagion had been clearly advanced as early as 1546 by Girolamo Fracastoro. This provided the theoretical justification for the sort of quarantine regulations that had become standard in the Mediterranean against plague. But early in the nineteenth century the germ theory was put on the defensive. The occasion was the disaster that came to French troops sent to Santo Domingo in 1802 to suppress rebellion led by Toussaint L'Ouverture. Within a few months, yellow fever and other tropical diseases utterly destroyed a force of 33,000 veterans, and the resulting setback to Napoleon's imperial ambitions (among other things) made him willing to sell the Louisiana Territory to the United States in 1803. This dramatic demonstration of the power of disease to blunt European military force overseas gave a special fillip to study of tropical diseases among French doctors; and when yellow fever broke out in Barcelona in 1822, they seized the opportunity to make a definitive test of the contagionist as against the miasmatic school of thought. French experts, led by Nicholas Chervin, organized systematic and careful study of how the disease occurred. They concluded that there was no possibility of contact among the different persons who came down with yellow fever in Barcelona. Thus contagionism seemed to have been fully and finally discredited.

For the next fifty years medical reformers set out to dismantle the long-standing quarantine regulations of Mediterranean ports, arguing that they were mere survivals from a superstitious age. Lacking any empirical base—for no one as yet imagined that insects might be carriers of disease—the germ theory seemed destined for the scrap heap of history.[54] British liberals, in particular, saw quarantine regulations as an irrational infringement of the principle of free trade, and bent every effort toward the eradication of such traces of tyranny and Roman Catholic folly.

Yet in 1854 a London doctor, John Snow, neatly demonstrated how cases of cholera that broke out in a district of central London could all be traced to a single contaminated source of drinking water. But Snow's argument was merely circumstantial[55]; and since contagionism had been so recently and so definitively discredited by Europe's most meticulous and celebrated medical experts, Snow's interpretation of his data commanded little attention. Then in the 1880s the microscope abruptly reversed the balance of medical opinion with the dramatic discovery of disease-causing "germs."

The first such germs to be detected were the bacilli of anthrax and tuberculosis, discovered respectively by Louis Pasteur, between 1877 and 1879 and Robert Koch in 1882. Since neither of these infections spread in a dramatically epidemic fashion, their identification did not upset the miasmatic theory, which had come into existence to account for epidemics. It was otherwise when in 1883 Robert Koch claimed to have found a new bacillus responsible for cholera, for if Koch was right the miasmatic theory was wrong—at least in explaining cholera.[56]

Since many learned and respected doctors had committed themselves to the miasmatic theory as explanation of epidemic, it is not surprising to find that Koch's explanation for the cause of cholera met stout resistance among experts.[57] As late as 1892, a famous German doctor drank a beaker full of cholera bacilli to prove the falsity of the germ theory—and gleefully informed his professional rivals that he had experienced no ill effects.[58] No doubt he was lucky; but his act dramatized the uncertainties that still surround the question of what factors affect transmission of cholera infections. Perhaps in the professor's case, anger and nervousness provoked an extra charge of stomach acids which sufficed to kill the bacilli he swallowed.[59]

Long before Koch's microscope thus provided doctors with an empirical base for the modern view of how cholera spreads, the alarm it created in American and European cities provided essential leverage for those reformers who sought to improve urban sanitation, housing, health services, and water supply. Models of what to do and how to do it were readily at hand, for during the eighteenth century European governments discovered that soldiers' and sailors' lives were much too valuable to squander needlessly, when simple and not overly expensive measures could check the ravages of disease.

The most famous and significant of these health measures was the use of citrus juice to ward off scurvy. This disease haunted European ships on long voyages, when crews for weeks or months on end ate food that lacked essential vitamins. Its peculiar pattern of incidence provoked an abundant medical literature; and as early as 1611 the use of lemons and oranges as a cure was recommended in print, and repeated thereafter by respectable and important medical writers. But other cures were no less warmly recommended, and a supply of citrus fruit was often hard to come by. Hence the superior effectiveness of the cure was not clearly recognized until the end of the eighteenth century.

Indeed, even after a British naval surgeon, James Lind, published the results of his carefully controlled experiments that proved the efficacy of fresh lemons and oranges in curing scurvy (1753), the Admiralty did not act. The reason was partly pecuniary: citrus fruit was expensive and scarce and could not be stored for very long. Partly too, the naval authorities believed other cures were more suitable, e.g., the sauerkraut Captain James Cook fed his crews in the Pacific. Moreover, when in 1795 the Admiralty did decide on citrus juices as the best preventative for scurvy and prescribed a daily ration for all sailors on shipboard, the result was imperfect. The species of limes grown in the West Indies lacked the essential vitamins; but it soon proved that West Indian limes were cheaper than Mediterranean lemons, with the result that the British navy soon was drinking the almost valueless lime juice that gave them the nickname, "Limeys." As late as 1875, therefore, outbreaks of scurvy occurred on British naval vessels, despite the daily dose of lime juice prescribed by regulations.[60]

In spite of such confusion and inefficiency, James Lind and

other medical men in the British navy pioneered a number of other significant improvements in health administration during the latter decades of the eighteenth century. Lind was instrumental, for instance, in installing sea-water distilleries on board ship to assure a supply of fresh drinking water. The adoption of the practice of quarantining new recruits until they had been bathed and equipped with a new set of clothes was another simple procedure that reduced typhus dramatically. Use of quinine against malaria, and rules against going ashore after dark on malarial coasts, were also introduced under Lind's direction.

Parallel improvements in army health administration, with conscious attention to water supplies, personal cleanliness, sewage, and the like, met with larger obstacles, inasmuch as soldiers were never so well insulated from external sources of infection as sailors aboard ship could be. Yet there, too, eighteenth-century European armies, being the pets and playthings of Europe's crowned heads, were both too valuable in the eyes of authority and too amenable to control from above not to benefit from a growing corpus of sanitary regulations. From protection of soldiers to medical regulation of the public at large was an easy step which had been made on the Continent, in principle if not fully in practice, by systematically minded servants of German monarchs. The most influential was Johann Peter Frank, whose six volumes on medical policy, published between 1779 and 1819, attracted wide and favorable attention among rulers and government administrators who recognized that the number and vigor of their subjects was a fundamental component of state power.

Interaction between Europe's political history and the health of professionalized standing armies and navies deserves more consideration than historians have commonly devoted to the subject. Obviously, the rise of absolutism on the European continent hinged on the availability of well-trained armies to do the sovereign's will; and the preservation of such armies, in turn, rested on the development of rules of sanitation and personal hygiene that reduced losses by epidemic disease to relatively minor proportions, winter and summer, in the field and in cantonments. "Spit and polish" and ritual attention to cleanliness was, of course, the way European armies achieved this goal, and the eighteenth century was clearly the time when such practices became normal, altering the experiential reality of soldiering in far-reaching ways. But no one seems to have investigated the intersection of high medical theory, as expressed by doctors like Johann Peter Frank, with the routines that inconspicuous drill sergeants and junior officers invented to occupy soldiers' time, keep them healthy and train them to battle efficiency.

As in most matters of military administration, the French were pace-setters. Early in the eighteenth century, the French royal administration set up military hospitals and medical training schools. In the 1770s a medical corps of a modern type was established. The key innovation was that doctors served their entire careers in the new corps, and could aspire to ascend a ladder of rank just like regular officers, instead of coming, as before, into military service from civilian practice at the invitation of a regimental colonel when some emergency or impending campaign required it.

The benefit of the professionalization of the French military medical corps was demonstrated during the wars of the revolutionary and Napoleonic period. Young men conscripted from remote farms and from the slums of Paris mingled in the ranks of the new and vastly expanded armies of the French Republic. Yet despite the fact that the recruits brought widely different disease experience and resistances into the army, the medical corps was able to prevent massive epidemic outbreaks, and took swift advantage of new discoveries, like Jenner's vaccination (announced in 1798), to improve the health of the soldiers in their charge. The expanded scale of land warfare, characteristic of the Napoleonic period, could not have occurred otherwise. Equally, the capacity of the British navy to blockade French ports for months and years on end, depended quite as much on lemon juice as on powder and shot.[61]

In view of the achievements of military medicine, therefore, the problem as it presented itself to sanitary reformers of the 1830s and 1840s was less one of technique than of organization. In England, at any rate, a libertarian prejudice against regulations infringing the individual's right to do what he chose with his own property was deeply rooted; and as long as theories of disease and its propagation remained under dispute, clear imperatives were hard to agree upon. In this situation the fear of cholera acted as a catalyst. To do nothing was no longer sufficient; old debates and stubborn clashes had to be quickly resolved by public bodies acting literally under fear of death.

The first outbreak of cholera in Britain (1832) promoted establishment of local boards of health. Being unpaid and locally elected, the personnel of these boards often lacked expertise as well as legal power to alter living conditions; indeed, not everyone agreed that filth and ill health went together. Far more significant was the reaction to the reappearance of cholera in 1848. In that year Parliament authorized the establishment of a Central Board of Health exactly one week before cholera appeared in England for a second time. The dreaded approach of Asiatic cholera had been a matter of public notice for more than a year, and there can be no doubt that it was the expectation of its return that precipitated Parliament's action.

The Board of Health instituted far-reaching programs of public sanitation that had been championed by a noisy group of reformers for a decade or more. Being staffed with some of the most prominent advocates of sanitary reform, the board used its extensive legal powers to remove innumerable sources of defilement from British towns and cities, and began installation of water and sewer systems all over the country.

Sewers were nothing new, being at least as old as the Romans; but until the 1840s a sewer was simply an elongated cesspool with an overflow at one end. Such sewers collected filth and had to be dug out periodically. The flow of water through them, save in periods of cloudburst, was sluggish because water supplies were sharply limited. The new idea of the 1840s, championed principally by an earnest Benthamite reformer named Edwin Chadwick, was to construct narrow sewers out of smooth ceramic pipe and pass enough water through to flush the waste matter toward some distant depository, far removed from human habitation. There Chadwick expected that the sewage could be processed and sold to farmers for fertilizer.

To work, the plan required installation of completely new systems of water pipes and of sewer pipes; development of more powerful pumps to deliver water into houses under pressure; and compulsory elimination of older sewage systems. Intrusion upon private property to allow water mains and sewer pipes to maintain the straight lines needed for efficient patterns of flow was also necessary. To many Englishmen at the time this seemed an unwarranted intrusion on their rights and, of course, the capital expenditures involved were substantial. It therefore took the lively fear that cholera provoked to overcome entrenched opposition.[62]

Half of Chadwick's initial vision failed, for he was unable to make financially successful arrangements for the sale of sewage to farmers for fertilizer. The reason was that guano from Chile and artificially synthesized fertilizer became available in forms more convenient for farmers to use than anything Chadwick could do with sewage. The practical solution was to discharge the new sewer pipes into accessible bodies of water—often with unpleasant results. Development of effective ways of processing sewage to make effluvia inoffensive took another half century; and installation of such plants on a large scale waited until the twentieth century, even in prosperous and carefully administered cities.[63]

Yet even though Chadwick was unable to realize the full scope of his plan, the Central Board of Health, under his direction, did demonstrate during the years of its existence, 1848–54, how the new cities called into existence by the industrial revolution could be made far healthier than cities of earlier times had ever been. Moreover, the new arterial-venous system of water supply and sewage disposal was not so appallingly expensive as to be prohibitive for urban communities in Europe and lands of European settlement overseas. In Asia, however, where use of human excreta for fertilizer was of long standing, the new system of sewage disposal never became general.

Spread to other countries occurred relatively rapidly, though not infrequently it took the same stimulus of an approaching epidemic of cholera to compel local vested interests to yield to advocates of sanitary reform. Thus, in the United States, it was not until 1866 that a comparable Board of Health was established in New York City, modeled on the British prototype and inspired by identical apprehensions of the imminence of a new cholera epidemic.[64] In the absence of this sort of stimulus, such a great city as Hamburg persisted in postponing costly improvements of its water supply until 1892, when a visitation of cholera proved beyond all reasonable doubt that a contaminated water supply propagated the disease. What happened was this: as an old free city, Hamburg remained self-governing within the new German Reich and drew its water from the Elbe without special treatment. Adjacent lay the town of Altona, part of the Prussian state, where a solicitous government installed a water-filtration plant. In 1892, when cholera broke out in Hamburg, it ran down one side of the street dividing the two cities and spared the other completely. Since air and earth —the explanations preferred by the miasmatists—were identical across the boundary between the two cities, a more clear-cut demonstration of the importance of the water supply in defining where the disease struck could not have been devised.[65] Doubters were silenced; and cholera has, in fact, never returned to European cities since, thanks to systematic purification of urban water supplies from bacteriological contamination.

Obviously, there was always a considerable lag between decision to introduce improved water and sewage systems and the completion of necessary engineering work. But by the end of the nineteenth century all major cities of the western world had done something to come up to the new level of sanitation and water management that had been pioneered in Great Britain, 1848–54. Urban life became far safer from disease than ever before as a result. Not merely cholera and typhoid but a host of other less serious water-borne infections were reduced sharply. One of the major causes of infant mortality thereby trailed off toward statistical insignificance.

In Asia, Africa, and Latin America, cities seldom were capable of making sanitary water and sewage systems available to all the population; yet even there, as the risks of contaminated water became more widely known, simple precautions, like boiling drinking water, and periodical testing of water supplies for bacteriological contamination, introduced a quite effective guard against wholesale exposure to water-borne infections. Administrative systems were not always capable of sustaining an effective bacteriological watch, of course; and enforcement was even more difficult in many situations. But means and knowledge needed to escape large-scale outbreaks of lethal disease became almost universal. Indeed, when local epidemics of cholera or some other killing disease occurred, it soon became common for richer countries to finance international mobilization of medical experts to help local authorities in bringing the outbreak under control. Hence even in cities where a water-sewage circulatory system had never been installed, some of the benefits of public sanitation were swiftly brought to bear.

By 1900, therefore, for the first time since cities had come into existence almost five thousand years previously, the world's urban populations became capable of maintaining themselves and even increasing in numbers without depending on in-migration from the countryside.[66] This was a fundamental change in age-old demographic relationships. Until the nineteenth century, cities had everywhere been population sumps, incapable of maintaining themselves without constant replenishment from a healthier countryside. It has been calculated, for example, that during the eighteenth century, when London's Bills of Mortality permit reasonably accurate accountancy, deaths exceeded births by an average of 6,000 per annum. In the course of the century, London therefore required no less than 600,000 in-migrants for its mere maintenance. An even larger number of in-migrants was needed to permit the population increase that was a conspicious feature of the city's eighteenth-century history.[67]

Implications of this change are profound. As cities became capable of sustaining growing populations, older patterns of migration from rural to urban modes of life met new obstacles. Rural in-migrants had to compete with a more abundant, more thoroughly acculturated population of city-born individuals, capable of performing functions formerly relegated to newcomers from the countryside. Social mobility thereby became more difficult than in times when systematic urban die-off opened niches in the cities of the world for upwardly mobile individuals coming in from rural backgrounds. To be sure, in regions where industrial and commercial development proceeded rapidly, this new relation between country and city was masked by the fact that so many new occupations opened in urban contexts that there was room for city-born and rural in-migrants alike. In regions where industrialization has lagged, on the other hand, the problem of social mobility has already assumed visible form. In Latin America and Africa, for example, vast fringes of semi-rural slums commonly surround well-established cities. These are the squatting grounds for migrants from the countryside who are seeking to become urban, yet cannot find suitable employment and so must eke out a marginal existence amid the most squalid poverty. Such settlements give visible form to the collision between traditional patterns of migration from the countryside and an urban population that no longer, as aforetime, withers away so as to accommodate the newcomers crowding at the gate.

More significant still: in all stable rural communities, custom prescribed controls on marriage that had the effect of reducing birth rates to levels that more or less matched up with prevailing death rates and rates of migration away from the village. Various elaborations of dowry rules, for instance, had the effect of postponing marriage in many communities until bride and bridegroom had in hand enough property to assure the new family of a standard of living equivalent to that their parents had known. In city environments, where wastage of population had traditionally prevailed, similar restraints on early marriage and procreation were characteristically limited to propertied classes. Poor urban youths, among whom employment was not usually hereditary, had no reason to wait for their parents to attain an age for retirement, as peasant dowry rules in effect often provided.[68] Hence older restraints upon early marriage and procreation were weakened or decayed entirely in urban settings. This, together with the withdrawal of epidemic disease as a serious drain upon human populations since 1900 (or, in Asia, since 1945) underlies the truly extraordinary upsurge of human numbers in our own time.[69]

Other implications of the demographic relation between city and country extend to redefinitions of what work is; divorce between social rank and possession of land; psychological reactions to crowding, etc. To explore these further would take us too far from the theme of this book; but the transformation of traditional relationships between town and country is surely a fundamental axis of humanity's encounter with the twentieth century all around the globe. Behind this change lies the series of medical and administrative improvements in urban housekeeping triggered by Europeans' fear of cholera in the nineteenth century.

International medical co-operation also achieved new efficiency as a result of Europe's encounter with cholera. International medical congresses date back to 1851 when experts met in Paris to try to settle the disputed question of quarantine, and whether it was effective against cholera and other diseases. Mediterranean doctors and governments, inheriting the methods that had been developed against plague, continued, by and large, to believe in contagion and the effectiveness of quarantine; the sanitary reformers of Britain and northern Europe were scornful of such antiquated ideas, believing that miasma from stinking refuse and sewage was the principal cause of disease. The conference therefore effected nothing but an exchange of views.

Nevertheless, international co-operation against cholera and plague was not entirely fruitless. The main theatre of co-operation was at first in Egypt. As early as 1831, when cholera first approached, the consuls of the European powers stationed in Alexandria had been asked by Egypt's modernizing ruler, the Albanian adventurer, Mehemet Ali, to constitute themselves a Board of Health for the city.[70] They continued to constitute a sort of special health outpost for western Europe thereafter, keeping track of the epidemiological fate of the Mecca pilgrims, and issuing warnings of the appearance and disappearance of potentially dangerous outbreaks of disease in Egypt. Accordingly, when cholera returned to Egypt in 1883 it seemed no more than a prudent advance upon earlier prophylaxis to dispatch teams of European doctors to the scene, seeking to bring the new resources of bacteriology to bear upon the problem.

The result was spectacular: within a few weeks, the German, Robert Koch, announced that he had discovered the bacillus causing cholera, thereby, as we have seen, giving enormous new impetus to the germ theory of disease. Not only that: methods for guarding against cholera became self-evident as soon as the nature of the infection was known. Chemical disinfectants and heat could kill the bacillus; careful handling of sufferers could guard against passing the disease to others; and by 1893 a vaccine against cholera had been developed. Hence by the end of the nineteenth century, scientific medicine had discovered effective means to counter the dread disease.

Even quite simple administrative actions could have far-reaching consequences when they were guided by the new understanding of infection. Thus in Egypt, official regulation of the Moslem pilgrimage began in 1890, when smallpox vaccination was decreed for all pilgrims entering the country. This eliminated a formerly significant disease from the Moslem pilgrimage. In 1900, mandatory quarantine for all transients was ordered, and in 1913 Egyptian authorities instituted compulsory inoculation against cholera. Thereafter, cholera ceased to disfigure the Moslem pilgrimage.[71] The disease remained common in India and sporadically affected China and some other parts of Asia and Africa until after World War II. But as a world scourge, the infection that had transgressed its traditional bounds because of the application of scientific principles to mechanical transport early in the century, was effectively defeated by the application of similar scientific principles to health administration at its close. As such, the career of cholera offers an unusually tidy paradigm of the nineteenth century's intensified encounter with infectious disease and the triumphant

containment of the risks implicit in a megalopolitan, indus-
trialized style of life.

A number of other infectious diseases of long-standing importance also quickly succumbed to the new techniques bacteriologists had learned to command. Thus typhoid fever was first
identified as a distinct disease in 1829; its causative bacillus was
discovered and an effective vaccine developed by 1896; and in
the first decade of the twentieth century mass inoculations
against typhoid proved capable of checking the disease. Diphtheria bacilli were identified in 1883, and an antitoxin was
proved effective in 1891. Bacilli in milk were brought under
control by pasteurization, i.e., heating the milk to a temperature at which most potentially harmful bacteria were killed.
The city of Chicago made this method of guarding infants and
others against milk-borne infection legally compulsory in 1908.
It was the first major city to do so, but others swiftly followed
suit, so that this source of infection also ceased to be significant
before World War I.[72]

Other infections proved more difficult to deal with. From
the 1650s European doctors had been aware that the debilitating symptoms of malaria could be suppressed by drinking an
infusion prepared by soaking the bark of the quinchona tree, a
native of South America, in water or some other solvent. (The
medically active agent in the infusion was later known as quinine.) But confusion over the identity of the tree that actually
yielded the healing bark, together with commercial adultera-
tion of the supply, later discredited the cure. This was especially true among Protestants, whose suspicions of the Jesuits,
who spread knowledge of the bark around the world, extended
also to their cure for malaria.[73] Not until 1854, when the
Dutch established quinchona plantations in Java, did Europeans command a reliable supply of the right kind of bark. In
fact, the penetration of the interior of Africa that became a
prominent feature of Europe's expansion in the second half of

the nineteenth century would have been impossible without quinine from the Dutch plantations. They continued to supply the European world until World War II.[74] In 1942, when the Japanese seized Java, a concerted effort to discover substitute chemicals for suppressing malaria became necessary, and led to the synthesis of Atabrine and a number of other, and quite effective, drugs.

Regular ingestion of suitable quantities of quinine allowed human beings to survive in regions where malaria would otherwise have killed them off; but the drug merely suppressed the fever, and did not either prevent or cure the disease. The identity and intricate character of the life cycle of the malarial plasmodium was worked out in the 1890s. No vaccine or antitoxin could be developed, and mosquito control proved so difficult to organize that it was only attempted in a few strategically important places before the 1920s.

Yellow fever excited even greater attention than malaria, partly because it was more often lethal to susceptible adults, and partly because it threatened to disrupt American imperial expansion into the Caribbean. But yellow fever was a viral disease, so that its causative organism could not be identified by the techniques available to nineteenth-century bacteriologists. Nevertheless, an American medical team headed by Walter Reed went to Cuba to combat the disease, and proved that it was spread by mosquitoes. In 1901 a campaign was launched to eliminate yellow fever from Havana by attacking mosquito-breeding places. The effort proved successful, largely because the medical campaign was backed by the prestige and resources of the United States army.

In 1901, Havana had but recently broken away from Spanish imperial control as a result of the Spanish-American War (1898). Thereafter the United States' ambitions and strategic considerations turned decisively toward the Caribbean, as plans for building a canal across the Isthmus of Panama assumed a new vivacity. The French attempt to pierce the isthmus (1881–88) had been abandoned because costs escalated unbearably, as a result of the heavy die-off among the work force from malaria and yellow fever. If a canal were to be successfully constructed, therefore, control of these mosquito-borne diseases became critically important. Hence American political leaders and military commanders concurred in placing hitherto unexampled resources at the disposal of the medical officers entrusted with this task.

The result was indeed spectacular, for a rigorous and energetic sanitary police—supported and sustained by meticulous observation of mosquito numbers and patterns of behavior—did succeed in reducing these previously formidable killers to trifling proportions. After 1904, when the Canal Zone was legally constituted, United States troops survived quite successfully while garrisoning what had previously been one of the world's most notorious fever coasts.[75]

United States military administrators limited their responsibility to safeguarding the health of American soldiers and did not seriously entertain the larger ambition of combatting yellow fever on a world-wide basis. Yet the opening of the Panama Canal in 1914 offered the prospect—or seemed to, since the relationship between dengue fever and yellow fever was then not understood—that ships passing through the Canal Zone might by ill-chance pick up the yellow fever infection and spread it throughout the Pacific islands and to the coastlands of Asia, where the disease was totally unknown.

To try to head off such a disaster, the newly established Rockefeller Foundation in 1915 undertook a global program for the study and control of yellow fever. In the ensuing twenty years much was learned about the complexities of the disease. A number of spectacularly successful control programs eliminated foci of infection from the west coast of South America; and the tough ecological system that sustains the disease in its

African homeland was sufficiently explored to convince all concerned that elimination of the disease on a global basis was impractical. By 1937, however, the development of a cheap and effective vaccine deprived yellow fever of its former significance for human life.[76]

Success against yellow fever encouraged the Rockefeller Foundation to undertake a similar assault upon malaria in the 1920s. Mosquito control of the kind that had driven yellow fever from Caribbean cities proved locally successful in countries such as Greece. But it was not until after World War II, and the discovery of the insecticidal power of DDT, that methods of combatting mosquitoes became cheap enough to affect the world-wide incidence of malaria very significantly. After World War II, administration of anti-malarial campaigns passed from the private hands of the Rockefeller Foundation to the World Health Organization, established in 1948 to carry through just such operations on an official, international basis.

The sudden lifting of the malarial burden brought about by liberal use of DDT in the years immediately after World War II was one of the most dramatic and abrupt health changes ever experienced by humankind. In some localities resultant changes in population growth rates were both spectacular and in their way as difficult to live with as malaria itself had been.[77] In addition, massive distribution of DDT destroyed a wide spectrum of insect life, and sometimes poisoned animals that fed on organisms that had been tainted with the chemical. Another unwished-for and unintended effect was the development of DDT-resistant strains of mosquitoes. But chemists responded by developing new lethal compounds, and so far have been able to evolve such variants faster than insects have been capable of developing tolerances to the chemical assault. All the same, the long-range ecological consequences of this chemical warfare between humans and insects is by no means clear. Nor is it certain that malaria has been permanently subdued, despite the fact that the World Health Organization formally declared it (along with smallpox) to be a principal target for eradication from the face of the earth.[78]

Tuberculosis was another infectious disease that proved unusually tenacious. As we saw in Chapter IV, it is possible that pulmonary tuberculosis had acquired a new importance by displacing the bacillus of leprosy among European populations after the fourteenth century. Some authorities think the incidence of the disease among European populations reached a peak in the seventeenth century and declined in the eighteenth, only to crest a second time among the ill-housed and ill-fed inhabitants of industrial towns in the nineteenth century.[79] Upper classes were, of course, also liable to infection; and "consumption" actually became fashionable in literary and aesthetic circles in the early decades of the nineteenth century.

Nevertheless, after about 1850, deaths from tuberculosis, at least in England, had already begun to decline very markedly when Robert Koch won instant fame in 1882 by announcing the discovery of the causative bacillus. Almost fifty years later, in 1921, a partially effective vaccine against tuberculosis was finally produced. Long before then, new knowledge of how the disease propagated itself, and systematic efforts to isolate sufferers from consumption in sanatoria, together with such simple methods of prophylaxis as slaughtering milk cattle found to harbor tuberculosis bacilli and prohibiting spitting in public places, had done a good deal to hasten the retreat of pulmonary forms of the infection from western countries.

On the other hand, tuberculosis remained virulent among a wide variety of previously isolated and primitive peoples brought into contact with outsiders by the continuing evolution of mechanical transport; and in much of Oceania, Asia, and Africa, tuberculosis remains a major source of human debility and death. The development of antibiotic drugs, during and after World War II, that were capable of attacking the bacillus without doing much damage to the human body, meant that in places where modern medical services were available the disease lost its former importance. But since the dramatic retreat of malaria in the post-World War II years, tuberculosis has remained probably the most widespread and persistent human infection in the world at large, with an annual death toll of something like 3.5 million.[80]

Successes in discovering relatively cheap and efficacious ways to check these and other less well-known infectious diseases went hand in hand with spread of more efficient organizations for acting on the new knowledge medical researchers developed so spectacularly. National and local boards of health and medical services proliferated through the world; army medical corps marched alongside (and usually in advance) of their civilian counterparts.

Decisive breakthroughs in military medical administration came just after the turn of the twentieth century. Until then, in even the best-managed armies, disease was always a far more lethal factor than enemy action, even during active campaigns. In the Crimean War (1854–56), for example, ten times as many British soldiers died of dysentery as from all the Russian weapons put together; and half a century later, in the Boer War (1899–1902), British deaths from disease as officially recorded were five times as great as deaths from enemy action.[81] Yet a mere two years thereafter, the Japanese showed what systematic inoculation and careful sanitary police could accomplish. Their losses from disease in the Russo-Japanese war (1904–6) were less than a quarter of deaths from enemy action.[82]

This remarkable breakthrough was not lost on other countries. In the course of the next decade, all the world's important armies made it a standard practice to do what the Japanese had done, i.e., routinely inoculate recruits against a whole battery of common infections—typhoid, smallpox, tetanus, and sometimes others as well. Previously, some European armies had adhered to Napoleon's example and vaccinated recruits against smallpox as a matter of course. Oddly enough, after 1815 the French did not continue this practice into peacetime, whereas the Prussians did. As a result, in 1870–71, during the Franco-Prussian War, smallpox put about 20,000 French soldiers out of action, whereas their German foes remained immune from the disease.[83] What was new in military medicine was not the idea of immunization; rather it was the systematic way it now began to be applied to all infections against which convenient immunization procedures could be devised.

In the decade before World War I another important medical discovery altered the epidemiology of European armies profoundly, for it was between 1909 and 1912 that the role of the louse in spreading typhus fever was figured out. This, together with systematic immunization against other common infections, was what made the unexampled concentration of millions of men in the trenches of northern France, 1914–18, medically possible. Passing men and clothing through delousing stations became part of the ritual of going to and returning from the front; and this prevented typhus from playing the lethal role on the Western Front that it did, sporadically but dramatically, in the East. Even when typhus did break out on the Eastern Front in 1915, disease losses in the ranks remained well below losses from enemy action as long as organization and discipline remained intact.[84] Only when these cracked, as happened among the Serbs in 1915–16 or the Russians in 1917–18, did epidemic disease resume its accustomed lethality among soldiers and civilians alike. Syphilis was the only disease to flourish in the face of a functioning medical corps during World War I. That disease did attain epidemic proportions among British troops, and army doctors failed to handle it effectively at first, more from moral than for medical reasons.[85]

Similar successes occurred during World War II, when even

the epidemiological perils of the monsoon forests of southeastern Asia and the rigors of the Russian steppe proved incapable of paralyzing medically well-managed armies. New chemicals—DDT, sulfas, penicillin, Atabrine, for instance—made formerly formidable diseases easy to prevent or cure; and military command channels proved exceedingly effective in delivering the resulting medical miracles to the places where they were most needed. Soldiers and sailors regularly took precedence when shortages arose, but it was also true that military medical administration was extended to civilian communities whenever some infectious disease threatened to cause trouble for occupation authorities. Wholesale and compulsory delousing of civilians in Naples in 1943, for instance, stopped an incipient typhus epidemic in its tracks[86]; and innumerable refugee camps, slave labor camps, and other forms of official accommodation for displaced persons shared in some degree or other the pattern of medical administration that had proved so valuable for military units.

Another remarkable by-product of the administrative innovations of World War II was improvement in health through food rationing. During World War I rationing was managed in ignorance of exact human dietary requirements, and came to be associated, especially in Germany, with malnutrition and intense human suffering. During World War II, hunger wreaked its ravages among some populations as before; but in Germany itself and still more in Great Britain, special allowances of critically short foods for children, pregnant women, and other specially vulnerable elements of the population, and a more or less rational allocation of vitamin pills, protein, and carbohydrates in accordance with scientifically established physiological needs for different classes of the population, actually improved the level of health in Great Britain, despite severe shortages and stringencies; and allowed the Germans to maintain a generally satisfactory level of health until almost the end of the struggle.[87]

Such triumphs of administrative rationality prepared the way for the amazingly successful post-war international health programs that have fundamentally altered disease patterns in nearly all the inhabited world since 1948.

International medical organization of a formal and official kind dates back to 1909, when an International Office of Public Hygiene was set up in Paris to monitor outbreaks of plague, cholera, smallpox, typhus, and yellow fever. The office also attempted to define uniform sanitary and quarantine regulations for the European nations. Between the two great wars of the twentieth century, the League of Nations set up a Health Section. Several special commissions discussed world incidence of such diseases as malaria, smallpox, leprosy, and syphilis. But more important work was done during this period by the Rockefeller Foundation with its programs attacking yellow fever and malaria. Then in 1948, a new and more ambitious World Health Organization was set up. With substantial government support, WHO set out to bring the benefits of up-to-date scientific medical knowledge to backward parts of the world, wherever local governmental authorities would co-operate.[88]

Since the 1940s, therefore, the impact of scientific medicine and public health administration upon conditions of human life has become literally world-wide. In most places epidemic diseases have become unimportant, and many kinds of infection have become rare where they were formerly common and serious. The net increment to human health and cheerfulness is hard to exaggerate; indeed, it now requires an act of imagination to understand what infectious disease formerly meant to humankind, or even to our own grandfathers. Yet as is to be expected when human beings learn new ways of tampering with complex ecological relationships, the control over microparasites that medical research has achieved since the 1880s has also created a number of unexpected by-products and new crises.

One interesting and ironic development has been the appearance of new diseases of cleanliness. The chief example of this phenomenon was the rising prevalence of poliomyelitis in the twentieth century, especially among the hygienically most meticulous classes. It seems clear that in many traditional societies minor infection in infancy produced immunity to the polio virus without provoking any very pronounced symptoms; whereas persons whose sanitary regimen kept them from contact with the virus until later in life, often suffered severe paralysis or even death.[89] Fear of annual outbreaks of poliomyelitis crested in the United States in the 1950s, assisted by careful propaganda aimed at securing funds for research into its causes and cure. As in so many earlier cases, an effective vaccine was developed in 1954, whereupon the disease sank again to a marginal position in public attention, affecting only a very few who escaped or refused vaccination.

Another sort of epidemic disease whose future among mankind remains at least potentially significant is well illustrated by the influenza epidemic of 1918–19. Influenza has been around a long time,[90] and is remarkable both for the rapidity of its spread, the brevity of the immunity it confers, and the instability of the virus that causes the disease. In 1918–19, the confluence of American with European and African troops in northern France provided the milieu for the emergence of an epidemic of unprecedented scope. New strains of virus were responsible, strains that proved unusually destructive to their human hosts. The disease spread throughout the earth, infecting almost the entire population of the globe, and killing twenty million or more. When the flu hit, medical personnel and facilities were immediately overburdened and health services generally broke down; but the acute phase passed rapidly because of the very infectiousness of the virus, so that within a few weeks human routines resumed and the epidemic faded swiftly away.[91]

A generation of research subsequent to 1918 established the existence of three distinct virus strains; and it is possible to create vaccines against all of them. The problem, however, is complicated by the fact that the influenza virus is itself unstable and alters details of its chemical structure at frequent intervals. Any new and widespread epidemic is therefore almost sure to originate with a virus that has changed enough to escape the antibodies last year's vaccine can create in human bloodstreams.

Changes in the flu virus and mutations of other infectious organisms therefore remain a serious possibility. In 1957, for example, a new "Asian" strain of flu appeared in Hong Kong; but before it attained epidemic force in the United States, vaccine against the new variant had been produced in sufficient quantity to affect the incidence and intensity of the infection. This required, nonetheless, nimble footwork on the part of public health authorities and private entrepreneurs in recognizing the new influenza strain and starting vaccine manufacture on a large scale without delay.[92]

Even without mutation, it is always possible that some hitherto obscure parasitic organism may escape its accustomed ecological niche and expose the dense human populations that have become so conspicuous a feature of the earth to some fresh and perchance devastating mortality.[93] Recent cholera outbreaks in India and southeastern Asia, for example, are due to a new type of bacillus indigenous to the Celebes, which has been able to displace the "classical" cholera organism from nearly all of its original habitat in and around Bengal.[94] Other recent examples of this sort of unpredictable biological fluctuation are the mysterious careers of Lassa fever in Nigeria and of O'nyong nyong fever in Uganda, referred to above.[95]

A third unpleasant possibility is that biological research

aimed at discovering effective ways of paralyzing enemy populations by disseminating lethal disease organisms among them might succeed in unleashing epidemiological disaster on part—or perhaps on all—of the world.

Apart from such conceivable catastrophes, it is clear that humankind remains subject to the limitations inherent in our place in the food chain. Galloping increases in human numbers that have resulted from the success of public health measures in the past 150 years create pressures on food supply. Other stresses created by population increases may manifest themselves in innumerable ways—sociological, psychological, and political, as well as epidemiological.

Skill and knowledge, though they have profoundly transformed ordinary encounters with disease for most of humankind, have not and in the nature of things never can extricate humanity from its age-old position, intermediate between microparasites attacking invisibly and the macroparasitism of some men upon their fellows. To be sure, the simple polarity of older ages, whereby human societies were neatly divided between food producers and those who preyed upon them, has been profoundly altered by the development of scientific farming and the services and supplies food producers now receive from others who do not themselves directly produce food. Nevertheless, in a more complicated form the old problem of adjusting relations between producers and consumers remains, even in our mechanized and bureaucratized age. Certainly, no enduring and stable pattern has emerged that will insure the world against locally if not globally destructive macroparasitic excesses. World War I and World War II both led to locally destructive results; and wars or revolutions, launched with different purposes in mind, may again, as in times past, inflict starvation and death upon large segments of the world's population.

From the other side, the galloping increase in human numbers practically guarantees that existing margins between food supplies and human hunger will swiftly disappear, leaving less and less in reserve for times of unusual crisis. As that occurs, the skills of doctors, farmers, administrators, and all those who take part in sustaining the familiar yet enormously complex flow of goods and services characteristic of modern society become critical for the maintenance of existing levels of human population.

In view of the truly extraordinary record of the past few centuries, no one can say for sure that new and unexpected breakthroughs will not occur, expanding the range of the possible beyond anything easily conceived of now. Birth control may in time catch up with death control. Something like a stable balance between human numbers and resources may then begin to define itself. But for the present and short-range future, it remains obvious that humanity is in course of one of the most massive and extraordinary ecological upheavals the planet has ever known. Not stability but a sequence of sharp alterations and abrupt oscillations in existing balances between microparasitism and macroparasitism can therefore be expected in the near future as in the recent past.

In any effort to understand what lies ahead, as much as what lies behind, the role of infectious disease cannot properly be left out of consideration. Ingenuity, knowledge, and organization alter but cannot cancel humanity's vulnerability to invasion by parasitic forms of life. Infectious disease which antedated the emergence of humankind will last as long as humanity itself, and will surely remain, as it has been hitherto, one of the fundamental parameters and determinants of human history.

Appendix

EPIDEMICS IN CHINA:
A check list compiled by Joseph H. Cha, Professor
of Far Eastern History, Quincy College

The following list of epidemics in China is based on two much
older compilations, one the work of Ssu-ma Kuang, a scholar who
lived during the Sung Dynasty (960–1279), and the other the
work of a staff of researchers, who compiled a general encyclopedia
of traditional Chinese learning in the eighteenth century. These
two lists of human and natural calamities were republished in 1940,
but the editor made some errors in expressing traditional dates in
the modern calendar. Professor Cha corrected such mistakes when
he could, by checking against passages in ancient dynastic histories
and other documents, whenever such sources were cited. In addition, he translated traditional place names into the modern provincial geography of China.

The result is not without faults. The choice of which modern
province to equate with an ancient regional name that does not
coincide with today's provinces is sometimes arbitrary. Moreover,
there undoubtedly remain additional references to epidemics in
Chinese writings that escaped the previous compilers and are therefore missing here too. All statements about how many died are
paraphrases of ancient texts, and Professor Cha made no attempt
to assess the credibility of each such remark; and though some do
deserve credence, others may be wide of the mark. Yet despite such
defects, it is clear that the following list is more accurate than any

published before in any western language, and it seems unlikely that major disease disasters escaped being here recorded. Crude indication of major turning points ought therefore to be detectable from the following list, and for this reason it seemed well to reproduce it here.

The printed text from which Professor Cha worked may be transliterated as follows: Ch'en Kao-yung, *Chung Kuo Li Tai Tien Tsai Jen Huo Piao*, 2 vols., Shanghai, 1940.

Epidemics in China to A.D. *1911*

B.C. 243 Epidemic throughout the empire

B.C.   48 Epidemic, flood and famine "east of the pass," i.e., probably in Honan, Shansi and Shantung

A.D.   16 Epidemic; a general attacking barbarians to the south lost six to seven tenths of his troops from disease.

      37 Epidemic in Kiangsu, Kiangsi, Anhui, Chekiang and Fukien

      38 Epidemic in Chekiang

      46 Famine and epidemic in Mongolia; two thirds of population died.

      50 Epidemic, location undefined

  119 Epidemic in Chekiang

  125 Epidemic in Honan

  126 Epidemic in Honan

  151 Epidemic in Honan, Anhui, Kiangsi

  161 Epidemic, location undefined

  162 Epidemic broke out in ranks of army in Sinkiang and Kokonor; three or four out of ten died.

  171 Epidemic, location undefined

  173 Epidemic, location undefined

  179 Epidemic, location undefined

  182 Epidemic, location undefined

  185 Epidemic, location undefined

  208 Epidemic in an army in Hupeh; two thirds of troops died of disease and famine.

  217 Epidemic, location undefined

  223 Epidemic, location undefined

  234 Epidemic, location undefined

275 Epidemic in Honan; tens of thousands died.

291 Epidemic in Honan

296 Epidemic in Shensi

297 Epidemic in Hopei, Shensi, Szechwan

312 Epidemic, locality undefined; following on earlier disasters from locusts and famine, northern and central China became a "great wasteland"; in Shensi only one or two out of a hundred taxpayers survived.

322 Epidemic; two or three out of ten died; location undefined.

330 Epidemic, location undefined

350 Epidemic, location undefined

351 Epidemic following rebellion in Honan

353 Epidemic, location undefined

379 Epidemic in Shensi

423 Epidemic in North China; in Honan two or three out of ten died.

427 Epidemic in Kiangsu

447 Epidemic in Kiangsu

451 Epidemic in Kiangsu

457 Epidemic in Kiangsu

460 Epidemic in Kiangsu

468 Epidemic throughout the empire; during a second outbreak later in the year in Honan, Hopei, Shantung, Hupeh, and Anhui 140,000 to 150,000 died.

503 Epidemic, location undefined

504 Epidemic in North China

505 Epidemic in North China

510 Epidemic in Shensi; 2,730 died.

529 Epidemic in Shensi

546 Epidemic in Kiangsu

565 Epidemic in Honan

598 Epidemic in southern Manchuria during military campaign against Korea

612 Epidemic in Shantung and elsewhere

636 Epidemic in Shansi, Kansu, Ninghsia, and Shensi

641 Epidemic in Shansi

642 Epidemic in Shansi and Honan

643 Epidemic in Shansi and Anhui

644 Epidemic in Anhui, Szechwan, and Northeast

648   Epidemic in Szechwan

655   Epidemic in Kiangsu

682   Epidemic in Honan and Shantung; land covered with corpses.

707   Epidemic in Honan and Shantung; several thousand died.

708   Epidemic in Honan and Shantung; one thousand deaths.

762   Epidemic in Shantung; more than half the population died.

790   Epidemic in Fukien, Hupeh, Kiangsu, Anhui, Chekiang

806   Epidemic in Chekiang; more than half the population died.

832   Epidemic in Szechwan, Yunnan and Kiangsu

840   Epidemic in Fukien, Chekiang

874   Epidemic in Chekiang

891   Epidemic in Hupeh, Kiangsu and Anhui; in Hupeh three or four out of ten died.

892   Epidemic in Kiangsu

994   Epidemic in Honan

996   Epidemic in Kiangsu, Anhui and Kiangsi

1003   Epidemic in Honan

1010   Epidemic in Shensi

1049   Epidemic in Hopei

1052   Epidemic in Hupeh, Kiangsu and Anhui

1054   Epidemic in Honan

1060   Epidemic in Honan

1094   Epidemic in Honan

1109   Epidemic in Chekiang

1127   Epidemic in Honan; half population of capital died.

1131   Epidemic in Chekiang and Hunan

1133   Epidemic in Hunan and Chekiang

1136   Epidemic in Szechwan

1144   Epidemic in Chekiang

1146   Epidemic in Kiangsu

1199   Epidemic in Chekiang

1203   Epidemic in Kiangsu

1208   Epidemic in Honan and Anhui

1209   Epidemic in Chekiang

1210   Epidemic in Chekiang

1211	Epidemic in Chekiang
1222	Epidemic in Kiangsi
1227	Epidemics among Mongol armies in North China
1232	Epidemic in Honan; 90,000 died in less than fifty days.
1275	Epidemic with incalculable mortality, location undefined
1308	Epidemic in Chekiang; more than 26,000 died.
1313	Epidemic in Hopei
1320	Epidemic in Hopei
1321	Epidemic in Hopei
1323	Epidemic in Hopei
1331	Epidemic in Hopei; nine tenths died.
1345	Epidemic in Fukien and Shantung
1346	Epidemic in Shantung
1351–52	Epidemic in Shansi, Hopei, Kiangsi; 50 per cent mortality among troops in the Huai Valley.
1353	Epidemic in Hupeh, Kiangsi, Shansi, Suiyuan; in part of Shansi more than two thirds of the population died.
1354	Epidemic in Shansi, Hupeh, Hopei, Kiangsi, Hunan, Kwangtung, and Kwangsi. In part of Hupeh six or seven out of ten of the population died.
1356	Epidemic in Honan
1357	Epidemic in Shantung
1358	Epidemic in Shansi and Hopei; over 200,000 died.
1359	Epidemic in Shensi, Shantung, and Kwangtung
1360	Epidemic in Chekiang, Kiangsu, and Anhui
1362	Epidemic in Chekiang
1369	Epidemic in Fukien; corpses in heaps on the roads.
1380	Epidemic in Chekiang
1404	Epidemic in Hopei
1407	Epidemic in Hunan
1408	Epidemic in Kiangsi, Szechwan, and Fukien; 78,400 died.
1410	Epidemic in Shantung (6,000 died) and Fukien (15,000 households perished)
1411	Epidemic in Honan and Shensi
1413	Epidemic in Chekiang
1414	Epidemic in Hopei, Honan, Shansi, and Hupeh
1445	Epidemic in Chekiang, Shensi, and Fukien
1454	Epidemic in Kiangsi and Hupeh
1455	Epidemic in Shensi, Kansu, and Chekiang
1461	Epidemic in Hunan, Hupeh, Kwangtung, and Shensi

1471 Epidemic in Kweichow
1475 Epidemic in Fukien and Kiangsi
1480 Epidemic in Fukien
1481 Epidemic in Kiangsi and Kweichow
1486 Epidemic in Fukien
1489 Epidemic in Hunan; whole villages and towns perished.
1492 Epidemic in Chekiang
1495 Epidemic in southeastern China
1500 Epidemic in Kwangsi
1504 Epidemic in Shansi
1506 Epidemic in Hunan, Hupeh, Kwangtung, Kwangsi, Yunnan, and Fukien; extremely high mortality.
1511 Epidemic in Chekiang
1514 Epidemic in Yunnan
1516 Epidemic in Hupeh
1517 Epidemic in Fukien
1519 Epidemic in Hopei, Shantung, Chekiang
1522 Epidemic in Shensi
1525 Epidemic in Shantung; 4,128 persons died.
1528 Epidemic in Shansi
1529 Epidemic in Hupeh, Szechwan, Kweichow
1532 Epidemic in Shensi
1533 Epidemic in Hupeh, Hunan
1534 Epidemic in Chekiang, Hupeh, Hunan
1535 Epidemic in Fukien
1538 Epidemic in Kwangsi
1543 Epidemic in Shansi
1544 Epidemic in Shansi, Honan
1545 Epidemic in Fukien
1554 Epidemic in Hopei
1556 Epidemic in Fukien
1558 Epidemic in Kweichow
1560 Epidemic in Shansi
1561 Epidemic in Hupeh
1562 Epidemic in Fukien; seven tenths died.
1563 Epidemic in Kiangsi
1565 Epidemic in Hopei and Chekiang
1571 Epidemic in Shansi
1573 Epidemic in Hupeh
1579 Epidemic in Shansi

1580 Epidemic in Shansi
1581 Epidemic in Shansi
1582 Epidemic in Hopei, Szechwan, Shantung, and Shansi
1584 Epidemic in Hupeh
1585 Epidemic in Shansi
1587 Epidemic in Shansi and Kiangsi
1588 Epidemic in Shantung, Shensi, Shansi, Chekiang, and Honan
1590 Epidemic in Hupeh, Hunan, and Kwangtung
1594 Epidemic in Yunnan
1597 Epidemic in Yunnan
1598 Epidemic in Szechwan
1601 Epidemic in Shansi and Kweichow
1603 Epidemic in Chekiang
1606 Epidemic in Chekiang
1608 Epidemic in Yunnan
1609 Epidemic in Fukien
1610 Epidemic in Shansi and Shensi
1611 Epidemic in Shansi
1612 Epidemic in Shensi and Chekiang
1613 Epidemic in Fukien
1617 Epidemic in Fukien
1618 Epidemic in Shansi, Hunan, Kweichow, and Yunnan; corpses lying side by side in Shansi.
1621 Epidemic in Hupeh
1622 Epidemic in Yunnan
1623 Epidemic in Yunnan and Kwangsi
1624 Epidemic in Yunnan
1627 Epidemic in Hupeh
1633 Epidemic in Shansi
1635 Epidemic in Shansi
1640 Epidemic in Hopei and Chekiang
1641 Epidemic in Honan, Hopei, Shantung, and Shansi; corpses lying side by side throughout.
1643 Epidemic in Shensi
1644 Epidemic in Shansi, Kiangsu, and Inner Mongolia
1653 Epidemic in Inner Mongolia
1656 Epidemic in Kansu
1665 Epidemic in Shantung
1667 Epidemic in Kansu

1668   Epidemic in Hopei
1670   Epidemic in Inner Mongolia
1673   Epidemic in Manchuria
1677   Epidemic in Kiangsu and Shensi
1680   Epidemic in Kiangsu
1681   Epidemic in Yunnan
1683   Epidemic in Hupeh
1692   Epidemic in Shensi
1693   Epidemic in Shantung
1694   Epidemic in Chekiang and on the island of Hainan
1697   Epidemic in Kiangsu, Shansi, Kiangsi
1698   Epidemic in Shantung and Shansi
1702   Epidemic in Kwangtung
1703   Epidemic in Inner Mongolia, Shantung, and the island
       of Hainan
1704   Epidemic in Hopei, Shantung, Chekiang, and Shensi
1706   Epidemic in Hupeh
1707   Epidemic in Kwangsi, Kwangtung, Hopei, and Hupeh
1708   Epidemic in Hupeh, Inner Mongolia, Kiangsi, Kansu,
       and Shantung
1709   Epidemic in Chekiang, Kiangsu, Anhui, Shantung,
       Shensi, Kwangtung, Fukien, Kiangsi
1713   Epidemic in Kwangtung
1714   Epidemic in Kwangtung
1717   Epidemic in Chekiang
1721   Epidemic in Shensi
1722   Epidemic in Chekiang
1723   Epidemic in Hopei
1724   Epidemic in Shantung
1726   Epidemic in Kiangsu, Shansi, Kwangtung, and Hopei
1727   Epidemic in Kwangtung, Hupeh
1728   Epidemic in Kiangsu, Chekiang, Shansi, Shensi, Hopei,
       Hupeh, Anhui, and at the eastern end of the Great Wall
1733   Epidemic in Kiangsu
1742   Epidemic in Anhui
1746   Epidemic in Hupeh
1747   Epidemic in Hopei
1748   Epidemic in Shantung
1749   Epidemic in Kiangsu, Kiangsi
1756   Epidemic in Fukien, Kiangsu, Anhui

1757 Epidemic in Chekiang and Shansi; in Sinkiang, on the western border, everyone afflicted with the disease died without exception.

1760 Epidemic in Shansi, Chekiang, and Kansu

1767 Epidemic in Chekiang

1770 Epidemic in Kansu

1775 Epidemic in Hopei

1783 Epidemic in Chekiang

1785 Epidemic in Kiangsu

1786 Epidemic in Kiangsu, Anhui, Shantung, and Hopei

1790 Epidemic in Kansu and Yunnan

1792 Epidemic in Hopei

1793 Epidemic in Chekiang

1795 Epidemic in Chekiang

1797 Epidemic in Chekiang

1798 Epidemic in Shantung

1800 Epidemic in Chekiang

1806 Epidemic in Hopei and Shensi

1811 Epidemic in Kansu

1814 Epidemic in Hupeh

1815 Epidemic in Kiangsu, Anhui, and Shantung

1816 Epidemic in Hopei

1818 Epidemic in Shantung

1820 Epidemic in Chekiang, Shansi, Kiangsu

1821 Epidemic in Hopei, Shantung, Yunnan

1822 Epidemic in Hopei and Shensi

1823 Epidemic in Kiangsu and Hopei

1824 Epidemic in Hopei

1826 Epidemic in Shantung

1827 Epidemic in Shantung

1831 Epidemic in Chekiang

1832 Epidemic in Hupeh, Shensi, Shantung

1833 Epidemic in Shantung, Hopei, Chekiang

1834 Epidemic in Chekiang and Kiangsu

1835 Epidemic in Shantung

1836 Epidemic in Kansu, Kwangtung, and Shantung

1839 Epidemic in Hopeh

1842 Epidemic in Kiangsu, Hupeh

1843 Epidemic in Hupeh, Kiangsi, and Chekiang

1847 Epidemic in Shensi

1848   Epidemic in Shensi
1849   Epidemic in Chekiang
1853   Epidemic in Honan; more than 10,000 died.
1855   Epidemic in Kansu
1856   Epidemic in Shensi
1861   Epidemic in Shantung
1862   Epidemic in Hopei, Kiangsu, Chekiang, Hupeh, Shantung
1863   Epidemic in Kansu, Chekiang, and Shensi
1864   Epidemic in Hupeh, Chekiang, and Kiangsi
1866   Epidemic in Kansu
1867   Epidemic in Shantung and Hopei
1869   Epidemic in Hunan, Kansu, and Hupeh
1870   Epidemic in Hupeh and Hopei
1871   Epidemic in Shensi and Hupeh
1872   Epidemic in Chekiang and Hupeh
1895   Epidemic in Hopei
1911   Epidemic in Manchuria

Notes

Introduction

1. Cf. Thomas W. M. Cameron, *Parasites and Parasitism* (London, 1956), p. 225; Theobald Smith, *Parasitism and Disease* (Princeton, 1934), p. 70. When white blood corpuscles break down the cell structure of an invading organism, no usable energy or building material for human cells results. The process therefore corresponds only to the first phase of digestion.

2. Cf. the remarks of Wladimir A. Engelhardt, "Hierarchies and Integration in Biological Systems," The American Academy of Arts and Sciences, *Bulletin*, 27 (1974), No. 4, 11–23. Engelhardt attributes the capacity of proteins and similarly complex molecules to reconstitute themselves to the action of weak intermolecular forces, as yet little examined; he suggests, further, that increasing organization always consumes free energy.

From such a viewpoint, it appears that humanity's most recent caper, whereby free energy extracted from fossil fuels was employed to congregate millions of men into industrial cities, is but the most recent and complex example of the processes whereby millions of atoms are regularly assembled into the larger organic molecules. Indeed, as one would expect, human cities, being far newer and much fewer than proteins, are less precisely organized than are the larger organic molecules, not to mention cells and organisms generally. But it is at least arguable that similar rules apply up and down all the hierarchies of organization within which we appear to live and move and have our being.

303

3. Hereditary differences that set one human group off from another with respect to disease resistance presumably are a long-term, statistical result of ancestral exposure to particular disease organisms. Disproportionate survival of individuals whose genes somehow facilitated recovery or prevented initial infection from occurring will in time create a genetic resistance to the disease in question. Such evolutionary selection can sometimes be very rapid; indeed, the more lethal an infection, the more rapid selection for tolerance and/or resistance to the infection must be. Equally rigorous selection processes work on the side of the parasite too, of course, tending toward a more nearly stable adaptation to the host, as a result of genetic and behavioral modifications. Cf. Arno G. Motulsky, "Polymorphisms and Infectious Diseases in Human Evolution," *Human Biology*, 32 (1960), 28–62; J. B. S. Haldane, "Natural Selection in Man," *Acta Genetica et Statistica Medica*, 6 (1957), 321–32. Because genes raising resistance to a particular disease may also create various disadvantages for human beings, the optimal state for a population is "balanced polymorphism." This means that some individuals will have the disease-inhibiting gene and others lack it. The exact mix and proportion of persons carrying disease-inhibiting genes will vary, depending on how severe selection for resistance to the disease in question may be, and what other selection pressures may be exerted upon the population.

4. Modern techniques even allow experts to decipher the record of individual and group encounters with a number of infectious diseases. This is done by analyzing blood samples for the presence of "antibodies" specific to particular agents. The disease history of small, isolated communities can be quite accurately determined by these techniques. Cf. Francis L. Black et al., "Evidence for Persistence of Infectious Agents in Isolated Human Populations," *American Journal of Epidemiology*, 100 (1974), 230–50.

5. Cf. T. Aidan Cockburn, *The Evolution and Eradication of Infectious Diseases* (Baltimore and London, 1963), p. 150 and *passim*.

6. Cf. Theodor Rosebury, *Microorganisms Indigenous to Man* (New York, 1962).

7. Cf. Theobald Smith, *Parasitism and Disease*, pp. 44–65; Richard Fiennes, *Man, Nature and Disease* (London, 1964), pp. 84–102.

8. L. J. Bruce-Chwatt, "Paleogenesis and Paleoepidemiology of

Primate Malaria," World Health Organization, *Bulletin*, 32 (1965), 363–87. The term plasmodium, applied to the organism causing malaria at a time when its biological character was imperfectly known, has become standard. The organism is in fact a protozoon, but its forms differ markedly in the different phases of its life cycle.

9. Hans Zinsser, *Rats, Lice and History* (New York, Bantam edition, 1965; original publication, 1935), pp. 164–71.

CHAPTER I

1. Richard Fiennes, *Zoonoses of Primates: the Epidemiology and Ecology of Simian Diseases in Relation to Man* (Ithaca, New York, 1967), pp. 121–22 and *passim*. Arbo is an abbreviation for arthropod-borne.

2. Authorities differ as to the exact count. Fiennes, op. cit., p. 73, tabulates five malarial species for apes and ten for monkeys; L. J. Bruce-Chwatt, "Paleogenesis and Paleoepidemiology of Primate Malaria," World Health Organization, *Bulletin*, 32 (1965), 368–69, mentions twenty kinds of malarial infection among apes and monkeys, and says that as may as twenty-five species of anopheles mosquitoes may serve as vectors for malaria among men and primates.

3. Fiennes, op. cit., p. 42.

4. Bruce-Chwatt, op. cit., pp. 370–82.

5. Cf. F. L. Dunn, "Epidemiological Factors: Health and Disease in Hunter-Gatherers," in Richard B. Lee and Irven DeVore, eds., *Man the Hunter* (Chicago, 1968), pp. 226–28; N. A. Croll, *Ecology of Parasites* (Cambridge, Massachusetts, 1966), p. 98.

6. F. Boulière, "Observations on the Ecology of Some Large African Mammals," in F. Clark Howell and François Boulière, eds., *African Ecology and Human Evolution* (New York, 1963). [Viking Fund Publication in Anthropology No. 36], pp. 43–54, calculates that the biomass (i.e. kilograms/hectare) of African ungulates and other prey available to early man is far greater on the African savanna today than in any other kind of natural environment. Moreover, under modern conditions, competition among carnivores for this enormous reservoir of food is not very severe. Lions, for instance, are far less numerous than their potential food supply is ca-

pable of sustaining. If modern conditions match those of the distant age when mankind's ancestors first began to venture onto the grasslands in search of larger game than they had been accustomed to encounter in the safety of tree branches, it seems clear that our predecessors moved into what might be called a partial vacuum, ecologically speaking, and profited accordingly.

7. A standard example is the elongation of the giraffe's neck, which allowed grazing upon otherwise inaccessible vegetation. Cf. C. D. Darlington, *The Evolution of Man and Society* (London, 1969), pp. 22–27.

8. Cf. the excellent essay by Frank L. Lambrecht, "Trypanosomiasis in Prehistoric and Later Human Populations: A Tentative Reconstruction," in Don Brothwell and A. T. Sandison, *Diseases in Antiquity* (Springfield, Illinois, 1967), pp. 132–51. Lambrecht argues that one form of sleeping sickness resulting from infection by *Trypanosoma gambiense* has evolved toward accommodation to human hosts, thus producing a milder, more chronic form of disease; but in the savanna, where ungulate hosts are abundant, evolutionary pressure to accommodate to antelopes rather than to *anthropos* perpetuated a death-dealing form of the disease for humankind. Accommodation to human hosts in such a circumstance would in fact have diminished (or even destroyed) the hospitable herds and therefore damaged the trypanosome's over-all biological success.

9. Mary Douglas, "Population Control in Primitive Peoples," *British Journal of Sociology*, 17 (1966), 263–73; Joseph B. Birdsell, "On Population Structure in Generalized Hunting and Collecting Populations," *Evolution*, 12 (1958), 189–205.

10. Cf. lists of species extinctions in Darlington, op. cit., p. 33. These (and later North American extinctions) may or may not have been due to human agency. Cf. the debate as presented in Paul S. Martin and H. E. Wright, eds., *Pleistocene Extinctions, the Search for a Cause* (New Haven, 1967). Among the species that suffered extinction Darlington does not list the diverse humanoid forms of life that once existed in Africa; but it is clear that less formidable variants within the humanoid family were among the most vulnerable, with the result that by 20,000 B.C., if not earlier, only one species, *Homo sapiens*, survived.

11. On the peculiar concentration of protozoal and helminthic

infestations in sub-Saharan Africa, see table in Darlington, op. cit., p. 662.

12. I have consulted David Pilbeam, *The Ascent of Man: An Introduction to Human Evolution* (New York, 1972); Frank E. Poirier, *Fossil Man: An Evolutionary Journey* (St. Louis, Missouri, 1973); and B. J. Williams, *Human Origins, an Introduction to Physical Anthropology* (New York, 1973) in connection with these remarks.

13. Joseph B. Birdsell, "Some Population Problems Involving Pleistocene Man," *Cold Spring Harbor Symposium on Quantitative Biology*, 20 (1957), 47–69, estimates that a mere 2,200 years sufficed to populate Australia. Cf. also Joseph B. Birdsell, "On Population Structure in Generalized Hunting and Collecting Populations," *Evolution*, 12 (1958), 189–205; ———, "Some Predictions for the Pleistocene Based on Equilibrium Systems Among Recent Hunters-Gatherers," in Richard B. Lee and Irven DeVore, eds., *Man the Hunter*, pp. 229–40.

14. For Australian rabbits, cf. the very instructive book, Frank Fenner and F. N. Ratcliffe, *Myxomatosis* (Cambridge, 1965). For the American scene, cf. Alfred W. Crosby, *The Columbian Exchange: Biological and Cultural Consequences of 1492* (Westport, 1972). More generally, Charles S. Elton, *The Ecology of Invasions by Animals and Plants* (New York, 1958).

15. Paul S. Martin, "The Discovery of America," *Science*, 179 (1973), 969–74.

16. N. A. Croll, *Ecology of Parasites* (Cambridge, Massachusetts, 1966), pp. 98–104 and *passim*. Croll is concerned mainly with multicellular parasites, but his observations are applicable to all parasitic forms of life, though, as we will see, the distribution of the viral and bacterial organisms that cause the most important forms of infectious disease among civilized populations is governed mainly by the density of potential hosts, and thus diverges widely from climatically regulated patterns. F. L. Dunn, "Epidemiological Factors: Health and Disease in Hunter-Gatherers," in Richard B. Lee and Irven DeVore, eds., *Man the Hunter*, pp. 226–28, also has some interesting things to say about biological diversity and human infections in different climates. Cf. also René Dubos, *Man Adapting* (New Haven, 1965), p. 61.

17. Study of Cro-Magnon and Neanderthal skeletons allows tentative assignment of ages at time of death. According to the data

assembled on this basis in Paul A. Janssens, *Paleopathology: Diseases and Injuries of Prehistoric Man* (London, 1970), pp. 60–63, 88.2 per cent of Cro-Magnon remains were less than forty years of age at the time of death, and 61.7 per cent were less than thirty. Corresponding figures for Neanderthal remains were 95 per cent and 80 per cent. Such calculations are, however, based on statistically unsatisfactory samples, and criteria for the assignment of age at death are often ambiguous.

18. Cf. Saul Jarcho, "Some Observations on Diseases in Prehistoric America," *Bulletin of the History of Medicine*, 38 (1964), 1–19; T. D. Stewart, "A Physical Anthropologist's View of the Peopling of the New World," *Southwestern Journal of Anthropology*, 16 (1960), 265–66, and Lucille E. St. Hoyme, "On the Origins of New World Paleopathology," *American Journal of Physical Anthropology*, 21 (1969), 295–302. J. V. Neel et al., "Studies of the Xavante Indians of the Brazilian Mato Grosso," *American Journal of Human Genetics*, 16 (1964), 110, speaks of the "exuberant health" of the men of the tribe he studied, although he found the women not so vigorous or free from infestation. Travelers' reports emphasizing the health of primitive peoples on first contact with the outside world abound, though their accuracy is suspect. Cf. Robert Fortuine, "The Health of the Eskimos as Portrayed in the Earliest Written Accounts," *Bulletin of the History of Medicine*, 45 (1971), 97–114. On the other hand, in and near the presumed original tropic home of earliest mankind, diseases of many kinds flourish among remote and isolated communities as well as in larger ones. Cf. Ivan V. Polunin, "Health and Disease in Contemporary Primitive Societies," in Don Brothwell and A. T. Sandison, *Diseases in Antiquity*, pp. 69–97. On the presumed good health of Australian aborigines before European contact, cf. B. P. Billington, "The Health and Nutritional Status of the Aborigines," in Charles P. Mountford, ed., *Records of the American-Australian Expedition to Arnhem Land* (Melbourne, 1960), I, 27–59.

Chapter II

1. The list is long (two hundred genera of herbivores and dependent carnivores), and includes such potentially useful animals as horses and camels in North America. Cf. Paul Schultz Martin

and H. E. Wright, *Pleistocene Extinctions*, pp. 82–95 and *passim*. Recent calculations of biomass in Africa, where extinctions of large-bodied animals were far less catastrophic than elsewhere, show how very great a food loss the disappearance of large-bodied prey could be. Elephants and hippopotamuses alone, for instance, constitute about 70 per cent of the entire animal biomass of African savanna lands. Even in places where zebra and wildebeest are the two largest herbivores, those two species constitute at least 50 per cent of the total estimated animal biomass. Cf. F. Clark Howell and François Boulière, *African Ecology and Human Evolution*, pp. 44–48.

For an interesting effort to bring economic analysis to bear on the phenomenon of extinction through overkill, see Vernon L. Smith, "The Primitive Hunter Culture, Pleistocene Extinctions, and the Rise of Agriculture," *Journal of Political Economy*, 83 (1975), 727–56. If Pleistocene extinctions were the work of human hunters, that catastrophic ancient overkill closely parallels our modern industrial squandering of fossil fuels. There is a difference: moderns will probably require fewer centuries to destroy the principal energy base of their existence than our prehistoric forebears needed to kill off theirs.

2. Cf. Sherwood Washburn and C. Lancaster, "The Evolution of Hunting," in Richard C. Lee and Irven DeVore, *Man the Hunter*, pp. 293–303; Kent V. Flannery, "Origins and Ecological Effects of Early Domestication in Iran and the Near East," in Peter Ucko and G. W. Dimbleby, eds., *The Domestication and Exploitation of Plants and Animals* (Chicago, 1969), pp. 77–87.

3. On the special conditions of early Chinese agriculture see Ping-ti Ho, "The Loess and the Origins of Chinese Agriculture," *American Historical Review*, 75 (1969), 1–36. For Amerindian cultivation see R. S. MacNeish, "The Origins of American Agriculture," *Antiquity*, 39 (1965), 87–93.

4. For instructive remarks on hyperinfestation and its relation to human activities, see N. A. Croll, *Ecology of Parasites*, pp. 115ff.

5. Ivan V. Polunin, "Health and Disease in Contemporary Societies," in Don Brothwell and A. T. Sandison, *Disease in Antiquity*, pp. 74, 84.

6. Estimates of ancient populations are entirely speculative, based on assumptions about density per square mile. For two such

global estimates see Kent V. Flannery, "Origins and Ecological Effects of Early Domestication in Iran and the Near East," in Peter Ucko and G. W. Dimbleby, *The Domestication and Exploitation of Plants and Animals*, p. 93; D. R. Brothwell, "Dietary Variation and the Biology of Earlier Human Populations," Ibid., pp. 539–40.

7. For details see C. A. Wright, "The Schistosome Life Cycle," in F. K. Mostofi, ed., *Bilharziasis* (New York, 1967), pp. 3–7.

8. Today Egypt is the best-known home of schistosomiasis; but much of eastern and western Africa, together with western Asia, the rice paddies of eastern Asia, and offshore areas like the Philippines and parts of Brazil are also infected. Three different varieties of blood flukes are involved; and local strains are often specific to local mollusks, making a very complex and still imperfectly understood series of local variations in the character and, for humans, the severity of the disease. Cf. Louis Olivier and Nasser Ansari, "The Epidemiology of Bilharziasis," in F. K. Mostofi, ed., *Bilharziasis*, pp. 8–14.

9. Marc Armand Ruffer, *Studies in Paleopathology of Egypt* (Chicago, 1921), p. 18, reports the discovery of schistosome eggs in the kidneys of two mummies from the XXth dynasty. He found such eggs in two out of six kidneys examined; and since the kidneys are not the organ blood flukes are most likely to infect (their usual home being the bladder and soft viscera that were discarded by ancient embalmers) it seems likely that schistosomiasis was as common in ancient as it is in modern Egypt.

10. J. V. Kinnier Wilson, "Organic Diseases of Ancient Mesopotamia," in Brothwell and Sandison, *Diseases in Antiquity*, pp. 191–208, tries to fit cuneiform terminology into modern medical classifications of disease. This is a hopeless enterprise and nothing he reports sounds in the least like schistosomiasis. Cf. also Georges Contenau, *La Médicine en Assyrie et la Babylonie* (Paris, 1938), and Robert Biggs, "Medicine in Ancient Mesopotamia," *History of Science*, 8 (1969), 94–105. On early contacts between Mesopotamia and Egypt, cf. Helene J. Kantor, "Early Relations of Egypt with Asia," *Journal of Near Eastern Studies*, 1 (1942), 174–213.

11. "A Lady from China's Past," *The National Geographic*, 145 (May 1974), 663. The corpse, which was of high social rank, also carried tuberculosis scars in the lungs.

12. Cf. J. N. Lanoix, "Relations Between Irrigation Engineering

and Bilharziasis," World Health Organization, *Bulletin*, 18 (1958), 1011–35.

13. In modern Egypt, hookworm was and remains almost or quite as important as schistosomiasis in debilitating the population. Globally, hookworm is more widespread than schistosomiasis, since it only requires moist soils and a barefoot population to spread from host to host.

14. Karl A. Wittfogel, *Oriental Despotism: A Comparative Study of Total Power* (New Haven, Connecticut, 1957) is the principal modern scholar to develop the notion that there was a peculiar type of totalitarianism associated with what he calls hydraulic civilizations.

15. What modern diseases correspond to biblical leprosy is a much disputed and quite insoluble question. Cf. Vilhelm Møller-Christensen, "Evidences of Leprosy in Earlier Peoples," in Brothwell and Sandison, *Diseases in Antiquity*, pp. 295–306; Olaf K. Skinsnes, "Notes from the History of Leprosy," *International Journal of Leprosy*, 41 (1973), 220–37.

16. Olivier and Ansari, op. cit., p. 9.

17. See below, p. 262.

18. René Dubos, *Man Adapting*, p. 237; George Macdonald, *The Epidemiology and Control of Malaria* (London, 1957), p. 33 and *passim*.

19. Frank B. Livingstone, "Anthropological Implications of Sickle Cell Gene Distribution in West Africa," *American Anthropologist*, 60 (1958), 533–62.

20. Detailed accounts of events in five different regions of Africa may be found in John Ford, *The Role of the Trypanosomiases in African Ecology: A Study of the Tsetse Fly Problem* (Oxford, 1971). Cf. also Charles N. Good, "Salt, Trade and Disease: Aspects of Development in Africa's Northern Great Lakes Region," *International Journal of African Historical Studies*, 5 (1972), 43–86; H. W. Mulligan, ed., *The African Trypanosomiases* (London, 1970), pp. 632ff. According to Mulligan, the outbreaks of sleeping sickness in the twentieth century are by-products of a sharp initial disturbance of ecological relationships in Africa arising from the catastrophic spread of rinderpest among African game animals in the 1890s. Die-off of herds was so extensive as to compel a shrinkage of tsetse range, together with a simultaneous reduction in domesticated herds and their ranges. As wild and domesticated

herds recovered and began to expand their territories, interpenetration began to occur, allowing transfer of the trypanosome to human populations at many points along the expanding frontier of herding and agriculture. Such a view puts less blame on colonial administration, more weight on ecological processes, than Ford's book does, though the two authorities agree as to fundamental data.

21. Cf. R. Edgar Hope-Simpson, "Studies on Shingles: Is the Virus Ordinary Chicken Pox?" *Lancet*, 2 (1954), 1299–1302; R. Edgar Hope-Simpson, "The Nature of *Herpes Zoster*: A Long-Term Study and a New Hypothesis," *Proceedings of the Royal Society of Medicine*, 48 (1965), 8–20.

22. Francis L. Black, "Infectious Diseases in Primitive Societies," *Science*, 187 (1975), 515–18. T. Aidan Cockburn, *The Evolution and Eradication of Infectious Diseases* (Baltimore and London, 1963), pp. 84ff; Macfarlane Burnet and David O. White, *Natural History of Infectious Disease*, 4th edition (Cambridge, 1972), pp. 147–48; T. W. M. Cameron, *Parasites and Parasitism* (London, 1956), pp. 284ff.

23. Francis L. Black, "Measles Endemicity," *Journal of Theoretical Biology*, 11 (1966), 207–11; T. Aidan Cockburn, "Infectious Diseases in Ancient Populations," *Current Anthropology*, 12 (1971), 51–56. Smallpox has a particularly complex and well-known set of relatives that affect cattle, sheep, pigs, horses, mice, birds, mollusks, and rabbits. In addition there are two forms prevalent among humans and in recent years man-made attenuated strains constitute yet another variety of the variola virus. Cf. Jacques M. May, ed., *Studies in Disease Ecology* (New York, 1961), p. 1.

24. Thomas G. Hull, *Diseases Transmitted from Animals to Man*, 5th ed. (Springfield, Illinois, 1963), pp. 879–906.

25. Extensive work has been done in the USSR to detect natural disease pools capable of affecting human populations. Cf. Evgeny N. Pavlovsky, *Natural Nidality of Transmissible Diseases* (Urbana and London, 1966). According to Pavlovsky, some infections are shared by as many as a dozen animal species, wild and domesticated alike. Hull, op. cit., pp. 907–9, tabulates 110 diseases shared by humans and wild animals or birds. The total we share with domesticated animals as listed in the same book is 296.

26. T. W. M. Cameron, *Parasites and Parasitism*, p. 241.

27. Richard Fiennes, *Zoonoses of Primates: The Epidemiology and Ecology of Simian Diseases in Relation to Man* (Ithaca, New York, 1967), p. 126.

28. John G. Fuller, *Fever! The Hunt for a New Killer Virus* (New York, 1974); John D. Frame et al., "Lassa Fever, a New Virus Disease of Man from West Africa," *American Journal of Tropical Hygiene*, 19 (1970), 670–96.

29. Cf. Kent V. Flannery, "The Origins of the Village as a Settlement Type in Mesoamerica and the Near East: A Comparative Study," in Peter J. Ucko, et al., *Man, Settlement and Urbanism* (London, 1972), pp. 23–53; and Kent V. Flannery, "The Cultural Evolution of Civilizations," *Annual Review of Ecology and Systematics*, 3 (1972), 399–426, for interesting discussion of the genesis of village social structures and of civilized governments or, as he calls them, states.

30. Alteration of virulence, that is, alteration of the type and severity of symptoms that a disease organism provokes, is a normal result of any transfer of parasitism to a new host species. Cf. Burnet and White, *Natural History of Infectious Disease*, pp. 150–51. On disease and gregariousness, cf. T. W. M. Cameron, *Parasites and Parasitism*, p. 237.

31. Frank Fenner and F. N. Ratcliffe, *Myxomatosis* (Cambridge, 1965), pp. 251, 286, and *passim*. Myxomatosis was also introduced into France and England in the 1950s with drastic and somewhat different results, owing largely to differences in the insect vectors that spread the infection.

32. Even here there are analogies. Careful observers reported that English rabbits reacted to the outbreak of myxomatosis by living more above ground, and spending less time in burrows. Fenner and Ratcliffe, op. cit., p. 346.

33. See below, p. 210.

34. Fenner and Ratcliffe, op. cit., p. 42.

35. Andre Siegfried, *Routes of Contagion* (New York, 1960), p. 18.

36. M. S. Bartlett, "Deterministic and Stochastic Models for Recurrent Epidemics," *Proceedings of the Third Berkeley Symposium in Mathematical Statistics and Probability*, 4 (Berkeley and Los Angeles, 1956), 81–109; M. S. Bartlett, "Epidemics," in Janet Tanur et al., *Statistics: A Guide to the Unknown* (San Francisco, 1972), pp. 66–76; M. S. Bartlett, "Measles Periodicity

and Community Size," *Journal of the Royal Statistical Society,* 120 (1957), 48–70; Francis L. Black, "Measles Endemicity in Insular Populations: Critical Community Size and its Evolutionary Implications," *Journal of Theoretical Biology,* 11 (1966), 207–11.

37. Cf. René Dubos, *Man Adapting,* p. 134.

38. Robert J. Braidwood and Charles A. Reed, "The Achievement and Early Consequences of Food Production: A Consideration of the Archaeological and Natural-Historical Evidence," *Cold Spring Harbor Symposium on Quantitative Biology,* 22 (1957), 28–29.

39. On this linguistic shift and the absence of any signs of military conflict in connection with it, cf. Thorkild Jacobsen, "The Assumed Conflict between Sumerians and Semites in Early Mesopotamian History," *Journal of the American Oriental Society,* 59 (1939), 485–95.

40. Emil Schultweiss and Louis Tardy, "Short History of Epidemics in Hungary until the Great Cholera Epidemic of 1831," *Centaurus,* 11 (1966), 279–301, estimate 1831 cholera deaths in Hungary at 250,000. Not all of these were urban; but a majority were. Such a sudden die-off obviously opened places in town for scores of thousands of peasants, who brought their languages with them.

41. For modern examples of devastating disease encounters of this kind and an easily comprehensible outline of factors affecting immunity to infectious disease, see René Dubos, *Man Adapting* (New Haven and London, 1965), pp. 171–85.

42. Burnet and White, *Natural History of Infectious Disease,* pp. 79–81, 97–100. The influenza epidemic of 1918–19 was the most recent disease to manifest this surprising preference for killing off young adults.

43. Cf. William H. McNeill, *The Rise of the West* (Chicago, 1963), Chs. 4, 5.

CHAPTER III

1. *Epic of Gilgamesh,* Tablet 11, line 184; "Story of Si-nuhe," J. B. Pritchard, ed., *Ancient Near Eastern Texts Relating to the Old Testament* (Princeton, New Jersey, 1950), p. 19.

2. Translated by Joseph Cha.

3. Exodus 9:9, J. M. P. Smith translation.
4. Exodus 12:30.
5. I Samuel 5:6-6:18.
6. II Samuel 24.
7. Isaiah 37:36.
8. Georg Sticker, *Abhandlungen aus der Seuchengeschichte und Seuchenlehre* (Giessen, 1908), 1, 17, falls into this trap in listing antecedents to the plagues he chronicles.
9. Marc Armand Ruffer and A. R. Ferguson, "Note on an Eruption Resembling That of Variola in the Skin of an Egyptian Mummy of the Twentieth Dynasty (1200-1100 B.C.)," *Journal of Pathology and Bacteriology* 15 (1911), 1-3, tentatively diagnose smallpox on the basis of microscopic examination of a small section of skin. Their techniques were clumsy compared to methods of microscopic and chemical analysis available today and results are not always dependable. Modern techniques have been used only sporadically and without notable results as yet. Cf. T. Aidan Cockburn, "Death and Disease in Ancient Egypt," *Science*, 181 (1973), 470-71.
10. As sidelight and confirmation: medical specialists were of ancient standing in Egypt and Mesopotamia; and Babylonian medical texts accepted the notion that some diseases were contagious as early as the seventeenth century B.C. One letter, indeed, says that since a lady is suffering from a contagious disease, no one should drink from her cup, sit on her seat, sleep in her bed, or visit her quarters. The concept of contagion may have been magical, but magic sometimes had a solid empirical base. Cf. Robert Biggs, "Medicine in Ancient Mesopotamia," *History of Science*, 8 (1969), 96.
11. Cf. William H. McNeill, *The Rise of the West*, Ch. V, for remarks on the definition of the Greek, Indian, and Chinese civilizations.
12. The river made this sort of drastic change of course as long ago as A.D. 11 and as recently as 1937. For the disaster of A.D. 11 and its population consequences cf. Hans Bielenstein, "The Census of China During the Period 2-742 A.D.," Museum of Far Eastern Antiquities, *Bulletin*, 19 (1947), 140.
13. The population maps appended to Bielenstein's article, cited above, show how preponderant the Yellow River flood plain remained until after the eighth century A.D.

315

14. *Shih-chi*, Ch. 129, translated by Ping-ti Ho.

15. For literary records of the unhealthiness of the South, see the collection of references assembled in Edward H. Schafer, *The Vermilion Bird: T'ang Images of the South* (Berkeley and Los Angeles, 1967), "Miasmas," pp. 130–34.

16. I counted five diseases as plotted in Ernst Rodenwaldt et al., eds., *World Atlas of Epidemic Diseases* (Hamburg, 1952–56), that were present in southern China and absent in the North. This atlas attempts to describe twentieth-century disease distributions, but data from China were so defective that for many diseases the compilers simply treated the entire country as a single whole. Thus the real differential in disease incidence in modern China is by no means recorded in this *Atlas*; and the distinctions it does make between north and south are doubtless liable to correction whenever more accurate and abundant data become available. I should also point out that one disease, Kala Azar, caused by a protozoal infection, is recorded only for northern China, so not everything intensifies in softer climes!

17. Lu Gwei-Djen and Joseph Needham, "Records of Diseases in Ancient China," in Brothwell and Sandison, eds., *Diseases in Antiquity*, pp. 222–37, assign modern names to a long list of Chinese terms, but their confidence in an easy convertibility between ancient and modern nosology remains unconvincing.

18. Mark F. Boyd, ed., *Malariology: A Comprehensive Survey of all Aspects of this Group of Diseases from a Global Standpoint* (Philadelphia and London, 1949), II, 816.

19. C. A. Chamfrault, *Traité de Médicine Chinoise*, 5 vols., 2nd ed. (Angoulême, 1964), I, 697–706.

20. Cf. C. A. Gordon, *An Epitome of the Reports of the Medical Officers of the Chinese Imperial Customs Service from 1871 to 1882* (London, 1884), p. 118.

21. "A Lady from China's Past," *The National Geographic*, 145 (May, 1974), 663.

22. Hippocrates, *Epidemics* I, 1.

23. Hippocrates, *Epidemics* I, vi; cf. W. H. S. Jones, *Malaria and Greek History* (Manchester, 1909), pp. 62–64.

24. Cf. Angelo Celli, *The History of Malaria in the Roman Campagna from Ancient Times* (London, 1933), pp. 12–30.

25. For a non-technical introduction to the complexities of malarial ecology of the Mediterranean, L. W. Hackett, *Malaria in*

Notes

Europe: An Ecological Study (London, 1937) can be warmly recommended. More recent, and more difficult, are George Macdonald, *The Epidemiology and Control of Malaria* (London, 1957), and Marston Bates, "Ecology of Anopheline Mosquitoes," in Mark F. Boyd, ed., *Malariology*, I (Philadelphia, 1949), 302–330.

26. *Airs, Waters, Places*, VII.

27. According to J. Szilagyi, "Beiträge zur Statistik der Sterblichkeit in der Westeuropäischen Provinzen des Romischen Imperium," *Acta Archaeologica Academica Scientiarum Hungaricae*, 13 (1961), 126–56, average age of death for a sampling of persons buried in Roman times comes out as follows:

City of Rome	29.9
Iberia	31.4
N. Africa	46.7
Britain	32.5
Germany	35.0

These figures are based on study of statistically inadequate samples, and the medical judgment that assigns an age to imperfectly preserved skeletal remains is liable to error as well. Hence no great store should be placed in such statistics, though the enhanced risk of early death inherent in megapolitan living seems clear enough.

28. M. L. W. Laistner, *Greek History* (Boston, 1931), p. 250.

29. Julius Beloch, *Die Bevölkerung der Griechische-Römischen Welt* (Leipzig, 1886), remains fundamental, summarizing all that can be deduced from written records in a very sensible way. For more recent and specialized population studies, see A. W. Gomme, *The Population of Athens in the Fifth and Fourth Centuries B.C.* (Oxford, 1933), and Tenney Frank, *An Economic Survey of Ancient Rome*, 5 vols. (Baltimore, 1933–40).

30. On Chinese population cf. Michel Cartier and Pierre-Etienne Will, "Demographie et Institutions en Chine: Contribution à l'Analyse des Recensements de l'Époque Imperiale (2 ap. J.C.-1750)," *Annales de Démographie Historique* (1971), 161–235, and the review of this work by Hans Bielenstein in *T'oung Pao*, 61 (1975) 181–85. The divergence between the two quoted figures reflects two different manuscript sources, and there seems no basis to prefer one as against the other. In his earlier work, Hans Bielenstein, "The Census of China During the Period 2–

742 A.D.," Museum of Far Eastern Antiquities, Stockholm, *Bulletin*, 19 (1947), 125–63, cited only the lesser of the two figures.

31. On probable underestimation by Beloch, cf. Adolphe Landry, "Quelques aperçus concernant la Dépopulation dans l'Antiquité Greco-romaine," *Revue Historique*, 177 (1936), 17.

32. II, 47–55.

33. A. W. Gomme, *Population of Athens*, p. 6.

34. J. F. D. Shrewsbury, "The Plague of Athens," *Bulletin of the History of Medicine*, XXIV (1950), 1–25, rejects typhus, smallpox, typhoid, and bubonic plague suggested by various and sundry predecessors, and declares that the affliction was measles. The whole debate is misguided, since symptoms must be presumed to have evolved for infections as unstable in their adaptation to humanity as the "civilized" diseases. Even today, familiar infections encountering a virgin population exhibit symptoms far different from those manifest in a population already exposed. Cf. above, Ch. I.

35. II, 48, R. Crawley translation.

36. Since measles requires a population of over 400,000 to achieve a stable pattern of infection in modern times, and since the population of Athens was only about 155,000 in 430 B.C., according to Gomme, op. cit., p. 47, the behavior of the disease does match well with that of modern measles, as Shrewsbury argues. Yet this does not suffice to identify it, since smallpox or some other kind of infection that has no contemporary descendant might also have behaved in the same way.

37. Ancient Chinese medical writers have little to say about contagious eruptive fevers, according to A. Chamfrault, *Traité de Médicine Chinoise*, I, 722. Historians, however, often mentioned unusual epidemics among other natural disasters. At my behest, Dr. Joseph Cha prepared a digest of such mentions which appears in the Appendix.

38. For an estimate of when and how the two canonical texts of ancient Indian medicine took shape, see H. R. Zimmer, *Hindu Medicine* (Baltimore, 1948), p. 45.

39. So far as I can tell, this tradition arose among British medical officers in India in the nineteenth century who accepted uncritically claims made by practitioners of traditional Indian medicine to an immemorial antiquity for their authoritative texts. But once having entered the English-speaking world, such views, in the ab-

sence of any countervailing tradition, attained an enhanced virulence. For recent reaffirmations of this view, Cf. T. Aidan Cockburn, *The Evolution and Eradication of Infectious Diseases*, p. 60; C. W. Dixon, *Smallpox* (London, 1962), p. 188.

40. Cf. the multiple designations of syphilis in the sixteenth century.

41. Traditional Indian medical writers refer clearly to malaria, to skin diseases, and to infection by worms, but none of the important civilized diseases—smallpox, measles, diphtheria, and the rest —are clearly recognizable from the Sanskrit phrases. Cf. Jean Filiozat, *La Doctrine Classique de la Médicine Indienne, Ses Origines et Ses Parallèles Grecs* (Paris, 1949); G. B. Mukhapadhaya, *History of Indian Medicine*, 3 vols. (Calcutta, 1923–29); O. P. Jaggi, *Indian Systems of Medicine* [History of Science and Technology in India, 4], (Delhi, 1973).

42. Imperfect sixteenth-century records of how infections spread among Amerindians of North America, far outrunning direct contacts with infection-bearing whites, proves that in suitable circumstances an infection can propagate itself among quite thinly scattered human settlements across hundreds and perhaps (depending on where the infection started), even thousands of miles. On evidences of this phenomenon, cf. below, Chapter IV.

43. Pliny, *Natural History*, XIX, 1, records a few unusually speedy voyages: Alexandria to Puteoli in less than nine days; Cadiz from Ostia in seven days; Ostia to Africa in two.

44. Albert Herrmann, *Die Alten Seidenstrassen zwischen China und Syrien* (Berlin, 1910), pp. 3–9, 126. It is not entirely clear what China imported from the West. "Blood sweating horses" were the main imperial *desiderata* in the first years; the resumption of trade in the first century A.D. may have led to an export mainly of metals (including precious metals) from Roman territory eastward.

45. W. McGovern, *Early Empires of Central Asia* (Chapel Hill, 1939), and René Grousset, *L'Empire des Steppes* (Paris, 1939).

46. Herrmann, op. cit., p. 9.

47. G. Coedès, *Les États Hindouisés d'Indochine et d'Indonésie*, (Paris, 1948), and H. G. Quaritch-Wales, *The Making of Greater India* (London, 1951), give political and cultural details.

48. R. E. M. Wheeler, *Rome Beyond the Imperial Frontiers*, (London, 1954), pp. 174–75; Coedès, op. cit., p. 38.

49. Wheeler, op. cit., pp. 146–50.

50. Strabo, *Geography*, 17, 1.13, "In earlier times, at least, not so many as twenty vessels would dare to traverse the Arabian Gulf . . . but at the present time even large fleets are despatched as far as India and the extremities of Aethiopia, from which most valuable cargoes are brought to Aegypt. . . ." H. L. Jones, trans., Loeb Library edition.

51. Diffusion of disease along caravan routes continued to occur in the nineteenth to twentieth centuries, and was sometimes more or less accurately recorded by European medical officers. For details of one such process—the spread of relapsing fever with the salt trade of east Africa—see Charles M. Good, "Salt, Trade, and Disease: Aspects of Development in Africa's Northern Great Lakes Region," *International Journal of African Historical Studies*, 5 (1972), 543–86. This offers a quite exact analogy to the way in which other diseases presumably must have spread along ancient caravan routes of Central Asia.

52. Thorkild Jacobsen and Robert M. Adams, "Salt and Silt in Ancient Mesopotamian Agriculture," *Science*, 128 (1958), 1251.

53. Conveniently catalogued by Georg Sticker, *Abhandlungen aus der Seuchengeschichte* I, 20–21.

54. Suetonius, *Lives of the Caesars*, "Nero" 39:1, says 30,000 persons died in the city of Rome in the autumn of that year.

55. So Sticker, op. cit., p. 21, following the weighty opinion of August Hirsch, *Handbook of Geographical and Historical Pathology*, Charles Creighton, trans., 3 vols. (London, 1883–86) I, 126.

56. In recent times when such a familiar disease as measles penetrated a previously unaffected community, initial die-off of up to 25 per cent has been observed, due largely to a breakdown of elementary nursing services. The classic example of this sort of disaster was recorded by William Squire, "On Measles in Fiji," Epidemiological Society of London, *Transactions*, 4 (1877), 72–74. What happened in Fiji in the 1870s corresponds well enough to what seems to have happened in a small Egyptian town, where records show a 33 per cent decrease of population between A.D. 144–46 and 171–74. Cf. A. E. R. Boak, "The Populations of Roman and Byzantine Karanis," *Historia*, 4 (1955), 157–62. For an account of how lethal measles still can be among primitive peoples, see James V. Neel et al., "Notes on the Effect of Measles and Measles

Vaccine in a Virgin Soil Population of South American Indians," *American Journal of Epidemiology*, 91 (1970), 418–29.

57. Scholarly opinion is now pretty well agreed that decay of Roman population began under the Antonine emperors. Cf. A. E. R. Boak, *Manpower Shortage and the Fall of the Roman Empire in the West* (Ann Arbor, 1955), pp. 15–21; J. F. Gilliam, "The Plague under Marcus Aurelius," *American Journal of Philology*, 82 (1961), 225–51.

58. So Boak, *Manpower Shortage*, p. 26.

59. It is customary to call the disease al-Razi described smallpox, and so it may have been. Cf. August Hirsch, *Handbook of Geographical and Historical Pathology*, I, 123. But confusion between smallpox, measles, and scarlet fever remained chronic among Arabic and European medical writers from al-Razi's time until the sixteenth century. Ibid., I, 154–55.

60. Gregory of Tours, *History of the Franks*, O. M. Dalton, trans. (Oxford, 1927), V, 8:14. "A great pestilence raged among the people during this year, great numbers were carried off by various malignant diseases, the symptoms of which were pustules and tumors. . . ."

61. For a clear reference to pustules and fever, cf. Galen, *Methodi Medendi*, XII. For a defense of Galen's behavior during the epidemic (he left Rome and returned home to Asia Minor), see Joseph Walsh, "Refutation of the Charges of Cowardice against Galen," *Annals of Medical History*, 3 (1931), 195–208. This is a better article than its title might suggest.

62. By definition, with the breakup of effective central administration, data disappear upon which estimates of population over wide territories might be based. An effort to guess at the decay of Roman population by projecting from the putative size of populations within walled cities has been made by J. C. Russell, "Late Ancient and Medieval Population," *American Philosophical Society Transactions*, 48 (1958), 71–87. He finds a population decay of 50 per cent between Augustan times and A.D. 543, but his method is open to objection, and the data on which his calculations are based remain both fragmentary and dubiously accurate.

63. For example, Eusebius, *Ecclesiastical History*, VII, 21–22.

64. Cyprian, *De Mortalitate* [Mary Louise Hannon, trans.] (Washington, D.C., 1933), pp. 15–16.

65. Procopius, *Persian Wars*, II, 22.6–39. Justinian himself fell ill but recovered.

66. Cf. the chart and admirable maps of the periodicity and geographic extent of epidemics between 541 and 750 presented in J. N. Biraben and Jacques LeGoff, "La Peste dans le Haut Moyen Age," *Annales: Economies, Sociétés, Civilisations*, 24 (1969), 1492–1507.

67. Hirsch, op. cit., I, 494–95.

68. Cf. M. A. C. Hinton, *Rats and Mice as Enemies of Mankind* (London, 1918), p. 3.

69. Cf. J. F. D. Shrewsbury, *A History of Bubonic Plague in the British Isles* (Cambridge, 1970), pp. 71–31; Biraben and LeGoff, op. cit.; J. C. Russell, "That Earlier Plague," *Demography*, 5 (1968), 174–84. For details of modern understanding of the epidemiology of plague, R. Pollitzer, *Plague* (World Health Organization, Geneva, 1954) is the best source.

70. For maps of twentieth-century plague endemicity see Geddes Smith, *Plague on Us* (New York, 1941), p. 320; D. H. S. Davis, "Plague in Africa from 1435 to 1949," World Health Organization, *Bulletin*, 9 (1953), 665–700; Robert Pollitzer, *Plague and Plague Control in the Soviet Union: History and Bibliography to 1964* (New York, 1966).

71. Cf. J. F. D. Shrewsbury, *The Plague of the Philistines* (London, 1964); Hans Zinsser, *Rats, Lice and History*, pp. 80–81.

72. Procopius, *Persian Wars*, 23:1.

73. Michael W. Dols, "Plague in Early Islamic History," *Journal of the American Oriental Society*, 94 (1974), 371–83. Cf. also Biraben and LeGoff, op. cit., maps on pp. 1504, 1506.

74. Biraben and LeGoff, op. cit., pp. 1499, 1508, make these suggestions and appropriate tentativeness.

75. Cf. Charles Creighton, *A History of Epidemics in Britain*, 2 vols., 2nd edition (New York, 1965) [original publication Cambridge, 1891–94], I, 409; J. F. S. Shrewsbury, "The Yellow Plague," *Journal of the History of Medicine*, 4 (1949), 15–47; Wilfrid Bonser, "Epidemics During the Anglo-Saxon Period," *Journal of the British Archaeological Association*, 3rd series, 9 (1944), 48–71.

76. Bonser, op. cit., pp. 52–53.

77. Cf. the classic report, Peter Ludwig Panum, *Observations Made During the Epidemic of Measles on the Faroe Islands in the*

Year 1846, reproduced in English translation in *Medical Classics,* III (1938–39), 829–86. In this epidemic, 6,000 of 7,782 inhabitants got the measles, which had not visited the islands since 1781; but only about 102 died. Ibid., p. 867.

78. This task was performed for me by Dr. Joseph Cha. This compilation is by no means perfect: further combing of ancient sources would probably add to the roster of epidemics and might alter the apparent pattern of frequencies this table suggests. On the other hand, really major epidemic disasters are probably here recorded fully; and it is these that principally interest me. For this reason and because Dr. Cha's list is clearly superior to either of the older lists of Chinese epidemics available in print, it seemed well to reproduce it here.

79. K. Chimin Wong and Wu Lien-teh, *History of Chinese Medicine: Being a Chronicle of Medical Happenings in China from Ancient Times to the Present Period,* 2nd ed. (Shanghai, 1936), p. 82.

80. Translation by Joseph Cha. Wong and Wu Lien-teh simply skip the passage referring to A.D. 653, no doubt on the ground that it is a later interpolation; but since the text has clearly been tampered with, the whole passage might also be late. The time of Chien-wu is a regnal title: but unfortunately two Chinese emperors took this regnal name; the second occupied the throne for a single year—A.D. 317; the first reigned thirty years, A.D. 25–55. I have been unable to pin down the reference to fighting barbarians at Nan-yang; this would perhaps settle the choice between A.D. 317 and A.D. 25–55. Western medical men have accepted A.D. 317 as the date for the arrival of smallpox in China since at least the 1860s. Cf. C. A. Gordon, *An Epitome of the Reports of the Medical Officers of the Chinese Imperial Customs from 1871 to 1882* (London, 1884), p. 74. But no really scholarly investigation seems to underlie this view.

81. Wu Lien-teh, *Plague,* p. 11. He translates the 610 text by Ch'ao Yuan-fang as follows: The disease "comes on abruptly with high fever together with the appearance of a bundle of nodes beneath the tissues. The size of the nodes ranges from a bean to a plum. . . . The nodes may be felt to move from side to side under the skin. If prompt treatment is not given, the poison will enter the system, cause severe chill and end in death."

82. See Appendix for details.

83. Cartier and Will, op. cit., p. 178.

84. Ping-ti Ho, "An Estimate of the Total Population of Sung-Ching China," in *Etudes Song I: Histoire et Institutions* (Paris, 1970), pp. 34–52.

85. Ibid.

86. My remarks on Japanese encounters with epidemic diseases are based on Fujikawa Yu, *Nihon Shippei Shi*, Matsuda Michio, ed. (Tokyo, 1969), pp. 11–66. His admirably learned and critically assembled chronological table of epidemic disease in Japan was translated for me by Dr. Joseph Cha.

87. The Japanese term used for this disease is the modern one for smallpox; and Fujikawa Yu accepts the term as describing a single infection. This may be so: certainly the chronology of its early appearances in Japan fits very well what would happen if the same disease were repeatedly introduced to an islanded population at intervals of thirty to fifty years, i.e., when antibodies had had time to disappear.

88. Irene Taeuber, *The Population of Japan* (Princeton, 1958), p. 14.

89. Josiah Cox Russell, *British Medieval Population* (Albuquerque, 1948), pp. 54, 146, 246, 269, 270.

90. Or so Procopius reports, *Persian Wars*, 23:21.

91. Cf. Thorkild Jacobsen and Robert M. Adams, "Salt and Silt in Ancient Mesopotamian Agriculture," *Science*, 128 (1958), 1251ff; Robert M. Adams, "Agriculture and Urban Life in Southwestern Iran," *Science*, 136 (1962), 109–22.

92. Vilhelm Møller-Christensen, "Evidence of Leprosy in Earliest Peoples," in Brothwell and Sandison, *Diseases in Antiquity*, pp. 295–306.

93. Erwin H. Ackerknecht, *History and Geography of the Most Important Diseases* (New York, 1965), p. 112.

CHAPTER IV

1. Christopher Dawson, ed., *The Mongol Mission* (London and New York, 1955), pp. 165–69.

2. V. N. Fyodorov, "The Question of the Existence of Natural Foci of Plague in Europe in the Past," *Journal of Hygiene, Epidemiology, Microbiology and Immunology* [Prague] 4 (1960),

135–41, asserts an age-old antiquity for bubonic infection solely on the ground that conditions were suitable for rodents in Europe in geologically distant ages. N. P. Mironov, "The Past Existence of Foci of Plague in the Steppes of Southern Europe," *Journal of Microbiology, Epidemiology and Immunology*, 29 (1958), 1193–98, makes the same assertion on the same grounds. This is absurd, for the mere existence of a rodent community suitable to sustain a plague infection does not guarantee that the plague bacillus will in fact be present, as the spread of endemic plague to the rodents of North America in the twentieth century amply proves.

3. For details, see K. Chimin Wong and Wu Lien-teh, *History of Chinese Medicine*, 2nd ed. (Shanghai, 1936), pp. 508ff.

4. Cf. R. Pollitzer, *Plague* (Geneva, 1954), p. 26.

5. These remarks are based on L. Fabian Hurst, *The Conquest of Plague: A Study of the Evolution of Epidemiology* (Oxford, 1953).

6. Howard M. Zentner, *Human Plague in the United States* (New Orleans, 1942).

7. Wu Lien-teh, J. W. H. Chun, R. Pollitzer and C. Y. Wu, *Plague: A Manual for Medical and Public Health Workers* (Shanghai, 1936), pp. 30–43; Carl F. Nathan, *Plague Prevention and Politics in Manchuria 1910–1931* (Cambridge, Massachusetts, 1967). In Yunnan, too, whence the plague had initially come, local folkways prescribed behavior that minimized human exposure— including temporary abandonment of houses in which unusual numbers of rats had died. Cf. C. A. Gordon, *An Epitome of the Reports of the Medical Officers of the Chinese Imperial Customs Service from 1871 to 1882* (London, 1884), p. 123. This report is especially interesting since Colonel Gordon was himself entirely ignorant of how plague infection occurred.

8. According to Charles E. A. Winslow, *Man and Epidemics* (Princeton, 1952), p. 206, no fewer than eight minor epidemics of bubonic plague broke out in the United States between 1908 and 1950 as a result of contagion from wild rodents. In the U.S.S.R. plague has been officially abolished, but scraps of evidence strongly suggest that similar outbreaks continue to occur there too. Cf. Robert Pollitzer, *Plague and Plague Control in the Soviet Union: History and Bibliography to 1964* (New York, 1966), pp. 6–8.

9. J. N. Biraben and Jacques LeGoff, "La Peste dans le Haut

Moyen Age," *Annales: Economies, Sociétés, Civilisations,* 24 (1969), 1508.

10. Michael Walter Dols, 'The Black Death in the Middle East (unpublished Ph.D. dissertation, Princeton, 1971), p. 29.

11. The roster of recorded plague episodes down to 1894 is conveniently assembled in Georg Sticker, *Abhandlungen aus der Seuchengeschichte und Seuchenlehre,* I (Giessen, 1908). Sticker's erudite register shows that the plague was never absent from Europe for as much as fifteen years after 1346—and since many outbreaks assuredly escaped Sticker's attention, we must believe that human infections were even more prevalent than his list shows.

12. Daniel Panzac, "La Peste à Smyrne au XVIIIᵉ Siècle," *Annales: Economies, Sociétés, Civilisations,* 28 (1973), 1071–93. This article proves, I think, that the plague was not endemic in Smyrna but arose though recurrent reinfection from the hinterland, i.e., from rats, fleas, and human beings who picked up infection from wild rodents of the grasslands. Reading this article provoked my hypothesis about the background of the fourteenth-century plague presented here.

13. Suitably populous burrowing rodent communities exist only in semi-arid grasslands; and cultivation, by destroying their burrows, tends to push such communities back from lands where enough rain falls to support a grain crop. Hence the exact geographical limit of plague endemicity among the rodents of the steppe has undoubtedly shifted across the centuries, and may in the fourteenth century have extended westward from twentieth-century boundaries throughout much or all of the Ukraine. Cf. N. P. Mironov, "The Past Existence of Foci of Plague in the Steppes of Southern Europe," *Journal of Microbiology, Epidemiology and Immunology,* 29 (1958), 1193–98.

14. Cf. Appendix.

15. Ping-ti Ho, *Studies on the Population of China, 1368–1953* (Cambridge, Massachusetts, 1959), p. 10. For a useful graphic summation of recent scholarly opinion about China's fluctuating population, see John D. Durand, "The Population Statistics of China, A.D. 2–1953," *Population Studies,* 13 (1960), 247. Durand's graph is also reproduced in R. Reinhard et André Armengaud, *Histoire Générale de la Population Mondiale* (Paris, 1961), p. 107.

16. Cf. A. von Kremer, "Uber die grossen Seuchen des Orients

nach arabischen Quellen," Oesterreich, Kaiserlichen Akademie, *Sitzungsberichte, Phil-Hist. Klasse,* 96 (1880), 136. Von Kremer transliterates the author in question as Ibn Wardy, referring, presumably, to Abu Hafs Umar ibn al-Wardi, who died in 1349 of plague.

17. Sticker, *Abhandlungen,* I, 43.

18. I owe recognition of the role of rat-flea concentrations at caravanserais and gristmills in the propagation of the plague to correspondence with Barbara Dodwell of Reading University. She found it necessary to hypothesize concentrations of rats around European gristmills to explain the propagation of the disease inland away from cities and ships; the same clustering of susceptibles (whether of rats or humans) is required to explain a rapid propagation across Eurasia through thinly populated landscapes.

19. Cf. Pollitzer, *Plague,* p. 14.

20. D. H. S. Davis, "Plague in Africa from 1935 to 1949," *World Health Organization Bulletin,* 9 (1953), 665–700.

21. For details of this key event in European history see Roberto Lopez, *Genova Marinara nel Duecento: Benedetto Zaccaria, ammiraglio e mercanti* (Messina-Milan, 1933).

22. David Herlihy, "Population, Plague and Social Change in Rural Pistoia, 1201–1430," *Economic History Review,* 18 (1965), 225–44.

23. In Europe, a "Little Ice Age" starting about 1300 climaxed between 1550 and 1850 and has been succeeded by warmer temperatures in the twentieth century. Cf. Emmanuel Le Roy Ladurie, *Times of Feast, Times of Famine: A History of Climate Since the Year 1000* (New York, 1971), and the speculative explanation of long-term fluctuations offered by H. H. Lamb, *The Changing Climate* (London, 1966), pp. 170–94. Roughly parallel alterations in climate can be inferred also from Chinese records. See the graph of fluctuating temperatures in Chu K'o-chen, "Chung kuo chin wu ch'ien nien lai ch'i hou pien ch'ien te ch'u pu yen chiu" [Initial researches into changes in the Chinese climate during the past five thousand years], *K'ao ku hsüeh pao* (1972), p. 37. Hugh Scogin brought this chart to my attention and translated the Chinese headings for me. The principal basis for Chu K'o-chen's graph is local records of years when the Yangtze lakes froze over in wintertime.

24. Conditions under which this "pneumonic" form of plague

occur remain obscure. There are experts who deny the importance of pneumonic plague in Europe in the fourteenth century. Cf. J. F. D. Shrewsbury, A *History of Bubonic Plague on the British Isles* (Cambridge, 1970), p. 6 and *passim*; and the rebuttal by C. Morris, "The Plague in Britain," *Historical Journal*, 14 (1971), 205–15. Barbara Dodwell's explanation for the propagation of the infection via rat concentrations at gristmills is probably a satisfactory reconciliation of Shrewsbury's epidemiology and the historical facts. She developed the hypothesis to explain how the plague could penetrate thinly populated regions as records attested but which Shrewsbury had declared impossible on epidemiological grounds. Being a meticulous scholar, Miss Dodwell has not yet published anything to resolve the problem, but generously shared her ideas with me in correspondence.

25. Shrewsbury, op. cit., p. 406. As a bacteriologist, Shrewsbury is an expert guide to the medical aspects of plague, even if his historical judgments remain controversial. The last outbreak of plague that ran its course without benefit of penicillin and related antibiotics (which destroy the infection rapidly) occurred in Burma in 1947, where 1,192 reported deaths from a total of 1,518 cases made a lethal percentage of 78. Pollitzer, *Plague* (Geneva, 1954), p. 22.

26. August Hirsch, *Handbook of Geographical and Historical Pathology*, I, 498.

27. Josiah C. Russell, "Late Ancient and Medieval Population," *American Philosophical Society Transactions*, 48 (1958), 40–45; Philip Ziegler, *The Black Death* (New York, 1969), pp. 224–31. Shrewsbury, op. cit., p. 123, vehemently argues for a mere 5 per cent die-off in Great Britain from bubonic plague—on the assumption that pneumonic plague did not manifest itself; but he allows an undiagnosed typhus, following in the rear of the plague, to raise mortality toward the 40–50 per cent die-off recorded among English clergy for the years 1346–49. Whether the well-attested and extraordinarily high death rates among English clergy can be projected upon the population at large has been the focus of considerable debate from the time F. A. Gasquet, *The Black Death of 1348 and 1349*, 2nd ed. (London, 1908), first discovered them by perusing monastic and diocesan records.

28. Italian records are potentially very rich but have only begun

to be carefully studied. Cf. William M. Bowsky, "The Impact of the Black Death upon Sienese Government and Society," *Speculum,* 39 (1964), 1–34; David Herlihy, "Population, Plague and Social Change in Rural Pistoia, 1201–1430," *Economic History Review,* 18 (1965), 225–44; Elisabeth Carpentier, *Une Ville Devant la Peste: Orvieto et la Peste Noire de 1348* (Paris, 1962). Some French towns also have abundant notarial records that can yield data on plague losses. Cf. Richard W. Emery, "The Black Death of 1348 in Perpignan," *Speculum,* 42 (1967), 611–23, who estimated a die-off of 58–68 per cent among the notaries of Perpignan from the plague.

29. The plague was, however, serious in Russia. Cf. the discussion of plague losses in Russia and their socio-political effects in Gustave Alef, "The Crisis of the Muscovite Aristocracy: A Factor in the Growth of Monarchical Power," *Forschungen zur osteuropaischen Geschichte,* 15 (1970), 36–39; Lawrence Langer, "The Black Death in Russia: Its Effects upon Urban Labor," *Russian History,* II (1975), 53–67.

30. A useful sampling of recent scholarly opinions about the effects of the plague on European history may be found in William M. Bowsky, ed., *The Black Death: A Turning Point in History?* (New York, 1971), pp. 65–121.

31. John Saltmarsh, "Plague and Economic Decline in the Later Middle Ages," *Cambridge Historical Journal,* 7 (1941), 23–41; J. M. W. Bean, "Plague, Population and Economic Decline in England in the Late Middle Ages," *Economic History Review,* 15 (1963), 423–36; J. C. Russell, "Effects of Pestilence and Plague, 1315–1385," *Comparative Studies in Society and History,* 8 (1966), 464–73; Sylvia Thrupp, "Plague Effects in Medieval Europe," Idem., 474ff; A. R. Bridbury, "The Black Death," *Economic History Review,* 26 (1973), 577–92.

32. Cf. Roger Mols, *Introduction à la Démographie Historique des Villes d'Europe du XIVᵉ au XVIIIᵉ Siècle* (Louvain, 1956), II, 426–59.

33. Cf. J. C. Russell, *Late Ancient and Medieval Population,* pp. 113–31. Russell summarizes his often flimsy data as follows: "The effects of the plague were very much the same everywhere they can be tested. Upon the basis of evidence of an earlier chapter we assume a 40 percent decline of the 1346 population, except for the drier areas, by the end of the fourteenth century. The numbers

reached then were generally static until well into the fifteenth century although some places declined further and others improved their position. . . . The population of the whole area [Europe and North Africa] about 1500 was still markedly smaller than it had been just before the Black Death. By 1550 it had risen to about the pre-plague figure." Ibid., p. 131.

34. For Australian rabbits, cf. above, Chapter II; for Amerindians, cf. below, Ch. V; for Pacific island populations, cf. Macfarlane Burnet, "A Biologist's Parable for the Modern World," *Intellectual Digest* (March 1972), p. 88.

35. George Rosen, A *History of Public Health* (New York 1958), p. 67.

36. For Ragusa cf. Miodrag B. Petrovich, A *Mediterranean City State: A Study of Dubrovnik Elites, 1592–1667* (Unpublished Ph.D. dissertation, University of Chicago, 1974); for Venice, Frederic C. Lane, *Venice: A Maritime Republic* (Baltimore, 1973), p. 18.

37. Daniel Panzac, "La Peste à Smyrne au XVIIIᵉ Siècle," *Annales: Economies, Sociétés, Civilisations,* 28 (1973), 1071–93, is fundamental. Paul Cassar, *Medical History of Malta* (London, 1964), pp. 175–90, documents plague visitations to that Mediterranean port until the nineteenth and twentieth centuries; and describes the traditional quarantine methods in full detail.

38. Cf. Erwin R. Ackerknecht, "Anticontagionism between 1821 and 1867," *Bulletin of the History of Medicine,* 22 (1948), 562–93.

39. Georg Sticker, *Abhandlungen aus der Seuchengeschichte,* I, 222–36, calculates deaths at 87,666, or 35 per cent of the population in affected localities of Provence. For details see Paul Gaffarel et Mis de Duranty, *La Peste de 1720 à Marseille et en France* (Paris, 1911); J. N. Biraben, "Certain Demographic Characteristics of the Plague Epidemic in France, 1720–22," *Daedalus* (1968), pp. 536–45.

40. For an overview, see Roger Mols, *Introduction à la démographie historique des villes d'Europe du XIVᵉ au XVIIIᵉ siècle,* 3 volumes (Louvain, 1954–56).

41. Daniele Beltrami, *Storia della Popolazione di Venezia* (Padua, 1954). For details of public measures to meet the emergency of the plague of 1575–77, cf. Ernst Rodenwalt, *Pest in Venedig, 1557–77:*

Notes

Ein Beitrag zur Frage der Infektkette bei den Pestepidemien West Europas (Heidelberg, 1953).

42. Cf. Bartolème Bennassar, *Recherches sur les Grandes Épidémies dans le Nord de l'Espagne à la Fin du XVI* Siècle (Paris, 1969).

43. René Baehrel, "Épidémie et terreur: Histoire et Sociologie," *Annales Historiques de la Révolution*, 23 (1951), 113–46, argues that the public manifestations in Paris and other cities of France during the Terror of 1793–94 derived from patterns for the expression of popular excitement that had become semi-ritualized as responses to plague and fear of plague in the seventeenth century, and which had been revivified throughout much of France in response to the plague outbreak in 1720–22. Similar problems of social control in time of plague alarmed Catherine II of Russia. Cf. John T. Alexander, "Catherine II, Bubonic Plague, and the Problem of Industry in Moscow," *American Historical Review*, 79 (1974), 637–71.

44. For details of this event, cf. Charles F. Mullett, *The Bubonic Plague and England*, pp. 105–222; Walter George Bell, *The Great Plague in London in 1665* (rev. ed., London, 1951).

45. Cf. R. Pollitzer, *Plague*, pp. 282–85, 298–99.

46. Cf. Mirko D. Grmek, "Maladies et morts: Préliminaires d'une étude historique des maladies," *Annales: Economies, Sociétés, Civilisations*, 24 (1969), 1473–83; R. Pollitzer, *Plague*, pp. 92, 448.

47. The canonical exposition may be found in Pollitzer, op. cit., pp. 11–16.

48. Wu Lien-teh, et al., *Plague: A Manual for Public Health Workers* (Shanghai, 1936), p. 14, claims that plague was also disappearing from China in the latter seventeenth century; but as an associate of Dr. Pollitzer and other public health experts, he simply assumed that the pandemic of the fourteenth century was fading out by the seventeenth century. Any search of Chinese literary records he may have made to support this assertion was minimal. There is no reason therefore to put much credence in Dr. Wu's remark.

49. Vilhelm Møller-Christensen, "Evidence of Leprosy in Earlier Peoples," in Brothwell and Sandison, *Disease in Antiquity*, pp. 295–306.

50. Hirsch, op. cit., 2, 7; Folke Henschen, *The History and Geography of Diseases* (English trans., New York, 1966), pp. 107–13.

51. Personal letter from Dr. Olaf Skinsnes, May 21, 1975.

52. Cf. T. Aidan Cockburn, *The Evolution and Eradication of Infectious Diseases*, pp. 219–23; Mirko D. Grmek, op. cit., p. 1478.

53. M. Pièry et J. Roshem, *Histoire de la Tuberculose* (Paris, 1931), pp. 5–9. Cf. also Vilhelm Møller-Christensen, "Evidence of Tuberculosis, Leprosy and Syphilis in Antiquity and the Middle Ages," *Proceedings of the XIX International Congress of the History of Medicine* (Basel, 1966). The Chinese corpse from the second century B.C., referred to above in Chapter II, offers one of the few evidences for the existence of pulmonary tuberculosis from ancient times.

An amazing variety of animals suffer from one or another form of tuberculosis. Indeed, on chemical grounds it is commonly believed that the bacillus became parasitic when all life was still oceanic. This hypothesis is based on peculiar acidic properties of tuberculosis bacilli. Cf. Dan Morse, "Tuberculosis," in Brothwell and Sandison, *Disease in Antiquity*, pp. 249–71.

54. René Dubos, *The White Plague: Tuberculosis, Man and Society* (Boston, 1952), pp. 197–207.

55. The principal advocate of this view is C. J. Hackett. Cf. C. J. Hackett, "On the Origin of the Human Treponematoses," *Bulletin of the World Health Organization*, 29 (1963), 7–41; C. J. Hackett, "The Human Treponematoses," in Brothwell and Sandison, *Diseases in Antiquity*, pp. 152–69. Others have accepted and elaborated upon the convertibility between pinta, yaws, and syphilis proposed by Hackett. Cf. E. H. Hudson, "Treponematosis and Man's Social Evolution," *American Anthropologist*, 67 (1965), 885–901; Theodor Rosebury, *Microbes and Morals: The Strange Story of Venereal Disease* (New York, 1971); Thomas Aidan Cockburn, "The Origin of the Treponematoses," *Bulletin of the World Health Organization*, 24 (1961), 221–228; T. D. Stewart and Alexander Spoehr, "Evidence on the Paleopathology of Yaws," *Bulletin of the History of Medicine*, 26 (1952), 538–53.

56. See below, p. 226.

57. The term was coined by Girolamo Fracastoro who published a poem, *Syphilis sive Morbus Gallicus*, in 1530.

58. Cf. A. W. Crosby, Jr., "The Early History of Syphilis: A Reappraisal," *American Anthropologist*, 71 (1969), 218–27.

59. Cf. Ziegler, *The Black Death*, pp. 84–100.

60. Raymond Crawfurd, *Plague and Pestilence in Literature and Art* (Oxford, 1914); A. M. Campbell, *The Black Death and Men of Learning* (New York, 1931); George Deaux, *The Black Death, 1347* (London, 1969).

61. Millard Meiss, *Painting in Florence and Siena after the Black Death* (Princeton, 1951), pp. 89–93 and *passim*; Henri Mollaret et Jacqueline Brossolet, *La Peste, Source Méconnue d'Inspiration Artistique* (Antwerp, 1965).

62. Cf. James E. Thorold Rogers, *Six Centuries of Work and Wages: the History of English Labour*, 2nd ed. (London, 1886), pp. 239–42.

63. For a useful summary of current views, see Elizabeth Carpentier, "Autour de la Peste Noire: Famines et Épidémies dans l'Histoire du XIVᵉ Siècle," *Annales: Economies, Sociétés, Civilisations*, 17 (1962), 1062–92. Charles F. Mullett, *The Bubonic Plague and England: An Essay in the History of Preventive Medicine* (Lexington, Kentucky, 1956), pp. 17–41, offers a less iconoclastic digest of older opinions.

64. Cf. Yves Renouard, "Conséquences et Interêt Démographique de la Peste Noire de 1348," *Population*, 3 (1948), 459–66; William L. Langer, "The Next Assignment," *American Historical Review*, 63 (1958), 292–301.

65. Cf. the remarks in J. F. D. Shrewsbury, *The Plague of the Philistines* (London, 1964), pp. 127ff. St. Sebastian was first invoked against pestilence in Rome in 680; but his cult remained insignificant until the sixteenth century. St. Roch was a Franciscan friar who died in 1327 after a career of caring for the sick.

66. The autonomy of French and English towns was also very broad, and in health matters remained almost total until the eighteenth century. The first time the French royal government intervened in plague prophylaxis was 1720–21, when the plague, having outrun the boundaries of Marseilles, came to be treated as a national problem. Cf. Paul Delaunay, *La Vie Médicale aux XVIᵉ, XVIIᵉ et XVIIIᵉ Siècles* (Paris, 1935), pp. 269–70.

67. Abraham L. Udovitch, "Egypt: Crisis in a Muslim Land," reproduced in William L. Bowsky, *The Black Death: A Turning Point in History?* (New York, 1971), p. 124.

68. M. W. Dols, *The Black Death in the Middle East* (Unpublished Ph.D. dissertation, Princeton, 1971), pp. 56–64, tabulated no fewer than fifty-seven outbreaks of plague between 1349 and 1517; of these, thirty-one afflicted Egypt, twenty afflicted Syria, and only two afflicted Iraq. An earlier scholar derived the following chronologically more extensive results from perusal of Arabic sources:

Epidemic Outbreaks in Egypt, Syria, and Iraq according to Arabic Sources:

	Number of episodes mentioned		
Time span	Syria	Egypt	Iraq
632–719	7	2	6
719–816	3	0	5
816–913	0	0	3
913–1010	0	0	3
1010–1107	2	2	5
1107–1204	2	2	2
1204–1301	1	5	0
1301–1398	3	5	1
1398–1495	5	17	0

Table derived from A. von Kremer, "Über die grossen Seuchen des Orients nach arabischen Quellen," Oesterreich, Kaiserlichen Akademie, *Sitzungsberichte, Phil-Hist. Klasse,* 96 (1880), 110–42. Von Kremer does not indicate how broad his search of Arabic literature may have been; and clearly what he calls "Pest" covers diseases other than bubonic plague. Nevertheless, the sudden increase in the number of epidemics Egypt experienced in his last period, which corresponds to the first full century of rule by the Circassian Mamelukes, surely suggests a new vulnerability to infection.

The monumental scholarly record of literary mentions of plague, Georg Sticker, *Abhandlungen aus der Seuchengeschichte I: Die Pest* (Giessen, 1908), records only eighteen outbreaks of plague in Egypt between 1399 and 1706; but his data are entirely at the mercy of information available to him in European languages, and von Kremer's compilation obviously escaped his attention. Generally, Sticker's results are fragmentary and undependable, since most European scholars who had explored Chinese, Indian, Islamic, and other exotic literatures in the nineteenth century were completely

Notes

uninterested in plague or other diseases. The result is whimsical and erratic: no plague in China until 1757, for example, or in East Africa until 1696. I conclude that it is useless to try to derive a valid world picture from the listings Sticker so energetically (and sometimes uncritically) collected. Only for Europe is he reasonably reliable and complete.

69. Cf. Robert Tignor, *Public Health Administration in Egypt Under British Rule, 1882–1914* (Unpublished Ph.D. dissertation, Yale University, 1960), p. 87. The last important outbreak, in 1835, reached Alexandria from Syria, and then traveled up the Nile.

70. In Persia, for example, plague outbreaks are reported between 1500 and 1800 as follows:

1535	in Gilan only.
1571–75	General outbreak. This coincided with a similarly general plague in the Mediterranean.
1595–96	General, including also Iraq.
1611–17	Plague coming from east via Afghanistan.
1666	Coincided with Great Plague of London.
1684–86	General and severe plague.
1725	
1757	
1760–67	Severe and general plague.
1773–74	General plague, also affecting Iraq. Coincided with plague in Moscow.
1797	

Data derived from Cyril Elgood, *Medical History of Persia and the Eastern Califate* (Cambridge, 1951) and Sticker, op. cit. Both depend on J. D. Tholozan, *Histoire de la Peste Bubonique en Perse, en Mésopotamie et au Caucase* (Paris, 1874), which I have been unable to see. Tholozan was a French doctor, interested in cures; how reliable his data may be I cannot tell.

Appropriate search of earlier Persian and Arabic texts would probably establish a similar pattern of plague in Iran from 1346; and if epidemic patterns from about that date differ from earlier recorded disease experience, the hypothesis here advanced would find important confirmation. But no one has tried to search Persian materials with this question in mind; and since many of the relevant texts have not even been printed, the task will not be easy.

71. My rendition of the French translation of Muhammad ibn Isma'il al-Bukhari Sahih, available as El Bokhari, *Les Traditions Islamiques*, O. Houdas, trans. [Publications de l'école des langues orientales vivantes], 4th series, VI (Paris, 1914), Titre lxxxvi, "De La Médicine," chs. 30, 31.

72. For Moslem attitudes toward plague see Jacqueline Sublet, "La Peste Prise aux Rets de la Jurisprudence: la Traité d'Ibn Hagar al-Asqalani sur la Peste," *Studia Islamica*, 33 (1971), 141–49; M. W. Dols, *The Black Death in the Middle East* (Unpublished Ph.D. dissertation, Princeton, 1971), pp. 131–46. On the interrelation of epidemic outbreaks (smallpox?) and Arab conquests, see Hirsch, *Handbook of Geographical and Historical Pathology*, I, 126. M. W. Dols, "Plague in Early Islamic History," *Journal of the American Oriental Society*, 94 (1974), 371–83, accepts the notion that the epidemics accompanying early Arab conquests were bubonic. This depends on whether or not the Arabic term used after 1346 for bubonic infection was used for the same infection seven hundred years earlier. This may or may not be true, since Moslem writers had not used the term to describe current afflictions for at least 150 years before the disastrous irruption of the Black Death in the fourteenth century. Or so Dols's own search of Arabic texts concludes. Cf. M. W. Dols, *The Black Death*, p. 29.

73. Ogier Ghislain de Busbecq, *Travels in Turkey* (London, 1744), p. 228.

74. See Appendix, and above, p. 163.

75. Michael W. Dols, *The Black Death in the Middle East*, p. 30.

76. I have been unable to locate any discussion of steppe demography; but David Neustadt, "The Plague and its Effects upon the Mameluke Army," *Journal of the Royal Asiatic Society* (1946), p. 67, remarks that diminution of the steppe population north of the Black Sea, whence the Mamelukes recruited their ranks, caused difficulties in the period after 1346.

77. No satisfactory history of the Crim Tartars exists. General histories of the steppe, of which the best is René Grousset, *The Empire of the Steppes: A History of Central Asia* (New Brunswick New Jersey, 1970), do not consider disease at all.

78. Cf. William H. McNeill, *Europe's Steppe Frontier*, 1500–1800 (Chicago, 1964).

79. On Russian population, cf. the convenient summary of

widely differing estimates for the period 1570–1715, in Richard Hellie, *Enserfment and Military Change in Muscovy* (Chicago, 1971), p. 305. On Ottoman population, cf. Halil Inalcik, *The Ottoman Empire in the Classical Age* (London, 1973), p. 46.

Chapter V

1. Alfred W. Crosby, Jr., *The Columbian Exchange* (Westport, Conn., 1972), pp. 73–121. This author goes so far as to state: "Today an American botanist can easily find whole meadows in which he is hard put to it to find a single species of plant that grew in the Americas in pre-Columbian times." (P. 74.)

2. Saul Jarcho, "Some Observations on Diseases in Prehistoric America," *Bulletin of the History of Medicine*, 38 (1964), 1–19; G. W. Goff, "Syphilis," in Brothwell and Sandison, *Diseases in Antiquity*, 279–94; Abner I. Weisman, "Syphilis: Was it Endemic in Pre-Columbian America or Was it Brought Here from Europe?" *New York Academy Medical Bulletin*, 24 (1966), 284–300.

3. Ernest Carrol Faust, "History of Human Parasitic Infections," *Public Health Reports*, 70 (1955), 958–65.

4. Sherburne F. Cook, "The Incidence and Significance of Disease Among the Aztecs and Related Tribes," *Hispanic American Historical Review*, 36 (1946), 320–35. Cook calculates the dates at 780, 1320, 1454; but the decipherment of Aztec codices is an inexact science at best.

5. "There was then no sickness; they had no aching bones; they had then no high fever; then had they no smallpox . . . At that time the course of humanity was orderly. The foreigners made it otherwise when they arrived here." *Book of Chilam Balam of Chumayel*, Ralph L. Roy, trans. (Washington, D.C., 1933), p. 83, quoted in Alfred W. Crosby, Jr., "Conquistador y Pestilencia: The First New World Pandemic and the Fall of the Great Indian Empires," *Hispanic American Historical Review*, 47 (1967), 322. This article is reproduced in Crosby's *The Columbian Exchange*, pp. 36–63.

6. On wild habitat of alpaca and llama, see F. F. Zeuner, *A History of Domesticated Animals* (London, 1963), pp. 437–38. I was unable to find any literature on the diseases of guinea pigs, llamas, or alpacas.

7. Cf. Daphne A. Roe, A *Plague of Corn: The Social History of Pellagra* (Ithaca and London, 1973), pp. 15–30 and *passim*.

8. Clifford Thorpe Smith, "Depopulation of the Central Andes in the 16th Century," *Current Anthropology*, 5 (1970), 453–60; Alfred W. Crosby, *The Columbian Exchange*, pp. 112–13.

9. Cf. the interesting summary of the evolution of opinion in Henry F. Dobyns, "Estimating Aboriginal American Population: An Appraisal of Techniques with a New Hemispheric Estimate," *Current Anthropology*, 7 (1966), 395–416.

10. Sherburne F. Cook led this revision of opinion beginning with his essay, "The Extent and Significance of Disease among the Indians of Baja California, 1697–1773," *Ibero-Americana*, 12 (1937). Thereafter appeared: Sherburne F. Cook and Lesley Byrd Simpson, "The Population of Central Mexico in the 16th Century," *Ibero-Americana*, 31 (1948); Sherburne F. Cook and Woodrow Borah, "The Indian Population of Central Mexico, 1531–1610," *Ibero-Americana*, 45 (1963); and as a sort of climatic demonstration of statistical and critical sophistication, Sherburne F. Cook and Woodrow Borah, *Essays in Population History: Mexico and the Caribbean*, 2 vols. (Berkeley, 1971–73).

11. Cf. convenient summaries in Woodrow Borah, "America as Model: The Demographic Impact of European Expansion upon the Non-European World," *Actas y Memorias del XXXV Congresso Internacional de Americanistas* (Mexico, 1964), III, 379–87; Henry F. Dobyns, "Estimating Aboriginal American Population," *Current Anthropology*, 7 (1966), 395–416.

12. Ibid., p. 413. For an impassioned (yet epidemiologically uninformed) account of similar demographic destruction among Eskimo in the Canadian Arctic, see Farley Mowat, *The Desperate People* (Boston, 1959).

13. John F. Marchand, "Tribal Epidemics in the Yukon," *Journal of the American Medical Association*, 23 (December 18, 1943) pp. 1019–20; George Catlin, *The Manners, Customs and Condition of the North American Indians* (London, 1841), I, 80, II, 257. I owe these references to Alfred W. Crosby, Jr., "Virgin Soil Epidemics as a Factor in Aboriginal Depopulation in America," *William and Mary Quarterly* (forthcoming, April 1976).

14. So Hans Zinsser, *Rats, Lice and History*, pp. 194–95, tentatively identifies this affliction; but definitive description of typhus

in America comes only in 1576 with an epidemic restricted to Mexico. Not only humans suffered: the epidemic of 1546 was preceded by an epizootic, 1544–45, which drastically reduced llama flocks. Cf. Nathan Wachtel, *La Vision des Vaincus: Les Indiens du Perou Devant de Conquête Espagnole* (Paris, 1971), p. 147.

15. Typhus fever is due to a rickettsial infection. As with plague, rats and their fleas constitute a reservoir of typhus infection; but in epidemic situations a simpler cycle involving only men and human lice prevails. Zinsser, op. cit., pp. 167ff.

16. F. J. Fisher, "Influenza and Inflation in Tudor England," *Economic History Review*, 18 (1965), 120–29. The Elizabethan poor law and Statute of Artificers were, Fisher suggests, legislative responses to the resulting dislocations of English society.

17. Fujikawa Yu, *Nikon Shippei Shi* (Tokyo, 1969) as abstracted for me by Dr. Joseph Cha. Chinese records, however, do not seem to mention anything unusual in the 1550s.

18. Sherburne F. Cook, "The Extent and Significance of Disease Among the Indians of Baja California, 1697–1773," *Ibero-Americana*, 12 (1937). Cook calculated that a population of 41,500 *after* the first pestilence shrank to a mere 3,972 by 1775.

19. But not altogether impossible, since digging up burial grounds and statistical analysis of age patterns among skeletons, etc., can reconstruct demographic disasters. Cf. Thomas H. Charlton, "On Post-conquest Depopulation in the Americas," *Current Anthropology*, XII (1971), 518.

20. William Wood, *New England's Prospect* (London, 1634), wrote that the "Lord put an end to this quarrel by smiting them with smallpox . . . Thus did the Lord allay their quarrelsome spirit and make room for the following part of his army." Quoted in Esther Wagner Stearn and Allen E. Stearn, *The Effect of Smallpox on the Destiny of the Amerindian* (Boston, 1945), p. 22.

21. Joseph Stocklein, *Der Neue Welt Bott* (Augsburg and Graz, 1728–29), quoted in Stearns and Stearns, op. cit., p. 17.

22. Percy M. Ashburn, *The Ranks of Death: A Medical History of the Conquest of America* (New York, 1947), pp. 57–79, analyzed details of several such expeditions and concluded that famine and scurvy were the two principal killers of European colonists and conquistadors.

23. Frederick L. Dunn, "On the Antiquity of Malaria in the Western Hemisphere," *Human Biology*, 37 (1965), 385–93.

Other experts have argued differently, e.g., L. J. Bruce-Chwatt, "Paleogenesis and Paleo-epidemiology of Primate Malaria," World Health Organization, *Bulletin,* 32 (1965), 377–82. The Amerindian testimony, cited above, to the effect that fevers were unknown before the white men came, would of course also support Dunn's conclusion.

24. Ashburn, op. cit., pp. 112–15.

25. Marston Bates, "The Ecology of Anopheline Mosquitoes," in Mark F. Boyd, ed., *Malariology* (Philadelphia, 1949), I, 302–30; L. W. Hackett, *Malaria in Europe: An Ecological Study* (Oxford, 1937), 85–108.

26. For current data on the distribution of malaria in the New World, cf. Ernest Carroll Faust, "Malaria Incidence in North America," in Mark F. Boyd, *Malariology,* I, 748–63; Arnaldo Gabaldon, "Malaria Incidence in the West Indies and South America," ibid., I, 746–87. Though we are tempted to think of malaria as a disease of tropical and subtropical climates, it was in fact prevalent in the whole Mississippi Valley in the nineteenth century and extended its range northward into Canada as well. Cf. E. H. Ackerknecht, "Malaria in the Upper Mississippi Valley," Supplement ⅄ 4, *Bulletin of the History of Medicine* (Baltimore, 1945). For malaria as a probable killer of coastal Amerindian populations of the Caribbean, cf. Woodrow Borah and Sherburne F. Cook, "The Aboriginal Population of Central Mexico on the Eve of the Spanish Conquest," *Ibero-Americana,* 45 (1963), 89.

27. Henry Rose Carter, *Yellow Fever: An Epidemiological and Historical Study of Its Place of Origin* (Baltimore, 1931), p. 10. When Carter published this book he was arguing against the fact that yellow fever was first identified in the Americas, and was recognized in Africa only in 1782. This led to the idea that it was an import to the Old World from the Caribbean. Subsequent study, including the observation that American monkeys are liable to epidemic death from yellow fever, whereas those of the African rain forest exhibit a well-adjusted tolerance for the infection, have confirmed Carter's view. Cf. Richard Fiennes, *Zoonoses of Primates* (Ithaca, New York, 1967), p. 13; Macfarlane Burnet and David O. White, *Natural History of Infectious Disease,* 4th ed. (Cambridge, 1972), pp. 242–49.

28. The contrast in environments was sharpest in Peru, and the survival differential between *altiplano* and coastlands was corre-

spondingly greater there than in Mexico—or so imperfect statistics seem to show. Thus Clifford Thorpe Smith, "Depopulation of the Central Andes in the 16th century," *Current Anthropology,* 11 (1970), 453–60, finds the following ratios of depopulation between 1520 and 1571:

Sierra   3.4:1
Coast   58.0:1

Sherburne F. Cook and Woodrow Borah, *Essays in Population History: Mexico and the Caribbean* (Berkeley and Los Angeles, 1971), I, 79–89, present graphs and tables illustrating the speedier and greater destruction of Amerindian population in the tropical coastal zones of Mexico. Translated into ratios like those used by Smith, these become, for the years 1531–1610:

Plateau   14:1
Coast   16:1

The Peruvian data are affected by the breakdown of irrigation required to keep agriculture going on the arid coasts; the Mexican cover a longer time span and thus reflect a longer impact of unfamiliar disease upon the native inhabitants.

29. Philip Curtin, "Epidemiology and the Slave Trade," *Political Science Quarterly,* 83 (1968), 190–216; Francisco Guerra, "The Influence of Disease on Race, Logistics, and Colonization in the Antilles," *Journal of Tropical Medicine,* 49 (1966), 23–35; Wilbur Zelinsky, "The Historical Geography of the Negro Population of Latin America," *Journal of Negro History,* 34 (1949), 153–221.

30. Henry F. Dobyns, "Estimating Aboriginal American Population," *Current Anthropology,* 7 (1966), 395–416; Sherburne F. Cook, "The Significance of Disease in the Extinction of the New England Indians," *Human Biology,* 45 (1973), 485–508. For a naive but recent survey of the matter, see Wilbur R. Jacobs, "The Tip of an Iceberg: Pre-Columbian Indian Demography and Some Implications for Revisionism," *William and Mary Quarterly,* 31 (1974), 123–32.

31. *The Annals of the Cakchiquels and Title of the Lords of Totonicapan,* Adrian Recinos, et al., trans. (Norman, Oklahoma, 1953), p. 116, quoted in Crosby, *The Columbian Exchange,* p. 58.

32. Early nineteenth-century figures for mortality among native African troops serving in the British army show about a 50 per cent increase in disease mortality as a consequence of moving within tropical Africa to a new region with new disease exposures and, of course, a radically new way of life. Philip D. Curtin, "Epidemiology and the Slave Trade," *Political Science Quarterly*, 83 (1968), 204–5. Death rates for white personnel, however, remained far above those of Africans.

33. Philip D. Curtin, *The Atlantic Slave Trade: A Census* (Madison, Wisconsin, 1969), pp. 270–71.

34. P. Huard, "La Syphilis Vue par les Médicins Arabo-Persans, Indiens et Sino-Japonais du XVᵉ et XVIᵉ Siècles," *Histoire de la Médicine*, 6 (1956), 9–13. Recommended cures were also of world-wide distribution, with the Chinese pharmacopeia taking the lead. Cf. K. Chimin Wong and Wu Lien-teh, *History of Chinese Medicine*, 2nd ed. (Shanghai, 1936), pp. 136, 215–16. These authors are of the opinion that despite contemporary testimony to the novelty of the disease in the sixteenth century, ancient Chinese texts reveal familiarity with syphilitic sores. Symptoms and language being as variable as they are, the facts seem completely irrecoverable.

35. Cf. the judicious summary in Alfred W. Crosby, Jr., *The Columbian Exchange*, pp. 122–56. Evidence of adaptation among isolated Amerindian tribes of the Amazon basin to syphilitic infection is ambiguous. Some tribes show widespread positive reactions to tests designed to tell whether they had been exposed to such infection; other tribes showed no such reactions, except among individuals who were known to have had contact with the outside world. Those tribes where positive reactions were widespread, however, showed no clinical signs of either yaws or syphilis or a third form of the infection, known as pinta. This remarkable result may indicate lengthy adaptation between host and parasite, and would be compatible with the theory of a Columbian introduction of syphilis into the Old World, for among a new population, inexperienced with the infectious agent in question, entirely different and far more fulminant symptoms are to be expected. Yet the erratic distribution of exposure to spirochetic infection among Amazonian Indians remains puzzling. Cf. Francis L. Black, "Infectious Diseases in Primitive Societies," *Science*, 187 (1975), 517.

36. Hans Zinsser, *Rats, Lice and History*, pp. 183–92, 210–28.

Notes

37. Cf. Charles Creighton, *History of Epidemics in Britain,* I, 237–81.

38. Cf. Albert Colnat, *Les Épidémies et l'Histoire* (Paris, 1937), p. 108.

39. Karl F. Helleiner, "The Population of Europe from the Black Death to the Eve of the Vital Revolution," *Cambridge Economic History of Europe,* IV (Cambridge, 1967), 20–40.

40. For plague, see Chapter IV above; for malaria, L. W. Hackett, *Malaria in Europe: An Ecological Study* (Oxford, 1937), pp. 53–96; and below, Chapter VI.

41. Cf. D. E. C. Eversley, "Population, Economy and Society," in D. V. Glass and D. E. C. Eversley, *Population in History: Essays in Historical Demography* (London, 1965), p. 57: "Everyone is agreed that the expectation of life was greater at the beginning of the modern statistical era [ca. 1750] than it had been in the seventeenth century. Yet we cannot pinpoint the improvement by time, area or cause . . . If people lived longer, it must have been partly because they were cleaner, partly because some effective medical practice was known, partly because famines were no longer severe, but *mostly because the great killer epidemics failed to return,* for reasons which might not be connected with human actions at all." (Italics added.) It seems obvious to me that the reason for the decay of the force of epidemics was their increased frequency, until epidemic became merely endemic childhood disease.

K. F. Helleiner, "The Vital Revolution Reconsidered," in D. V. Glass and D. E. C. Eversley, eds., *Population in History: Essays in Historical Demography* (London, 1965), pp. 79–86, arrives at essentially the same conclusion with reference to eighteenth-century European population growth: not any notable diminution of death rates in normal times but rather a leveling off of peaks of mortality in times of crisis was the major growth factor in Helleiner's opinion. Blunting of famine by improved marketing of food supplies plus increased food production had something to do with the reduction of crisis die-offs; but the changing pattern of epidemic incidence—which these authors seem unaware of—was surely at work also.

42. Temperature dropped in the seventeenth century; the peak of this "Little Ice Age" seems to have come in the first decade of the eighteenth century. Cf. Emmanuel LeRoy Ladurie, *Times of*

Feast, Times of Famine: A History of Climate Since the Year 1000 (New York, 1971).

43. This has been persuasively analyzed by Fernand Braudel, *La Méditerranée et le Monde Méditerranée au Temps de Phillippe II*, 2nd ed. (Paris, 1966), English translation, New York, 1972.

44. Despite the well-deserved obloquy that historians have lavished on the destructiveness of the soldieries in the Thirty Years' War, deaths from disease far outstripped deaths from weapons in this as in every European conflict prior to the twentieth century. For a few details, cf. R. J. G. Concannon, "The Third Enemy: The Role of Epidemics in the Thirty Years' War," *Journal of World History*, 10 (1967), 500–11.

45. Helleiner, op. cit., pp. 81–84.

46. For an instructive analysis of the Tuscan model see Carlo M. Cipolla, *Christofano and the Plague: A Study in the History of Public Health in the Age of Galileo* (Berkeley and Los Angeles, 1973); for the Venetian model see Brian Pullan, *Rich and Poor in Renaissance Venice: The Social Institutions of a Catholic State to 1620* (Cambridge, Massachusetts, 1971).

47. As whites advanced, Amerindian populations withered, much as a penicillin mold creates a bacteria-free zone around its edges. In the United States, it was only in 1907, when smallpox vaccinations became compulsory in Indian schools, that population decay among Amerindians was checked, according to E. S. Stearn and A. E. Stearn, *The Effect of Smallpox on the Destiny of the Amerindian* (Boston, 1945), pp. 71, 136.

48. Cf. A. Grenfell Price, *The Western Invasions of the Pacific and its Continents: A Study of Moving Frontiers and Changing Landscapes, 1513–1958* (Oxford, 1963); Douglas L. Oliver, *The Pacific Islands* (New York, 1961); J. Burton Cleland, "Disease amongst Australian Aborigines," *Journal of Tropical Medicine and Hygiene*, 31 (1928), 53–59, 66–70, 141–45, 173–77, 307–13; Bolton G. Corney, "The Behavior of Certain Epidemic Diseases in Natives of Polynesia with Especial Reference to the Fiji Islands," Epidemiological Society of London, *Transactions*, new series, 3 (1883–84), 76–95.

49. Unnumbered pages in the back of I. S. Gurvich, *Etnicheskaya Istoriya Severo-Vostoka Siberi*, Trudy Instituta Etnografiye, new series, 39 (1966), offer a series of graphs showing

how various Siberian peoples decayed and in some cases recovered their numbers between 1650 and 1940.

50. Philip Curtin, *The Atlantic Slave Trade: A Census*, p. 270; C. W. Dixon, *Smallpox* (London, 1962), p. 208.

51. P. Huard, "La Syphilis Vue par les Médicins Arabo-Persans, Indiens et Sino-Japonais du XVᵉ et XVIᵉ Siècles," *Histoire de la Médicine*, 6 (1956), 9–13.

52. Cf. Appendix for details.

53. Ping-ti Ho, *Studies in the Population of China, 1368–1953*, p. 277.

54. Chu K'o-chen, op. cit., p. 37.

55. Irene Taeuber, *The Population of Japan*, pp. 20–21.

56. Totals are of course not particularly significant, since some epidemics were serious, others not. But here they are:

1300–1399	27	epidemics
1400–1499	28	"
1500–1599	21	"
1600–1699	18	"
1700–1799	32	"
1800–1867	33	"

57. So says Kingsley Davis, *The Population of India and Pakistan* (Princeton, 1951), p. 25.

58. In Europe, maize and potatoes became significant only after 1650; in China, maize and sweet potatoes seem to have spread more rapidly, perhaps because the intensive hand labor characteristic of Chinese farming easily allowed experimentation with a new crop, whereas the rigidities of collective "open field" cultivation, which prevailed in most of northern Europe until the eighteenth century or later, powerfully inhibited any departure from custom. On spread of American food crops, cf. Berthold Laufer, *The American Plant Migration: I—The Potato* [Field Museum, Anthropological Series Publication ⩮418] (Chicago, 1938); William L. Langer, "Europe's Initial Population Explosion," *American Historical Review*, 69 (1963), 1–17; W. H. McNeill, *The Influence of the Potato on Irish History* (Unpublished Ph.D. dissertation, Cornell University, 1947); Traian Stoianovich, "Le Mais dans les Balkans," *Annales: Economies, Sociétés, Civilisations*, 21 (1966), 1026–40; Ping-ti Ho, "The Introduction of American Food Plants into China," *American Anthropologist*, 57 (1955), 191–201;

Philip Curtin, *The Atlantic Slave Trade: A Census* (Madison, Wisconsin, 1969), p. 270.

59. My colleague, Donald Lach, first called my attention to the vitamin value of American food crops, and their importance in the contemporary cuisine of India. Cf. also Alfred W. Crosby, *The Columbian Exchange*, p. 194. The significance of vitamin-deficiency diseases in traditional civilized societies was sometimes very great. European encounters with scurvy on shipboard are relatively well known; but prior to the spread of potatoes, which also contain important vitamins, European peasantries, especially in the North, often suffered from scurvy over the winter. Cf. August Hirsch, *Handbook of Geographical and Historical Pathology*, II, 521–25. As for China, cf. T'ao Lee, "Historical Notes on Some Vitamin Deficiency Diseases of China," in Brothwell and Sandison, *Disease in Antiquity*, pp. 417–22.

60. For a general conspectus of the rise of these empires see W. H. McNeill, *The Rise of the West*, Ch. XI.

Chapter VI

1. Wu et al., *Plague*, pp. 4–12.

2. Jacques M. May, ed., *Studies in Disease Ecology* (New York, 1961), p. 37.

3. See above, Chapter II, p. 45.

4. This statement may reflect lack of adequate information. Cf. Charles Leslie, "The Modernization of Asian Medical Systems," John J. Poggie, Jr., and Robert N. Lynch, eds., *Rethinking Modernization: Anthropological Perspectives* (New York, 1974), pp. 69–108.

5. J. Ehrard, "Opinions médicales en France au XVIIIe siècle: la Peste et l'idée de contagion," *Annales ESC*, 12 (1957), 46–59; Ernst Rodenwalt, *Pest in Venedig 1575–77: Ein Beitrag zur Frage der Infektkette bei den Pestepidemien West Europas* (Heidelberg, 1953); Brian Pullan, *Rich and Poor in Renaissance Venice: The Social Institutions of a Catholic State* (Cambridge, Massachusetts, 1971), pp. 315ff.

6. Cf. Allen Debus, *The English Paracelsians* (London, 1965), pp. 67–68.

7. One estimate puts the population of Oceania in 1522 at 3.5

million. By 1939 the number of natives had fallen to 2.0 million according to Douglas L. Oliver, *The Pacific Islands* (New York, 1961), p. 255.

8. Scholarly efforts to calculate world populations date from the seventeenth century, when a group of Englishmen, of whom John Graunt (d. 1674) and William Petty (d. 1687) were the most important, became interested in "political arithmetic" and in more theoretical matters like the mathematical regularities in London's patterns of birth and death. In the twentieth century speculation about world population took up where these seventeenth-century worthies had left off. Walter F. Willcox, "World Population Growth and Movement Since 1650," in Walter F. Willcox, ed., *International Migrations*, 2 vols. (New York, 1929–31), simply reproduced the opinions of John Graunt in his estimates of Asian and African populations as of 1650. These guesses were modified on an impressionistic basis by A. M. Carr-Saunders, *World Population, Past Growth and Present Trends* (Oxford, 1936).

More recent students, having elaborated mathematical tools for refining census data of our own time, are unwilling to endorse and unable to improve such loose "order of magnitude" guesswork. Cf. John D. Durand, "The Modern Expansion of World Population," *American Philosophical Society Proceedings*, 11 (1967), 136–59.

Yet however admirable and powerful mathematical analysis of census data can be, by confining attention to the most recent two centuries of the world's history demographers focus attention on what is a grossly atypical sample of demographic history as a whole. They confine their study to an age in which epidemic disease had ceased to be nearly as important as in earlier times and when public control and containment of local violence has attained unparalleled efficiency. Even the incidence of famine has been much reduced by organized relief and the potentiality of redistributing food stocks through mechanical transport on short notice and on a global scale. By working so closely with an untypical sample of human demographic history, the experts tend to forget—or even disdainfully dismiss—factors that had been determinant in earlier ages.

9. Ping-ti Ho, *Studies on the Population of China, 1386–1953*, pp. 277–78.

10. Durand, op. cit., p. 137, offers the figure of 125 million for Europe's population in 1750 and 152 million in 1800. Marcel R.

Reinhard et André Armengaud, *Histoire Générale de la Population Mondiale*, pp. 114–201, summarize recent results of local studies in Europe without offering any over-all figures.

11. Debate over the interrelation between the industrial revolution, population growth, good and bad crop years and disease incidence is lively among British historians, who, however, have mostly followed the scientific demographers into such fascination with the way quantitative data can be converted into birth and death rates, fertility indices, age and sex pyramids, price indices, and other such mathematical artifacts as to pay little attention to disease. See for instance Thomas McKeown, R. G. Brown, R. G. Record, "An Interpretation of the Modern Rise of Population in Europe," *Population Studies*, 26 (1972), 341–82. Some, however, of whom P. E. Razzell, "Population Change in Eighteenth Century England: A Reinterpretation," *Economic History Review*, 18 (1965), 312–32, is the most emphatic, have brought changing incidence of disease under consideration. For a recent and judicious summary, see Thomas McKeown, "Medical Issues in Historical Demography," in Edwin Clark, ed., *Modern Methods in the History of Medicine* (London, 1971), 57–74.

12. This figure is derived by adding totals offered for European settlement in different parts of America ca. 1800, listed in Reinhard and Armengaud, op. cit., pp. 202–6.

13. Georg Sticker, *Abhandlungen*, I, 176–77, 237ff. For interesting sidelights on other aspects of Russia's official reaction to the plague of 1771, see John T. Alexander, "Catherine II, Bubonic Plague, and the Problem of Industry in Moscow," *American Historical Review*, 79 (1974), 637–671.

14. Reinhard and Armengaud, *Histoire Générale de la Population Mondiale*, pp. 180–81.

15. On Irish population see Robert E. Kennedy, Jr., *The Irish: Emigration, Marriage, Fertility* (Berkeley and Los Angeles, 1973). For the role of the potato in the drama, my unpublished Ph.D. thesis, *The Influence of the Potato in Irish History* (Cornell, 1947), provides the background for my remarks.

16. L. W. Hackett, *Malaria in Europe, an Ecological Study*, pp. 53–96.

17. Gordon Philpot, "Enclosure and Population Growth in Eighteenth Century England," *Explorations in Economic History*, 12 (1975), 29–46, brought this idea to my attention.

Notes

18. Jean-Paul Desaive, ed., *Médecins, Climat et Epidemies à la Fin du XVIIIe Siècle* (Paris, 1972); Jean-Pierre Goubert, *Malades et Médecins en Bretagne, 1770–1970* (Paris, 1974).

19. P. E. Razzell, "Population Change in Eighteenth Century England: A Reinterpretation," *Economic History Review*, 18 (1965), 312–32; D. E. C. Eversley, "Epidemiology as Social History," Foreword to Charles Creighton, *A History of Epidemics in Great Britain*, 2nd ed. (New York, 1965), p. 29.

20. For details of the continued significance of smallpox in London, see William A. Grey, "Two Hundred and Fifty Years of Smallpox in London," *Journal of the Royal Statistical Society*, 45 (1882), 399–443.

21. Genevieve Miller, *The Adoption of Inoculation for Smallpox in England and France* (Philadelphia, 1957), pp. 194–240.

22. The principal early champion of inoculation was the famous Congregational minister, Cotton Mather (d. 1728). Cf. Genevieve Miller, "Smallpox Inoculation in England and America: A Reappraisal," *William and Mary Quarterly*, 13 (1956), 476–92. On epidemics in colonial America see John Duffy, *Epidemics in Colonial America* (Baton Rouge, 1953).

23. Cf. J. C. Long, *Lord Jeffrey Amherst, Soldier of the King* (New York, 1933), p. 186–87.

24. Sherburne F. Cook, "F. X. Balmis and the Introduction of Vaccination to Spanish America," *Bulletin for the History of Medicine*, 11 (1941), 543–60; 12 (1942), 70–101. Epidemics had been a serious administrative concern in Spanish America for a long time. Cf. Donald B. Cooper, *Epidemic Disease in Mexico City, 1761–1813: An Administrative, Social and Medical Study* (Austin, Texas, 1965).

25. Harry Wain, *A History of Preventive Medicine* (Springfield, Illinois, 1970), pp. 177, 185, 195.

26. Lady Mary can also be credited with introducing into England a quite new attitude toward an alien civilization. Instead of fear or scorn—or reluctant admiration for a recognized threat from afar—she and others became interested in Ottoman ways as a sample of the diversity of human behavior. Such disinterested, idle curiosity required leisure, and perhaps also a deep sense of the basic superiority of one's own inherited style of life—all of which Lady Mary's aristocratic circle enjoyed. Cf. Norman Daniel, *Islam and the West: The Making of an Image* (Edinburgh, 1960).

27. Inoculation may also have been practiced in Wales before 1721. Perrot Williams, M.D., "A Method of Procuring the Small Pox Used in South Wales," Royal Society of London, *Transactions Abridged III, Transactions to the Year 1732* [John Eames and John Martyn, eds.] (London, 1734), pp. 618–20. C. S. Dixon, *Smallpox.* p, 216, also mentions folk variolation reported from Poland (1671), Scotland (1715), Naples (1754).

28. Genevieve Miller, *The Adoption of Inoculation*, pp. 48–67.

29. K. Chimin Wong and Wu Lien-teh, *History of Chinese Medicine*, pp. 215–16.

30. There seems no sound basis for the story popularized by Voltaire, *Lettres Philosophiques* (reprinted in Paris, 1915), II, 130, to the effect that inoculation had been invented among Circassians seeking to preserve the fair complexions of their daughters for sale to Turkish harems.

31. C. W. Dixon, *Smallpox*, pp. 216–27; Genevieve Miller, *The Adoption of Inoculation for Smallpox in England and France.*

32. On Near Eastern practices with respect to smallpox inoculation, cf. Patrick Russell, "An Account of Inoculation in Arabia in a Letter from Dr. Patrick Russell, Physician at Aleppo to Alexander Russell, M.D., F.R.S.," *Philosophical Transactions of the Royal Society*, 18 (1768), 140–50. Russell's report was in response to inquiry from the Royal Society.

33. J. S. Chambers, *The Conquest of Cholera* (New York, 1938), p. 11.

34. Wu Lien-teh, "The Early Days of Western Medicine in China," *Journal of the North China Branch of the Royal Asiatic Society*, 1931, pp. 9–10; K. Chimin Wong and Wu Lien-teh, *History of Chinese Medicine*, pp. 276–80.

35. Private letter from Professor D. B. Shimkin, Department of Anthropology, University of Illinois.

36. Harry Wain, *A History of Preventive Medicine* (Springfield, Illinois, 1970), p. 206.

37. For a catalogue of recorded outbreaks, cf. Friedrich Prinzing, *Epidemics Resulting from Wars* (Oxford, 1916), pp. 92–164. Prinzing concludes that accurate totals are unattainable, but suggests that in the single campaign of 1813–14, one tenth of the population of Germany fell ill with typhus and one per cent of the population died in this single epidemic.

38. The fungus made it across the oceans because bigger and

faster ships plying between South America and Europe could traverse the tropics without allowing their holds to heat up past the critical temperature which the fungus could not survive.

39. One calculation concluded that one out of every forty-six New Yorkers died annually in 1810, whereas one out of twenty-seven did so in 1859. Cf. Howard D. Kramer, "The Beginnings of the Public Health Movement in the United States," *Bulletin of the History of Medicine*, 21 (1947), 352–76. In Paris the death rate increased between 1817 and 1835 from 31 to 34 per thousand. Cf. Roderick E. McGrew, *Russia and the Cholera, 1823–1832* (Madison and Milwaukee, Wisconsin, 1965), p. 6.

40. Cf. Aidan T. Cockburn, *The Evolution and Eradication of Infectious Diseases*, p. 196: ". . . there is no reason why the last case of smallpox should not disappear within two or three years." (1963).

41. Laverne Kuhnke, *Resistance and Response to Modernization: Preventive Medicine and Social Control in Egypt, 1825–1850* (Unpublished Ph.D. dissertation, Chicago, 1971), p. 51.

42. A number of casual references to sudden outbreaks of lethal disease in southern and western India that sound like cholera punctuate European records from the days of the first Portuguese residents at Goa. Cf. R. Pollitzer, *Cholera* (Geneva, 1959), pp. 12–13. C. Macnamara, *A History of Asiatic Cholera* (London, 1876), discovered no fewer than sixty-four such references dating between 1503 and 1817.

43. Cf. the bar graphs in Pollitzer, op. cit., p. 80.

44. Cf. C. H. Gordon, *An Epitome of the Reports of the Medical Officers of the Chinese Imperial Customs from 1871 to 1882* (London, 1884), p. 124.

45. Pollitzer, op. cit., pp. 17–21; McGrew, *Russia and the Cholera*, pp. 39–40; Norman Longmate, *King Cholera: The Biography of a Disease* (London, 1966), pp. 2–3; Hirsch, *Handbook of Geographical and Historical Pathology*, I, 394–97.

46. Estimates of mortality ranged from 12,000 to 30,000. Cf. Laverne Kuhnke, op. cit., p. 66.

47. There was a minor recurrence in 1930, but nothing was reported from Mecca itself on that occasion. Pollitzer, op. cit., p. 63.

48. Norman Longmate, *King Cholera*, p. 237.

49. Between 1910 and 1954, 10.2 million died of cholera in India according to official tabulation; to these should be added nearly 200,000 deaths in Pakistan since 1947. Pollitzer, op. cit., p. 204 and *passim.*

50. Kuhnke, op. cit., p. 204 and *passim.*

51. Asa Briggs, "Cholera and Society in the 19th Century," *Past and Present,* 19 (1961), 76–96.

52. McGrew, op. cit., pp. 67, 111, 125; Longmate, *King Cholera,* pp. 4–5; Louis Chevalier, ed., *Le Cholera, la Première Épidémie du XIX⁰ Siècle* (La Roche sur Yon, 1958).

53. Cf. Charles E. Rosenberg, "Cholera in 19th Century Europe: A Tool for Social and Economic Analysis," *Comparative Studies in Society and History,* 8 (1966), 452–63.

54. Erwin H. Ackerknecht, "Anti-contagionism between 1821 and 1867," *Bulletin of the History of Medicine,* 22 (1948), 562–93.

55. Reprinted as *Snow on Cholera, being a Reprint of Two Papers by John Snow, M.D.* (New York, 1936).

56. According to Norman Howard-Jones, "Choleranomalies: the Unhistory of Medicine as Exemplified by Cholera," *Perspectives in Biology and Medicine,* 15 (1972), 422–33, an Italian named Filippe Pacini anticipated Koch by some thirty years in identifying the "vibrio" as causing cholera; but his theory attracted almost no attention at the time and it was thus Koch's "discovery" that mattered as far as medical opinion and practice are concerned.

57. The motivation behind Charles Creighton's monumental book, *The History of Epidemics in Britain,* 2 vols. (Cambridge, 1891, 1894) was a passionate wish to disprove the germ theory of epidemic infection.

58. Longmate, *King Cholera,* p. 229.

59. Pollitzer, *Cholera,* pp. 202–372, offers a careful discussion of the complex factors that are currently believed to affect cholera infections.

60. It has long been customary to ridicule the way the Admiralty handled scurvy. On the surface it certainly looks like a classic case of bureaucratic bungling. When effective cure and prevention had been published by respectable medical men as early as 1611 and several times thereafter, how could official command wait till 1795? Cf. John Woodall, *The Surgeon's Mate or Military and Domestique Surgery,* 2nd ed. (London, 1639), p. 165. "Of the Cure of

the Scurvie," which reads in part as follows: "The use of the juyce of lemmons is a precious medicine and well tried, being sound and good, let it have the chief place, for it will deserve it. . . . Some Chirugeons also give this juyce daily to the men in health as a preservative, which course is good if they have store, otherwise it were best to keep it for need."

Yet it is a defect of historical perspective to assume from passages such as this that *the* cure for scurvy was apparent in London before the very end of the eighteenth century. For explanation of the reasons for delay and misinformation, see John Joyce Keevil, *Medicine and the Navy, 1200–1900,* 4 vols. (London, 1957–63) I, 151; Christopher Lloyd and Jack S. Coulter, ibid., III, 298–327.

61. On sanitation in European armies in the eighteenth century, see Paul Delaunay, *La Vie Médicale aux XVIe, XVIIe et XVIIIe Siècles* (Paris, 1935), pp. 84ff; 275–80 and *passim;* Charles Singer and A. E. Underwood, *A Short History of Medicine* (New York, 1928), pp. 169–71; George Rosen, *From Medical Police to Social Medicine: Essays on the History of Health Care* (New York, 1974), pp. 120–58, 201–45; David M. Vess, *Medical Revolution in France, 1789–1796* (Gainesville, Florida, 1975). On Frank, see Henry E. Sigerist, *Grosse Ärzte,* 4th ed. (Munich, 1959), pp. 217–29.

62. Cf. R. A. Lewis, *Edwin Chadwick and the Public Health Movement, 1832–1854,* (London, 1952), pp. 52–55 and *passim.* Chadwick's proposal for using urban sewage for fertilizer was not a new idea. It had, in fact, been projected as early as 1594. Allen G. Debus, "Palissy, Plat and English Agricultural Chemistry in the 16th and 17th centuries," *Archives int. hist. sci.,* 21 (1968), 67–88.

63. Cf. C. Fraser Brockington, *A Short History of Public Health* (London, 1966), pp. 34–43.

64. Cf. Charles E. Rosenberg, *The Cholera Years: The United States in 1832, 1849 and 1866* (Chicago, 1962), pp. 175–212; John Duffy, *A History of Public Health in New York City, 1625–1866* (New York, 1968).

65. Cf. Longmate, *King Cholera,* pp. 228–29.

66. In Cairo, Egypt, for example, the birth rate was 44.1 per thousand, the death rate only 36.9 per thousand in 1913, the year *before* a modern sewage system was inaugurated in part of the city. Cf. Robert Tignor, *Public Health Administration in Egypt under*

British Rule, 1882–1914 (Unpublished Ph.D. thesis, Yale University, 1960), pp. 115–21.

67. C. Fraser Brockington, *World Health*, 2nd ed. (Boston, 1968), p. 99.

68. For an incisive account of one of the most extreme examples of how dowry rules may postpone marriage and regulate population growth to economic circumstances, see Conrad Arensberg and Solon T. Kimball, *Family and Community in Ireland*, 2nd ed. (Cambridge, Massachusetts, 1968).

69. A couple of examples may be in order: Egypt's population, about 5.3 million in 1846, grew to 26 million in 1950; Java's population of 12.4 in 1860 grew to 40 million in 1940; world population is estimated to have grown:

1850	1 billion
1950	2.5 billion
1970	3.6 billion
1976	4 billion

Cf. Gabriel Baer, *Population and Society in the Arab East* (London, 1964), p. 3; Reinhard and Armengaud, *Histoire Générale de la Population Mondiale*, p. 379; *United Nations Demographic Yearbook, 1972*, p. 119; Ronald Freedman, ed., *Population, the Vital Revolution* (New York, 1964), pp. 18–19.

70. Laverne Kuhnke, op. cit., p. 70.

71. Cf. Robert Tignor, op. cit., pp. 91, 102.

72. Cf. Harry Wain, *A History of Preventive Medicine*, pp. 284–87, 353–58, 250–63.

73. Oliver Cromwell suffered from malaria for much of his life and malarial sweats played a part in his final illness. He is said to have refused the "Jesuit bark" as nothing but a popish plot to get rid of him. Antonia Fraser, *Cromwell, the Lord Protector* (New York, 1973), pp. 770ff; A. W. Haggis, "Fundamental Errors in the Early History of Cinchona," *Bulletin of the History of Medicine*, 10 (1941), 417–59, 568–92; Paul F. Russell, *Man's Mastery of Malaria* (London, 1955), pp. 93–102.

74. Russell, op. cit., pp. 96, 105–16. For illustrative details of the consequence of trying to penetrate Africa without malarial suppressant drugs, see Frederick F. Cartwright, *Disease and History* (London, 1972), pp. 137–39; Philip Curtin, *The Image of Africa:*

Notes

British Ideas and Action 1780–1850 (Madison, Wisconsin, 1964), pp. 483–87.

75. Cf. William Crawford Gorgas, *Sanitation in Panama* (New York, 1915); John M. Gibson, *Physician to the World: The Life of General William C. Gorgas* (Durham, North Carolina, 1950).

76. George K. Strohde, ed., *Yellow Fever* (New York, 1951), pp. 5–37.

77. Cf. W. A. Karunaratne, "The Influence of Malaria Control on Vital Statistics in Ceylon," *Journal of Tropical Medicine and Hygiene,* 62 (1959), 79–82.

78. Cf. the interesting discussion in R. Mansell Prothero, *Migration and Malaria* (London, 1965) of how migration patterns have helped to upset WHO plans for eliminating malaria from parts of Africa.

79. This is the opinion of René Dubos, *The White Plague: Tuberculosis, Man and Society* (Boston, 1952), pp. 185–207. He bases his estimate on the reported numbers seeking relief from scrofula (a form of tuberculosis) by the "King's Touch." But obviously, the number of sufferers who attended levees at which the King of England touched scrofulous persons in hope and expectation of a cure also depended on how vividly the populace believed in such magic. The supposed retreat of tuberculosis in the eighteenth century may therefore be a result of mounting skepticism as to the efficacy of the royal touch. After all, something went out of the mystique of monarchy in England with the Hanoverian succession; and Louis XV and his successor Louis XVI never commanded the charisma Louis XIV had done in France. The spread of American food crops and of the New Husbandry provided better nutrition for some Europeans; and this would tend to check tuberculosis, as the contrary experience of recent upsurges of tuberculosis rates in wartime when food rations run short amply shows. But exact statistics are irrecoverable and Dubos' opinion remains a possible but by no means a necessary interpretation of what is known.

80. René Dubos, *The White Plague,* p. vi and *passim*; T. Aidan Cockburn, *The Evolution and Eradication of Infectious Diseases,* pp. 219–30.

81. H. H. Scott, *A History of Tropical Medicine,* I, 44–54; A. J. P. Taylor, *English History 1914–1945* (New York, 1970), p. 121.

82. Ralph H. Major, *Fatal Partners: War and Disease* (New York, 1941), p. 240.

83. R. H. Shryock, *The Development of Modern Medicine* (Philadelphia, 1936), p. 309.

84. In the Austro-Hungarian army, for instance, despite prolonged exposure to the epidemic of typhus raging in Serbia, disease losses never exceeded 50 per cent of losses from enemy action, according to Clemens Pirquet, ed., *Volksgesundheit im Krieg* (Vienna and New Haven, 1926), I, 70.

85. Cf. R. S. Morton, *Venereal Disease* (Baltimore, 1966), p. 28.

86. Cf. Harry Wain, *A History of Preventive Medicine*, p. 306.

87. Cf. Thomas McKeown and C. R. Lowe, *An Introduction to Social Medicine* (Oxford and Edinburgh, 1966), p. 126.

88. For a conveniently brief summary, see Ernest L. Stebbins, "International Health Organization," in Philip E. Sartwell, ed., *Maxcy-Rosenau Preventive Medicine and Public Health*, 9th ed. (New York, 1965), pp. 1036–45.

89. Isolation of an islanded population could create similar vulnerability. Thus in Taiwan in the 1960s some 40,000 cases of crippling poliomyelitis came to official medical attention. Presumably what had happened was that the virus broke in upon a previously unexposed population, and attacked vulnerable adults and adolescents not because their sanitary regimens had previously shielded them from infection, but because the infection had been absent from the island entirely.

90. August Hirsch, *Handbook of Geographical and Historical Pathology*, I, 6–18, lists no fewer than ninety-four epidemics of influenza between 1173, the earliest he thought he could identify, and 1875. Of these he calculated at least fifteen had been pandemic, i.e., affected Asia as well as Europe. Given the imprecision of historical disease descriptions, there is no reason to suppose that influenza was new in 1173, however; and prior to the sixteenth century, when European doctors began to describe symptoms precisely enough to make identification reasonably sure, the history of the disease remains irrecoverable.

91. F. M. Burnet and E. Clark, *Influenza: A Survey of the Last Fifty Years in the Light of Modern Work on the Virus of Epidemic Influenza* (Melbourne and London, 1942); Edwin O. Jordan, *Epidemic Influenza* (Chicago, 1927), p. 229. I was also privileged to read a history of the flu epidemic of 1918–19 by Alfred W. Crosby, Jr., in manuscript.

Notes

92. Joseph A. Bell, "Influenza" in Ernest L. Stebbins, ed., *Maxcy-Rosenau Preventive Medicine and Public Health*, 9th ed., pp. 90–104.

93. Cf. the cataclysmic possibilities of up to a 90 per cent die-off outlined in Richard Fiennes, *Man, Nature and Disease* (London, 1964), p. 124.

94. See W. E. Woodward, et al., "The Spectrum of Cholera in Bangladesh," *American Journal of Epidemiology*, 96 (1972), 342–51.

95. See above, p. 52.

Index

Index

Ceremonial bathing, 46
Ceylon, 263
Cha, Dr. Joseph, 228
Chadwick, Edwin, 272
Chaldean empire, 77
Charlemagne, 139
Charles VIII, King, 218
Chaucer, Geoffrey, 183
Chekiang province (China), 134
Chervin, Nicholas, 266
Chicken pox, 13, 49–50
Chien-wu, Emperor, 133
Childhood diseases, 50–51, 61, 62, 63, 117, 130, 141, 180, 202
China, 44, 67, 79, 91, 228–29; breakdown of imperial administration, 135; Buddhism, 136–37; climatic differences in, 86; compared to India (first millennium B.C.), 95–96; Confucian culture in, 84; early Christian centuries, 132–40; epidemics in, 132, 293–301; humanoid hunters in, 25; marmot trappers, 155–56, 160–61; medical science and (since 1700), 236–37, 240, 241–44, 246, 253, 254, 262, 278; micro- and macroparasitic balances (500 B.C. to A.D. 1200), 81–90, 95–96, 98, 100, 104–5, 106, 107, 109–11, 113, 115, 125, 131–40, 145; millet farmers, 39, 42; Mongol conquest of (1213–79), 162–63; Mongol empire and (1200–1500), 149, 150, 151, 152–53, 156, 159, 162–63, 164, 187, 190, 194, 196; population decay, 134–35; population estimate (Han Dynasty), 104–5; trade, 110, 111; Warring States epoch of (403–221 B.C.), 87

Cholera, 46, 92, 107, 271; germ theory of, 267; impact of medical science on (since 1700), 261–67, 271–73, 277–78, 287, 289; sanitary water and sewage systems, 272–75; spread of (nineteenth century), 262–64; symptoms of, 261
Christianity, 136; advantage over pagans, 121–22; missionaries, 2, 208, 210, 211; rise and consolidation of, 121–23
Civilized societies, disease and (500 B.C. to A.D. 1200), 77–147; biblical texts, 79–80, 107, 126–27; breakthrough to history (before 500 B.C.), 62–76; Christian centuries, 109–47; first millennium B.C., 77–109; Ganges Valley, 82, 90–92, 112; Mediterranean coastland, 82, 96–104, 107, 109, 123; Middle East, 77–81, 98, 99, 104, 107, 110, 114, 143, 145; northern Europe, 128–29, 138; population (Roman world and Han China), 104–5; religious doctrines, 121–23, 136–37, 139; sea contacts, 112; trade development, 110–15, 124, 146; Yangtze Valley region, 85–87, 88, 89, 90, 137; Yellow River flood plain, 81–85, 86, 87, 89, 90, 137
Clothes, invention of, 26–27
Columbus, Christopher, 177, 199, 200, 203, 211, 219, 231
Confucianism, 94, 139, 244
Confucius, 84, 91, 94
Constantinople, 127, 253
Cook, Captain James, 268
Cortez, Hernando, 1, 2, 4, 204, 207
"Coughing violence" (Japan), 140, 209

Index

Index

About the Author

William H. McNeill is professor of history at the University of Chicago. He is the author of numerous books and articles, and is the editor of *The Journal of Modern History*. His most famous book, *The Rise of the West: A History of the Human Community*, won the National Book Award for History in 1964.